Topic relevant selected content from the highest rated entries, typeset, printed and shipped.

Combine the advantages of up-to-date and in-depth knowledge with the convenience of printed books.

A portion of the proceeds of each book will be donated to the Wikimedia Foundation to support their mission: to empower and engage people around the world to collect and develop educational content under a free license or in the public domain, and to disseminate it effectively and globally.

The content within this book was generated collaboratively by volunteers. Please be advised that nothing found here has necessarily been reviewed by people with the expertise required to provide you with complete, accurate or reliable information. Some information in this book maybe misleading or simply wrong. The publisher does not guarantee the validity of the information found here. If you need specific advice (for example, medical, legal, financial, or risk management) please seek a professional who is licensed or knowledgeable in that area.

Sources, licenses and contributors of the articles and images are listed in the section entitled "References". Parts of the books may be licensed under the GNU Free Documentation License. A copy of this license is included in the section entitled "GNU Free Documentation License"

All used third-party trademarks belong to their respective owners.

Contents

Articles

Richard Gere	1
Report to the Commissioner	7
Baby Blue Marine	9
Looking for Mr. Goodbar (film)	10
Bloodbrothers (1978 film)	12
Days of Heaven	14
Yanks	20
American Gigolo	22
An Officer and a Gentleman	25
The Honorary Consul (film)	32
Breathless (1983 film)	33
The Cotton Club (film)	36
King David (film)	40
No Mercy (film)	42
Power (1986 film)	44
Miles from Home	47
Internal Affairs (film)	49
Pretty Woman	51
Rhapsody in August	59
Final Analysis	62
Mr. Jones (film)	65
Sommersby	67
And the Band Played On (film)	71
Intersection (film)	75
First Knight	76
Primal Fear (film)	80
The Jackal (1997 film)	84
Red Corner	87
Runaway Bride (1999 film)	90
Dr. T & the Women	93
Autumn in New York (film)	95
Chicago (2002 film)	97
Unfaithful (2002 film)	105
The Mothman Prophecies (film)	111

Shall We Dance? (2004 film)	115
Bee Season (film)	118
The Hoax	121
The Hunting Party (2007 film)	125
I'm Not There	131
The Flock (film)	141
Nights in Rodanthe	143
Amelia (film)	146
Hachi: A Dog's Tale	151
Brooklyn's Finest	155
The Double (film)	160
Arbitrage (film)	162

References

Article Sources and Contributors	163
Image Sources, Licenses and Contributors	167

Article Licenses

License	168

Richard Gere

	Richard Gere
Born	Richard Tiffany Gere August 31, 1949 Philadelphia, Pennsylvania, U.S.
Nationality	American
Occupation	Actor
Years active	1973–present
Religion	Buddhist
Spouse	Cindy Crawford (1991–1995) Carey Lowell (2002–present)
Children	Son

Gere in Venice, 2007

Richard Tiffany Gere[1] (/ˈɡɪər/ *geer*; born August 31, 1949) is an American actor. He began acting in the 1970s, playing a supporting role in *Looking for Mr. Goodbar*, and a starring role in *Days of Heaven*. He came to prominence in 1980 for his role in the film *American Gigolo*, which established him as a leading man and a sex symbol. He went on to star in several hit films including *An Officer and a Gentleman*, *Pretty Woman*, *Primal Fear*, and *Chicago*, for which he won a Golden Globe Award as Best Actor, as well as a Screen Actors Guild Award as part of the Best Cast.

Early life

Born in Philadelphia, Pennsylvania, Gere is a descendant of *Mayflower* Pilgrims Francis Eaton, John Billington, George Soule, Richard Warren, Degory Priest, William Brewster, and Francis Cooke.[1] Gere's mother, Doris Ann (née Tiffany, born 1924),[1] was a homemaker, and his father, Homer George Gere (born 1922),[1] was an insurance agent for the Nationwide Mutual Insurance Company and had originally intended to become a minister.[2] Gere is their eldest son and second child.[1] In 1967, he graduated from North Syracuse Central High School, where he excelled at gymnastics and music, playing the trumpet.[2] He attended the University of Massachusetts Amherst on a gymnastics scholarship, majoring in philosophy, but did not graduate, leaving after two years.[2][3]

Career

Gere first worked professionally at the Provincetown Playhouse on Cape Cod in 1971 where he starred in *Rosencrantz and Guildenstern Are Dead*. His first major acting role was in the original London stage version of *Grease* in 1973.[2] He began appearing in Hollywood films in the mid 1970s, co-starring in the thriller *Looking for Mr. Goodbar* (1977) and playing the leading role in director Terrence Malick's well-reviewed 1978 film, *Days of Heaven*.[2] In 1980, Gere appeared in the Broadway production of *Bent*. He became a major star that year with the film *American Gigolo*, followed by the romantic drama *An Officer and a Gentleman*, which grossed almost $130 million in 1982.[4]

However, after 1982, Gere's career was dogged by several box office failures.[5][6] His career was somewhat resurrected after the release of both *Internal Affairs* and *Pretty Woman* in 1990. Gere's status as a leading man was again solidified, and he went on to star in several successful films throughout the 1990s, including *Sommersby* (1993), *Primal Fear* (1996), and *Runaway Bride* (1999) which reunited him with his *Pretty Woman* co-star Julia Roberts.[5] Richard also took a leading role in the 1997 action movie *The Jackal*, playing Declan Mulqueen.

People magazine named Gere the "Sexiest Man Alive" in 1999. In 2002, he appeared in three major releases: the horror thriller *The Mothman Prophecies*, the drama *Unfaithful*, and the Academy Award-winning film version of *Chicago*,[2] for which he won a Golden Globe as "Best Actor – Comedy or Musical". Gere's 2004 ballroom dancing drama *Shall We Dance?* was also a solid performer that grossed $170 million worldwide[7] though his next film, 2005's *Bee Season*, was a commercial failure.[8]

Gere was Harvard University's Hasty Pudding Theatricals' "Man of the Year" for 2006. In 2007, he co-starred with Jesse Eisenberg and Terrence Howard in *The Hunting Party*, a comic thriller in which he played a journalist in Bosnia. The same year he also starred with Christian Bale, Heath Ledger, and Cate Blanchett in Todd Haynes' semi-biographical film about Bob Dylan, *I'm Not There*.

Gere co-starred with Diane Lane in the romantic drama *Nights in Rodanthe*, released in 2008. The film was widely panned by critics[9] (even making #74 on *The Times* Worst Films of 2008 list),[10] but grossed over $84 million worldwide.[11]

In December 2010, Gere was honored for his lifetime achievement from the 34th Cairo International Film Festival.[12]

Gere remains one of the few actors, if not the only actor, to be nominated multiple times for the Golden Globe Award without ever being nominated for an Academy Award.

Personal life and activism

Gere was married to supermodel Cindy Crawford from 1991 to 1995. In 2002, he married model and actress Carey Lowell. They have a son, Homer James Jigme Gere, who was born in 2000 and is named after Gere's father.[2]

Gere was raised by Methodist parents;[13] his interest in Buddhism began when he traveled to Nepal in 1978 with the Brazilian painter, Sylvia Martins.[14] He is a practicing Buddhist and an active supporter of the Dalai Lama.[2] Gere is also a persistent advocate for human rights in Tibet; he is a co-founder of the Tibet House,

Gere presented with a Khata by the 14th Dalai Lama

creator of The Gere Foundation, and he is Chairman of the Board of Directors for the International Campaign for Tibet. Because he strongly supports the Tibetan Independence Movement, he is permanently banned from entering the People's Republic of China.[15][16] Gere was banned as an Academy Award presenter in 1993 after he denounced the Chinese government in his capacity as presenter.[17][18] In September 2007, Gere called for the boycott of the 2008 Beijing Olympic Games to put pressure on China to make Tibet independent. He starred in Free Tibet-themed Lancia commercial featuring the Lancia Delta.[19] On June 27, 2011 Richard Gere meditated in Borobudur temple.[20]

Gere Visits USAID HIV / AIDS "Operation Lighthouse" Project In Mumbai, as part of USAID.

Richard Gere actively supports Survival International, an organization dedicated to protecting the rights and lands of tribal peoples throughout the world.[14] He contributed some of his writing for the book, *We Are One: A Celebration of Tribal Peoples*, released in October 2009.[21] The book explores the culture of peoples around the world, portraying both its diversity and the threats it faces. Among other contributors, we can find several western writers, such as Laurens van der Post, Noam Chomsky, Claude Lévi-Strauss; and also indigenous peoples, such as Davi Kopenawa Yanomami and Roy Sesana. Richard Gere discusses the persecution and loss of land of the Jummas, as an example of a tragic story that repeats itself in different continents of the world. He calls attention to the crime against their peaceful culture and how it reflects on our own relationship with nature and capacity to survive.[22] The royalties from the sale of this book go to the indigenous rights organization, Survival International.

Gere campaigns for ecological causes and AIDS awareness. He currently serves on the Board of Directors for Healing the Divide, an organization that supports global initiatives to promote peace, justice and understanding.[23] He helped to establish the AIDS Care Home, a residential facility in India for women and children with AIDS, and also supports campaigns for AIDS awareness and education that country. In 1999, he created the Gere Foundation India Trust to support a variety of humanitarian programs in India.[24]

On April 15, 2007, Gere appeared at an AIDS awareness rally in Jaipur, India. During a live news conference to promote condom use among truck drivers, he embraced Bollywood superstar Shilpa Shetty, dipped her, and kissed her several times on the cheek.[25] As a result of that gesture, a local court ordered the arrest of Gere and Shetty, finding them in violation "public obscenity" laws. Gere, who quickly fled the country, has said the controversy was "manufactured by a small hard-line political party." About a month later, a two-judge bench headed by the Chief Justice of India, KG Balakrishnan, described the case as "frivolous" and believed that such complaints (against celebrities) were filed for "cheap publicity" and have brought a bad name to the country. They ruled that "Richard Gere is free to enter the country. This is the end of the matter."[26]

In June 2008, Gere appeared in a Fiat commercial for the European market, driving a new Lancia Delta from Hollywood to Tibet. The commercial concluded with a tagline of "New Lancia Delta: the power to be different". The commercial was reported in Chinese newspapers, and Fiat apologized to the PRC.[27] Branding expert John Tantillo argued that Fiat had foreseen the controversy the ad would cause and hoped to benefit from press coverage it would receive, labeling it "adpublitizing".[28]

Political views

Invasion of Iraq

Gere has stated that the decision to go to war in Iraq was one that the American people were not in support of and that the administration at the time "bullied" Americans into the decision. He blamed the situation on a very "poor president".[29]

"I'm very sorry about what the U.S. has done in Iraq. This war has been a tragedy for everyone. I hope that the people of Iraq can rebuild their country," Richard Gere said in a press conference, held on the sidelines of the 34th Cairo International Film Festival.[30]

Filmography

Year	Title	Role	Notes
1975	Report to the Commissioner	Billy	
1976	Baby Blue Marine	Raider	
1977	Looking for Mr. Goodbar	Tony Lo Porto	
1978	Bloodbrothers	Thomas Stony De Coco	
1978	Days of Heaven	Bill	David di Donatello Award for Best Foreign Actor
1979	Yanks	Matt Dyson	
1980	American Gigolo	Julian Kaye	
1982	An Officer and a Gentleman	Zack Mayo	Nominated — Golden Globe Award for Best Actor - Motion Picture Drama
1983	The Honorary Consul	Dr. Eduardo Plarr	
1983	Breathless	Jesse Lujack	
1984	The Cotton Club	Dixie Dwyer	
1985	King David	David	
1986	No Mercy	Eddie Jillette	

1986	*Power*	Pete St. John	
1988	*Miles from Home*	Frank Roberts, Jr.	
1990	*Internal Affairs*	Dennis Peck	
1990	*Pretty Woman*	Edward Lewis	Nominated — Golden Globe Award for Best Actor - Motion Picture Musical or Comedy
1991	*Rhapsody in August*	Clark	
1992	*Final Analysis*	Dr. Isaac Barr	
1993	*Mr. Jones*	Mr. Jones	
1993	*Sommersby*	John Robert 'Jack' Sommersby	
1993	*And the Band Played On*	The Choreographer	Nominated — CableACE Award for Supporting Actor in a Movie or Miniseries Nominated — Emmy Award for Outstanding Supporting Actor – Miniseries or a Movie
1994	*Intersection*	Vincent Eastman	
1995	*First Knight*	Lancelot	
1996	*Primal Fear*	Martin Vail	
1997	*The Jackal*	Declan Joseph Mulqueen	National Board of Review Freedom of Expression Award
1997	*Red Corner*	Jack Moore	
1999	*Runaway Bride*	Ike Graham	
2000	*Dr. T & the Women*	Dr. T	Nominated — Satellite Award for Best Actor - Motion Picture Musical or Comedy
2000	*Autumn in New York*	Will Keane	
2002	*Chicago*	Billy Flynn	Broadcast Film Critics Association Award for Best Cast Golden Globe Award for Best Actor - Motion Picture Musical or Comedy Screen Actors Guild Award for Outstanding Performance by a Cast in a Motion Picture Nominated — Phoenix Film Critics Society Award for Best Cast Nominated — Screen Actors Guild Award for Outstanding Performance by a Male Actor in a Leading Role
2002	*Unfaithful*	Edward Sumner	
2002	*The Mothman Prophecies*	John Klein	
2004	*Shall We Dance?*	John Clark	
2005	*Bee Season*	Saul Naumann	
2007	*The Hoax*	Clifford Irving	Nominated — Satellite Award for Best Actor - Motion Picture Musical or Comedy
2007	*The Hunting Party*	Simon	
2007	*I'm Not There*	Bob Dylan as Billy The Kid	Independent Spirit Robert Altman Award
2007	*The Flock*	Agent Erroll Babbage	
2008	*Nights in Rodanthe*	Dr. Paul Flanner	
2009	*Amelia*	George Putnam	
2009	*Hachi: A Dog's Tale*	Parker Wilson	
2010	*Brooklyn's Finest*	Eddie Dugan	
2011	*The Double*	Paul Shepherdson	

| 2012 | *Arbitrage* | Robert Miller | filming |

References

[1] Roberts, Gary Boyd. "The New England Ancestry of Actor Richard (Tiffany) Gere" (http://www.newenglandancestors.org/research/services/articles_gbr74.asp). New England Historic Genealogical Society. . Retrieved January 12, 2007.

[2] Stated in interview on *Inside the Actors Studio*, 2002

[3] "Richard Gere Biography" (http://www.thebiographychannel.co.uk/biography_story/105:713/1/Richard_Gere.htm), Carey Latimore, *The Biography Channel*. Retrieved May 1, 2008.

[4] "An Officer and a Gentleman" (http://www.boxofficemojo.com/movies/?id=officerandagentleman.htm). Box Office Mojo. . Retrieved May 4, 2009.

[5] "Richard Gere" (http://www.boxofficemojo.com/people/chart/?view=Actor&id=richardgere.htm). Box Office Mojo. . Retrieved May 4, 2009.

[6] "Richard Gere" (http://www.rottentomatoes.com/celebrity/richard_gere/). Rotten Tomatoes. . Retrieved May 4, 2009.

[7] "Shall We Dance" (http://www.boxofficemojo.com/movies/?id=shallwedance.htm). Box Office Mojo. . Retrieved May 4, 2009.

[8] "Bee Season" (http://www.boxofficemojo.com/movies/?id=beeseason.htm). Box Office Mojo. . Retrieved May 4, 2009.

[9] "Nights in Rodanthe (2008)" (http://www.rottentomatoes.com/m/nights_in_rodanthe/). Rotten Tomatoes. . Retrieved May 4, 2009.

[10] "Turkeys! The 100 Worst Movies of 2008" (http://entertainment.timesonline.co.uk/tol/arts_and_entertainment/film/article5245052.ece). *The Times*. December 8, 2008. . Retrieved May 4, 2009.

[11] "Nights in Rodanthe" (http://www.boxofficemojo.com/movies/?id=nightsinrodanthe.htm). Box Office Mojo. . Retrieved May 4, 2009.

[12] "Gere, Binoche honored at CIFF opening" (http://www.thedailynewsegypt.com/film/gere-binoche-honored-at-ciff-opening-dp1.html). *Daily News Egypt*. November 30, 2010. . Retrieved December 1, 2010.

[13] Jones, Chris (December 27, 2002). "Richard Gere: On guard" (http://news.bbc.co.uk/1/low/in_depth/uk/2000/newsmakers/2591237.stm). *BBC News*. . Retrieved May 22, 2010.

[14] "Richard Gere Biography" (http://www.thebiographychannel.co.uk/biography_story/105:713/1/Richard_Gere.htm), Carey Latimore, *The Biography Channel*. Retrieved May 12, 2007.

[15] Yahlin Chang, 'Red Corner,' (http://www.newsweek.com/1997/11/09/can-you-go-home-again.html) Newsweek November 10, 1997:"Gere has already been banned from entering China for his pro-Tibet activities.'

[16] Laurence Caracalla, *Harrison Ford*, Silverback Books, 2007 p.93

[17] An in-depth look at your favourite celebrity personalities – hellomagazine.com, HELLO! (http://www.hellomagazine.com/profiles/richardgere/)

[18] Richard Gere: Man of masks (http://www.independent.co.uk/arts-entertainment/films/features/richard-gere-man-of-masks-761587.html)

[19] Lancia Delta "Richard Gere" TV Commercial (http://paultan.org/2008/07/06/lancia-delta-richard-gere-tv-commercial/)

[20] http://www.mediaindonesia.com/read/2011/06/27/237640/65/10/Richard-Gere-Ingin-Kembali-ke-Candi-Borobudur

[21] Survival International – We Are One (http://www.survivalinternational.org/weareone)

[22] Eede, Joanna (2009). *We are One: A Celebration of Tribal Peoples*. Quadrille Publishing. ISBN 1844007294.

[23] Healing The Divide (http://www.healingthedivide.org)

[24] The Gere Foundation (http://www.gerefoundation.org/bio.html). Retrieved May 12, 2007.

[25] YouTube – Richard Gere kissing Shilpa Shetty (http://www.youtube.com/watch?v=kdnaHHns3c0)

[26] "Richard Gere cleared of obscenity" (http://news.bbc.co.uk/2/hi/south_asia/7295797.stm). *BBC News*. March 14, 2008. . Retrieved May 22, 2010.

[27] "Fiat apologizes to China for Richard Gere Commercial" (http://www.autoblog.com/2008/06/20/fiat-apologizes-to-china-for-richard-gere-commercial) Auto Blog. June 20, 2008.

[28] "Richard Gere Fiat Ad Is Just The Latest Saga In the Risky New World Of Global Branding" (http://blog.marketingdoctor.tv/2008/06/25/tantillo-on-the-news.aspx) Marketing Doctor Blog. June 25, 2008.

[29] Al-Masry Al-Youm. December 1, 2010. http://www.almasryalyoum.com/en/news/juliette-binoche-and-richard-gere-greet-press.

[30] *Egyptian Gazette*. December 27, 2010. http://213.158.162.45/~egyptian/index.php?action=news&id=13433&title=Seeing%20the%20stars%20in%20Cairo.

External links

- Richard Gere (http://www.imdb.com/name/nm152/) at the Internet Movie Database
- Richard Gere (http://www.ibdb.com/person.asp?ID=41996) at the Internet Broadway Database
- Richard Gere (http://www.lortel.org/LLA_archive/index.cfm?search_by=people&first=Richard&last=Gere&middle=) at the Internet Off-Broadway Database
- Defended India's nuclear tests (http://web.archive.org/web/19991009190431/http://www.tibet.ca/wtnarchive/1998/5/23_4.html)
- The Gere Foundation (http://gerefoundation.org/)
- The Druk White Lotus School (external link (http://dwls.org/)) of which Gere is an Honorary Patron.
- Shambhala Sun Interview (http://www.shambhalasun.com/index.php?option=com_content&task=view&id=1882&Itemid=0)

Report to the Commissioner

Report to the Commissioner is a 1974 crime drama film starring Michael Moriarty and based on a 1972 book by James Mills. The story involves a rookie cop in the New York City Police Department who is assigned a special missing person case but in fact is meant to be a wild-goose chase to back up an undercover female police officer, who is involved in a deadly accidentally shooting.

The film was directed by Milton Katselas and features a musical score by Elmer Bernstein.Richard Gere made his screen debut with a minor supporting role in this film as a pimp.

Cast

- Michael Moriarty - Bo Lockley
- Yaphet Kotto - Richard 'Crunch' Blackstone
- Susan Blakely - Patty Butler
- Héctor Elizondo - Captain D'Angelo
- Tony King - Thomas 'Stick' Henderson
- Michael McGuire - Lt. Hanson
- Edward Grover - Captain Strichter
- Dana Elcar - Chief Perna
- Bob Balaban - Joey Egan (as Robert Balaban)
- William Devane - Asst. D.A. Jackson
- Stephen Elliott - Police Commissioner
- Richard Gere - Billy
- Vic Tayback - Lt. Seidensticker
- Albert Seedman - Detective Schulman
- Noelle North - Samantha

External links

- *Report to the Commissioner* [1] at the Internet Movie Database

References

[1] http://www.imdb.com/title/tt0073620/

Baby Blue Marine

Baby Blue Marine	
Directed by	John D. Hancock
Starring	Jan-Michael Vincent
Release date(s)	1976
Running time	90 min.
Country	United States
Language	English

Baby Blue Marine is a 1976 film set during World War II that was directed by John D. Hancock. It stars Jan-Michael Vincent and Glynnis O'Connor.

Film critic Roger Ebert gave the film 2½ out of 4 stars.[1]

Plot

Marion, a Marine recruit during World War II is kicked out of the Corps and sent home in a blue fatigue uniform. As recruits sent their civilian clothes home or sold them, the Corps did not wish less than honourably discharged Marine recruits to wear a uniform they had not earned. In real life the Corps issued light blue uniforms used by Flying Cadets prior to Pearl Harbor; hence the name "Baby Blue Marine" for a failed recruit.

Ashamed, Marion meets a Marine Raider (Richard Gere in his second big screen appearance) a young, battle-scarred war hero back from the Pacific who has aged beyond his years with prematurely gray hair. As the Raider doesn't wish to return to the war, he knocks out Marion and changes uniforms with him.

Marion enters an idyllic small town where the decorations and Raider shoulder sleeve insignia of his uniform make him a hero to the community whose own young men are away at the war.

Film Locations

Baby Blue Marine was primarily shot in Siskiyou County, California. Most elements were filmed in McCloud, California with the scene at a local football game filmed in Weed, California at the high school. It showed one of the rare times Mount Shasta was shown in a motion picture. Other elements were shot in Hollywood.

References

[1] http://rogerebert.suntimes.com/apps/pbcs.dll/article?AID=/19760615/REVIEWS/606150301/1023

External links

- *Baby Blue Marine* (http://www.imdb.com/title/tt0074173/) at the Internet Movie Database

Looking for Mr. Goodbar (film)

Looking for Mr. Goodbar	
Directed by	Richard Brooks
Produced by	Freddie Fields
Written by	Richard Brooks
Based on	*Looking for Mr. Goodbar* by Judith Rossner
Starring	Diane Keaton Tuesday Weld Richard Gere
Cinematography	William A. Fraker
Editing by	George Grenville
Distributed by	Paramount Pictures
Release date(s)	October 19, 1977
Running time	135 minutes
Country	United States
Language	English
Budget	$5 million
Box office	$22,512,655

Looking for Mr. Goodbar is a 1977 film written for the screen and directed by Richard Brooks and starring Diane Keaton, Tuesday Weld, Richard Gere, and also features Tom Berenger. The film is based on the novel of the same name by Judith Rossner, which was in turn based on the real life murder of New York City schoolteacher Roseann Quinn.

Although the film was an award-nominated financial success and is considered a classic by some critics, it is out of print on VHS and to date has not been released on DVD or Blu-ray.[1][2]

Plot

The 1977 film, starring Diane Keaton as Theresa Dunn, traces the sexual awakening of a young teacher searching for excitement outside of her mundane existence. Suffering with severe body image issues and a sense of inadequacy following a childhood surgery that left a large scar on her back, Irish American Theresa finds first love with her older, married university professor, who ends the affair as her time in college comes to an end. The end of the affair leaves Theresa feeling used, and she begins daydreaming about being reunited with her professor.

Theresa enters the sexual revolution of the 1970s feeling confused, as she is simultaneously repelled and attracted to the sexual experimentation she witnesses going on around her. Although she continues to teach by day, developing a reputation as a gifted and caring teacher to deaf children, at night she goes clubbing at a series of increasingly seedy bars, picking up men for one-night stands. The recreational sexual encounters slowly become an addiction, as Theresa begins pursuing more dangerous men with violent sexual proclivities to enhance her "high".

An encounter with an Italian thug named Tony (Richard Gere) develops into a nascent relationship, and the two begin regularly meeting for increasingly rough and dangerous sex, culminating in Tony's introduction of a switchblade knife into their sex play. Meanwhile, Theresa attempts to date a boy from her neighborhood named James, whom her family holds up as the paragon of Irish-American youth. The relationship quickly falters, as James turns out to be just as shallow and emotionally manipulative as Tony.

Theresa ultimately breaks up with Tony following a disastrous "date" to his mother's birthday party, during which the volatile Tony verbally abuses his family and starts a fist fight. With the new year approaching, Theresa resolves to leave her clubbing behind and take control of her life. Seeking one final hookup on New Year's eve, Theresa picks up a man named Gary, who turns out to be a sexually confused war veteran. At Theresa's apartment, Gary finds himself unnable to attain an erection. Misreading Theresa's frustration as her questioning his sexuality, Gary attacks her and begins beating and raping her. After Theresa screams "Do it!" Gary stabs her to death. Theresa's dead face drifts farther away from the screen and into a black void as the film ends.

Cast

- Diane Keaton ... Theresa Dunn
- Tuesday Weld ... Katherine
- William Atherton ... James
- Richard Kiley ... Mr. Dunn
- Richard Gere ... Tony
- LeVar Burton ... Cap Jackson
- Brian Dennehy ... Surgeon
- Alan Feinstein ... Martin
- Tom Berenger ... Gary

Awards

Tuesday Weld received a nomination for the Academy Award for Best Supporting Actress for her performance in the film, and William A. Fraker received a nomination for the Academy Award for Best Cinematography.

Diane Keaton was nominated for the Golden Globe Award for Best Actress - Motion Picture Drama for her performance in the film. She was not nominated for an Academy Award for her performance in this film, although she was nominated (and won) the same year for *Annie Hall*.

References

[1] NoFlix: 23 great movies not available on region-1 DVD (http://www.avclub.com/articles/noflix-23-great-movies-not-available-on-region1-dv,16754/), Onion OV Club

[2] http://www.salon.com/entertainment/movies/andrew_ohehir/2011/07/19/10_greatest_missing_movies/index.html

External links

- *Looking for Mr. Goodbar* (http://www.imdb.com/title/tt0076327/) at the Internet Movie Database

Bloodbrothers (1978 film)

Bloodbrothers	
Directed by	Robert Mulligan
Produced by	Stephen J. Friedman
Written by	Walter Newman
Starring	Richard Gere Paul Sorvino Tony Lo Bianco Marilu Henner
Music by	Elmer Bernstein
Cinematography	Robert L. Surtees
Editing by	Sheldon Kahn
Distributed by	Warner Bros.
Release date(s)	October 6, 1978
Running time	116 minutes
Country	United States
Language	English
Budget	$4 million

Bloodbrothers is a 1978 coming-of-age film directed by Robert Mulligan. It stars Richard Gere, Paul Sorvino, Tony Lo Bianco and Marilu Henner. The film was also based on the novel of the same title by Richard Price. It was nominated for an Academy Award for Best Adapted Screenplay.

Plot

Set in a working class community, it tells the story of the De Coco family, a family of construction workers. Louis is the head of the family with three sons, but one, Stoney (Richard Gere) wants to be a teacher, not a hardhat. Then he accepts a job as a recreational assistant at a children's ward. Immediately, bitter divisions begin to surface.

Cast

- Paul Sorvino as Louis Chubby De Coco
- Tony Lo Bianco as Tommy De Coco
- Richard Gere as Thomas Stony De Coco
- Lelia Goldoni as Marie De Coco
- Yvonne Wilder as Phyllis De Coco
- Kenneth McMillan as Banion
- Floyd Levine as Dr. Harris
- Marilu Henner as Annette
- Michael Hershewe as Albert Tiger De Coco
- Jeffrey Jacquet as Derek
- Kristine DeBell as Cheri
- Paulene Myers as Mrs. Pitt
- Gloria LeRoy as Sylvia

- Bruce French as Paulie

Response

The movie opened to positive reviews, and though it would be forgotten about in later years, it was liked for the ensemble cast. As one of the De Coco sons, Richard Gere was especially praised. The film also introduced Marilu Henner, who would later star on the TV show *Taxi*.

External links

- *Bloodbrothers* [1] at the Internet Movie Database

References

[1] http://www.imdb.com/title/tt0078878/

Days of Heaven

Days of Heaven	
Theatrical release poster	
Directed by	Terrence Malick
Produced by	Bert Schneider Harold Schneider
Written by	Terrence Malick
Starring	Richard Gere Brooke Adams Sam Shepard Linda Manz
Music by	Ennio Morricone
Cinematography	Néstor Almendros Haskell Wexler
Editing by	Billy Weber
Distributed by	Paramount Pictures
Release date(s)	September 13, 1978
Running time	90 minutes
Country	United States
Language	English
Budget	$3,000,000[1]
Box office	$3,446,749[2]

Days of Heaven is a 1978 American romantic drama film written and directed by Terrence Malick and starring Richard Gere, Brooke Adams, Sam Shepard and Linda Manz. Set in the early 20th century, it tells the story of two poor lovers, Bill and Abby, as they travel to the Texas Panhandle to harvest crops for a wealthy farmer. Bill encourages Abby to claim the fortune of the dying farmer by tricking him into a false marriage. This results in an unstable love triangle and a series of unfortunate events.

Days of Heaven is widely recognized as a landmark of 1970s cinema.

Plot

The story is set in 1916.[3] Bill (Gere), a Chicago manual laborer, knocks down and kills a boss in the steel mill where he works. He flees to the Texas Panhandle with his girlfriend Abby (Adams) and younger sister Linda (Manz). Bill and Abby pretend to be siblings to prevent gossip.

The three hire on as part of a large group of seasonal workers with a rich, shy farmer (Shepard). The farmer learns that he is dying of an unspecified disease. When he falls in love with Abby, Bill encourages her to marry him so that they can inherit his money after he dies. The marriage takes place and Bill stays on the farm as Abby's "brother." The farmer's foreman suspects their scheme. The farmer's health unexpectedly remains stable, foiling Bill's plans.

Eventually, the farmer discovers Bill's true relationship with Abby. At the same time, Abby has begun to fall in love with her new husband. After a locust swarm and a fire destroy his wheat fields, the farmer goes after Bill with a gun, but Bill kills him. Bill then flees with Abby and Linda. The foreman and the police pursue and eventually find them, and the police kill Bill. Abby leaves Linda at a boarding school and goes off on her own.

Cast

- Richard Gere as Bill
- Brooke Adams as Abby
- Sam Shepard as The Farmer
- Linda Manz as Linda
- Robert J. Wilke as The Farm Foreman
- Jackie Shultis as Linda's Friend
- Stuart Margolin as Mill Foreman
- Timothy Scott as Harvest Hand
- Gene Bell as Dancer
- Doug Kershaw as Fiddler
- Richard Libertini as Vaudeville Leader

Production

Producer Jacob Brackman introduced fellow producer Bert Schneider to filmmaker Terrence Malick in 1975.[4] On a trip to Cuba, Schneider and Malick began conversations that would lead to the development of *Days of Heaven*. Malick had tried and failed to get Dustin Hoffman or Al Pacino to star in the film. Schneider agreed to produce the film. He and Malick cast a young Richard Gere, actor and playwright Sam Shepard and Brooke Adams. Paramount Pictures CEO Barry Diller wanted Schneider to produce films for him and agreed to finance *Days of Heaven*. At the time, the studio was headed in a new direction. They were hiring new production heads who had worked in network television, and, according to former production chief Richard Sylbert, "[manufacturing] product aimed at your knees".[4] Despite the change in direction, Schneider was able to secure a deal with Paramount by guaranteeing the budget and taking personal responsibility for all overages. "Those were the kind of deals I liked to make", Schneider said, "because then I could have final cut and not talk to nobody about why we're gonna use this person instead of that person."[4]

Malick admired cinematographer Nestor Almendros' work on *The Wild Child* and wanted him to shoot *Days of Heaven*.[5] He was impressed by Malick's knowledge of photography and willingness to use little studio lighting. The two men modeled the film's cinematography after silent films, which often used natural light. They also drew inspiration from painters such as Johannes Vermeer, Edward Hopper (particularly his *House by the Railroad*), and Andrew Wyeth, as well as photo-reporters from the turn of the century.[5]

Principal photography

Production began in the fall of 1976.[6] Though the film was set in Texas, the exteriors were shot in Whiskey Gap, a ghost town on the prairie of Alberta, Canada and a final scene shot on the grounds of Heritage Park Historical Village in Calgary.[7] Jack Fisk designed and built the mansion from plywood in the wheat fields and the smaller houses where the workers lived. The mansion was not a facade, as was normally the custom, but authentically recreated inside and out with period colors: brown, mahogany and dark wood for the interiors.[5] Patricia Norris designed and made the period costumes from used fabrics and old clothes to avoid the artificial look of studio-made costumes.[5]

According to Almendros, the production was not "rigidly prepared", allowing for improvisation.[5] Daily call sheets were not very detailed and the schedule changed to suit the weather. This upset some of the Hollywood crew members not used to working in such a spontaneous way. Most of the crew were used to a "glossy style of photography" and felt frustrated because Almendros did not give them much work.[5] On a daily basis, he asked them to turn off the lights they had prepared for him. Some crew members said that Almendros and Malick did not know what they were doing. Some of the crew quit the production. Malick supported what Almendros was doing and pushed the look of the film further, taking away more lighting aids, and leaving the image bare.[5] Due to union regulations in North America, Almendros was not allowed to operate the camera. With Malick, he would plan out and rehearse movements of the camera and the actors. Almendros would stand near the main camera and give instructions to the camera operators.[5]

Almendros was losing his eyesight by the time shooting began. To evaluate his setups, "he had one of his assistants take Polaroids of the scene, then examined them through very strong glasses".[4] According to Almendros, Malick wanted "a very visual movie. The story would be told through visuals. Very few people really want to give that priority to image. Usually the director gives priority to the actors and the story, but here the story was told through images".[8] Much of the film would be shot during "magic hour", which Almendros called

> "a euphemism, because it's not an hour but around 25 minutes at the most. It is the moment when the sun sets, and after the sun sets and before it is night. The sky has light, but there is no actual sun. The light is very soft, and there is something magic about it. It limited us to around twenty minutes a day, but it did pay on the screen. It gave some kind of magic look, a beauty and romanticism".[8]

This "magic look" would extend to interior scenes, which often utilized natural light.

Almendros said,

> "In this period there was no electricity. It was before electricity was invented and consequently there was less light. Period movies should have less light. In a period movie the light should come from the windows because that is how people lived."[8]

For the shot in the "locusts" sequence, where the insects rise into the sky, the filmmakers dropped peanut shells from helicopters. They had the actors walk backwards while running the film in reverse through the camera. When it was projected, everything moved forward except the locusts.[9] For the closeups and insert shots, thousands of live locusts were used which had been captured and supplied by the Canadian Department of Agriculture.[5]

While the photography yielded exquisite results, the rest of the production was difficult from the start.[6] The actors and crew reportedly viewed Malick as cold and distant. After two weeks of shooting, Malick was so disappointed with the dailies, he "decided to toss the script, go Leo Tolstoy instead of Fyodor Dostoyevsky, wide instead of deep [and] shoot miles of film with the hope of solving the problems in the editing room."[6] In addition, the harvesting machines constantly broke down, which resulted in shooting beginning late in the afternoon, allowing for only a few hours of daylight before it was too dark to go on. One day, two helicopters were scheduled to drop peanut shells that were to simulate locusts on film; however, Malick decided to shoot period cars instead. He kept the helicopters on hold at great cost. Production was lagging behind, with costs exceeding the budget by about $800,000, and Schneider had already mortgaged his home in order to cover the overages.[6]

The production ran so late that both Almendros and camera operator John Bailey had to leave due to a prior commitment on François Truffaut's *The Man Who Loved Women*. Almendros approached his friend and renowned cinematographer Haskell Wexler to complete the film. They worked together for a week so that Wexler could get familiar with the film's visual style.[5] Wexler was careful to match Almendros' work, but he did make some exceptions. "I did some hand held shots on a Panaflex", he said, "[for] the opening of the film in the steel mill. I used some diffusion. Nestor didn't use any diffusion. I felt very guilty using the diffusion and having (sic) the feeling of violating a fellow cameraman."[8] Though half the finished picture was footage shot by Wexler, he received only credit for "additional photography", much to his chagrin. The credit denied him any chance of an Academy Award for his work on *Days of Heaven*. He sent critic Roger Ebert a letter "in which he described sitting in a theater with a stopwatch to prove that more than half of the footage" was his.[10]

Post-production

After the production finished principal photography, the editing process took over two years to complete. Malick had a difficult time shaping the film and getting the pieces to go together.[11] Schneider reportedly showed some footage to director Richard Brooks, who was considering Gere for a role in *Looking for Mr. Goodbar*. According to Schneider, the editing for *Days of Heaven* took so long that "Brooks cast Gere, shot, edited and released [*Looking for Mr. Goodbar*] while Malick was still editing".[6] A breakthrough came when Malick experimented with voice-overs from Linda Manz's character, similar to what he had done with Sissy Spacek in *Badlands*. According to editor Billy Weber, Malick jettisoned much of the film's dialogue, replacing it with Manz's voice-over, which served as an oblique commentary on the story.[6]

After a year, Malick had to call the actors to Los Angeles to shoot inserts of shots that were necessary but had not been filmed in Alberta. The finished film thus includes close-ups of Shephard that were shot under a freeway overpass. The underwater shot of Gere's falling face down into the river was shot in a large aquarium in Sissy Spacek's living room.[7]

Meanwhile, Schneider was upset with Malick. He had confronted Malick numerous times about missed deadlines and broken promises. Due to further cost overruns, he had to ask Paramount for more money, which he preferred not to do. When they screened a demo for Paramount and made their pitch, the studio was impressed and reportedly "gave Malick a very sweet deal at the studio, carte blanche, essentially".[6]

Malick was not able to capitalize on the deal. He was so exhausted from working on the film that he moved to Paris with his girlfriend. He tried developing another project for Paramount, but after a substantial amount of work, he abandoned it. He did not make another film until 1998's *The Thin Red Line* twenty years later.[11]

Reaction

In his review for *The New York Times*, Harold C. Schonberg wrote, "*Days of Heaven* never really makes up its mind what it wants to be. It ends up something between a Texas pastoral and Cavalleria Rusticana. Back of what basically is a conventional plot is all kinds of fancy, self-conscious cineaste techniques."[12] Dave Kehr of *The Chicago Reader* wrote: "Terrence Malick's remarkably rich second feature is a story of human lives touched and passed over by the divine, told in a rush of stunning and precise imagery. Nestor Almendros's cinematography is as sharp and vivid as Malick's narration is elliptical and enigmatic. The result is a film that hovers just beyond our grasp—mysterious, beautiful, and, very possibly, a masterpiece".[13] Gene Siskel of *The Chicago Tribune* also wrote that the film "truly tests a film critic's power of description ... Some critics have complained that the *Days of Heaven* story is too slight. I suppose it is, but, frankly, you don't think about it while the movie is playing".[14] *Time* magazine's Frank Rich wrote, "*Days of Heaven* is lush with brilliant images".[15] The periodical went on to name it one of the best films of 1978.[16]

Nick Schager of *Slant Magazine* has called it "the greatest film ever made."[17] Roger Ebert described the movie as "one of the most beautiful films ever made" and added it on his list of Great Movies.[18]

Days of Heaven held a 93% approval rating at Rotten Tomatoes with an average rating of 8.2/10 based on 45 reviews.[19]

Awards

The film won an Academy Award for Best Cinematography. Per Academy custom the award was given in the name of principal photographer Nestor Almendros.[11] This was somewhat controversial as renowned cinematographer Haskell Wexler also received credit on the film. The film was also nominated for Academy Awards for Costume Design, Original Score, and Sound (John Wilkinson, Robert W. Glass, Jr., John T. Reitz and Barry Thomas).[20] Malick won the *Prix de la mise en scène* (Best Director award) at the 1979 Cannes Film Festival.[21] Furthermore, he was named the best director by the National Society of Film Critics.

In 2007, *Days of Heaven* was selected for preservation in the United States National Film Registry by the Library of Congress as being "culturally, historically, or aesthetically significant".

Notes

[1] http://www.imdb.com/title/tt0077405/business
[2] http://www.boxofficemojo.com/movies/?id=daysofheaven.htm
[3] The film shows a 1916 newspaper, and a scene late in the film shows American soldiers headed off for World War I.
[4] Biskind 1998, p. 296.
[5] Almendros 1986
[6] Biskind 1998, p. 297.
[7] Almereyda, Michael (April 13, 2004). "After The Rehearsal: Flirting with *Disaster*: Discussing *Days of Heaven* and Dylan classics with Sam Shepard" (http://www.webcitation.org/5vB9iCJez). *Village Voice*. Archived from the original (http://www.villagevoice.com/2004-04-13/film/after-the-rehearsal/) on December 23, 2010. . Retrieved April 17, 2006.
[8] Glassman, Arnold; Todd McCarthy, Stuart Samuels (1992). "Visions of Light: The Art of Cinematography". Kino International.
[9] Thompson, Rustin (June 30, 1998). "Myth-making With Natural Light" (http://www.webcitation.org/5vB9c8biT). *Moviemaker*. Archived from the original (http://www.moviemaker.com/directing/article/mythmaking_with_natural_light_3206/) on December 23, 2010. . Retrieved February 13, 2009.
[10] Ebert, Roger (December 7, 1997). "*Days of Heaven*: Great Movies" (http://www.webcitation.org/5vB9nB5PF). *Chicago Sun-Times*. Archived from the original (http://rogerebert.suntimes.com/apps/pbcs.dll/article?AID=/19971207/REVIEWS08/401010327/1023) on December 23, 2010. . Retrieved September 19, 2007.
[11] Biskind, Peter (August 1999). "The Runaway Genius" (http://www.webcitation.org/5vB9qbjx8). *Vanity Fair*. Archived from the original (http://www.vanityfair.com/hollywood/classic/features/runaway-genius-199812) on December 23, 2010. . Retrieved April 22, 2010.
[12] Schonberg, Harold C (September 14, 1978). "*Days of Heaven*" (http://movies.nytimes.com/movie/review?_r=2&res=EE05E7DF173EE767BC4C52DFBF668383669EDE&partner=Rotten Tomatoes). *The New York Times*. . Retrieved December 11, 2008.
[13] Kehr, Dave (1978). "*Days of Heaven*" (http://www.webcitation.org/5vB9tXN6P). *The Chicago Reader*. Archived from the original (http://onfilm.chicagoreader.com/movies/capsules/2482_DAYS_OF_HEAVEN) on December 23, 2010. . Retrieved December 11, 2008.
[14] Siskel, Gene (October 9, 1978). "*Days of Heaven*". *Chicago Tribune*.
[15] Rich, Frank (September 18, 1978). "*Days of Heaven*" (http://www.webcitation.org/5vBA4XKHV). *Time*. Archived from the original (http://www.time.com/time/magazine/article/0,9171,916396,00.html) on December 23, 2010. . Retrieved September 9, 2009.
[16] "Cinema: Year's Best" (http://www.webcitation.org/5vBA6v6Hh). *Time*. January 1, 1979. Archived from the original (http://www.time.com/time/magazine/article/0,9171,916590,00.html) on December 23, 2010. . Retrieved September 9, 2009.
[17] Schager, Nick (October 22, 2007). "Days of Heaven review" (http://www.webcitation.org/5vBAIbjN1). *Slant Magazine*. Archived from the original (http://www.slantmagazine.com/film/review/days-of-heaven/3213) on December 23, 2010. . Retrieved December 23, 2010.
[18] "Days of Heaven (1978)" (http://rogerebert.suntimes.com/apps/pbcs.dll/article?AID=/19971207/REVIEWS08/401010327/1023). *Chicago Sun-Times*. .
[19] "Days of Heaven (1978)" (http://www.rottentomatoes.com/m/days_of_heaven/). *Rotten Tomatoes*. . Retrieved October 15, 2011.
[20] "The 51st Academy Awards (1979) Nominees and Winners" (http://www.oscars.org/awards/academyawards/legacy/ceremony/51st-winners.html). *oscars.org*. . Retrieved 2011-10-06.
[21] "Sweeping Cannes" (http://www.webcitation.org/5vBATPd59). *Time*. June 4, 1979. Archived from the original (http://www.time.com/time/magazine/article/0,9171,946279,00.html) on December 23, 2010. . Retrieved September 9, 2009.

References

- Almendros, Nestor (1986) *A Man with a Camera*. Farrar, Straus and Giroux.
- Biskind, Peter (1998) *Easy Riders, Raging Bulls*. New York: Simon & Schuster.

Further reading

- Charlotte Crofts (2001), 'From the "Hegemony of the Eye" to the "Hierarchy of Perception": The Reconfiguration of Sound and Image in Terrence Malick's *Days of Heaven*', *Journal of Media Practice*, 2:1, 19-29.
- Terry Curtis Fox (1978), 'The Last Ray of Light', *Film Comment*, 14:5, Sept/Oct, 27-28.
- Martin Donougho (1985), 'West of Eden: Terrence Malick's *Days of Heaven*', *Postscript: Essays in Film and the Humanities*, 5:1, Fall, 17-30.
- Terrence Malick (1976), *Days of Heaven*, Script registered with the Writers Guild of America, 14 Apr; revised 2 Jun.

- Brooks Riley (1978), 'Interview with Nestor Almendros', *Film Comment*, 14:5, Sept/Oct, 28-31.
- Janet Wondra (1994), 'A Gaze Unbecoming: Schooling the Child for Femininity in *Days of Heaven*', *Wide Angle*, 16:4, Oct, 5-22.

External links

- *Days of Heaven* (http://www.imdb.com/title/tt0077405/) at the Internet Movie Database
- *Days of Heaven* (http://www.allrovi.com/movies/movie/v12659) at AllRovi
- *Days of Heaven* (http://www.rottentomatoes.com/m/days_of_heaven/) at Rotten Tomatoes
- *Days of Heaven* (http://www.boxofficemojo.com/movies/?id=daysofheaven.htm) at Box Office Mojo
- Essay by Katy Karpfinger for New Linear Perspectives (http://newlinearperspectives.wordpress.com/film/k2/)
- Essay by Adrian Martin for the Criterion Collection (http://www.criterion.com/current/posts/555-days-of-heaven-on-earth-as-it-is-in-heaven)

Yanks

Yanks	
Original theatrical poster of *Yanks*	
Directed by	John Schlesinger
Produced by	Joseph Janni Lester Persky
Written by	Colin Welland (story and screenplay) Walter Bernstein (screenplay)
Starring	Richard Gere Vanessa Redgrave William Devane Rachel Roberts Lisa Eichhorn
Music by	Richard Rodney Bennett
Cinematography	Dick Bush
Editing by	Jim Clark
Distributed by	Universal Pictures United Artists
Release date(s)	1979
Running time	141 minutes
Country	United Kingdom United States
Language	English

Yanks is a 1979 John Schlesinger film, set in World War II in the village of Dobcross, in Greater Manchester, England. Starring Richard Gere, Vanessa Redgrave, William Devane, Lisa Eichhorn, Rachel Roberts and Tony Melody.

The film focuses on three romances taking place as a result of the stationing of American troops in Britain in the build up to the Normandy Landings, plus the impact and reactions of the two different cultures on each other in rural 1940s England.

Plot

In the build-up to the Normandy landings, thousands of American troops descend upon England. Near a small Lancashire town, a large US Army base is established and soon houses the rambunctious "Yanks" as they are known to the English. On leave in the town, young Arizona man, Matt Dyson (Richard Gere), encounters pretty young Jean Moreton (Lisa Eichhorn) and asks her out to the cinema. She is the girlfriend of a British soldier fighting overseas, and initially rebuffs his advances. He is quite persistent, and she was having her doubts about her relationship with her fiancé anyway. The handsome, brash American sergeant is in stark contrast to the restrained Englishmen she has known. Soon, she is keeping company with Matt, though it is largely platonic at first.

For her part, Helen (Vanessa Redgrave) is a bit more worldly in her affairs. John (William Devane), an American Army captain, comes to her estate often, and a relationship develops, culminating in a semi-nude love scene featuring Redgrave. They are both married, but her Royal Navy officer husband is away at sea, and his wife is thousands of miles distant.

Eventually, the kind-hearted Matt Dyson is accepted by the Moreton family, though she is engaged to an English lad. They welcome his visits, when he often brings hard-to-find foods normally on wartime rationing and other presents. But when news of Ken's death in action arrives, Jean's mother condemns their relationship as a kind of betrayal.

Helen and John travel to a Welsh seaside resort, where they make love. Almost immediately after, the Americans ship out by troop train to southern England to prepare for D-Day. In a mad scene, many of the townswomen, some of them pregnant from liaisons with men they may never see again, scramble to catch one last glimpse of their American boyfriends before the train leaves town. Matt shouts from the train that he will return.

Locations

Much of the filming took place on location in northern England, especially in localities near Oldham, Stalybridge and surrounding areas. The opening shot of the film is of a war memorial and this is in Stalybridge town centre, and throughout Glossop. The dance party scene was filmed at Hyde Town Hall.

The sequence showing the troops boarding the train and making their farewells was filmed at Keighley railway station on the Keighley and Worth Valley Railway, making use of authentic World War II locomotives now preserved on the KWVR. A former Royal Ordnance Factory in nearby Steeton was also used.[1]

The exterior shots at the Welsh resort were filmed in Llandudno, North Wales.

References

[1] History Enthusiasts Launch Campaign to Save Rare Pillbox. (http://www.cravenherald.co.uk/news/4773588. History_enthusiasts_launch_campaign_to_save_rare_pillbox/)

External links

- *Yanks* (http://www.imdb.com/title/tt0080157/) at the Internet Movie Database
- *Yanks (Film)* (http://www.allrovi.com/movies/movie/v55700) at AllRovi

American Gigolo

American Gigolo	
Theatrical release poster	
Directed by	Paul Schrader
Produced by	Jerry Bruckheimer
Written by	Paul Schrader
Starring	Richard Gere Lauren Hutton Hector Elizondo Nina Van Pallandt Bill Duke
Music by	Giorgio Moroder
Cinematography	John Bailey
Editing by	Richard Halsey
Distributed by	Paramount Pictures
Release date(s)	February 8, 1980
Running time	117 min.
Country	United States
Language	English
Budget	$4,800,000
Box office	$22,743,674[1] (domestic)

American Gigolo is a 1980 crime drama film, written and directed by Paul Schrader. It is informally considered the second installment in his "lonely man" trilogy, following the Martin Scorsese directed *Taxi Driver* (1976) and preceding *Light Sleeper* (1992).[2]

Plot

Julian Kaye (Richard Gere) is a male prostitute in Los Angeles whose job supports his expensive taste in cars, stereophonic equipment, and clothes. He is, at times, blatantly narcissistic and superficial; however, he claims to take some pleasure in his work from being able to sexually satisfy women.

When on an assignment for his primary procuress, Anne (Nina Van Pallandt), he meets Michelle Stratton (Lauren Hutton), the unhappy wife of a local politician, who becomes interested in him. Julian's other pimp, Leon (Bill Duke), sends him to the house of a financier, Mr. Rheiman, who asks Julian to physically abuse and copulate with his wife while he watches them.

As Julian begins to get to know Michelle, he learns that the financier's wife, Mrs. Rheiman, was murdered. Los Angeles Police Department Detective Sunday (Hector Elizondo) investigates Julian as a primary suspect. Though he was with a client, Lisa Williams (K Callan), on the night of the murder, the client refuses to give Julian an alibi in order to protect her and her husband's reputations.

As Julian's relationship with Michelle deepens, suspicion of the murder mounts against him. He soon realizes that he is being framed and grows increasingly desperate. His decline is visually represented by a degeneration in style as his clothes become rumpled, he goes unshaven, and he even rents a cheap commuter car after his Mercedes SL has been tampered with.

Julian finally confronts Leon, who confesses that one of the other, younger gigolos who works for him had killed the wealthy man's wife, and Leon had conceived the plan to frame Julian. After an argument, Julian accidentally pushes Leon over the apartment balcony and he falls to his death.

With no one to help him, Julian ends up in jail, awaiting trial for the murder. However, when all seems lost, Michelle risks her reputation and that of her husband to provide Julian with the alibi that can save him from prison.

Production

John Travolta, after the successes of *Saturday Night Fever* (1977) and *Grease* (1978) had been offered the Julian Kaye role, but got "cold feet" and dropped out.[3] This is not the only role that Travolta has turned down only to be taken by Richard Gere; it had previously happened with *Days of Heaven* (1978)[4] and occurred again when Travolta was offered the lead in both *An Officer and a Gentleman* (1982) and *Chicago* (2002).[5] Christopher Reeve reportedly turned down the role despite a million dollar fee.[6] Julie Christie was attached to the role of Michelle Stratton at one stage but left the production when Gere was briefly replaced by Travolta.[7] When Gere returned to the project, Lauren Hutton had already been hired for the role. Meryl Streep was also offered the role of Michelle which she declined because she didn't like the tone of the film.[8] Schrader acknowledges that *Pickpocket* (1959) by the French director Robert Bresson was a direct influence on the film;[9][10] the composition of the final shot draws heavily from the film,[11][12] as does the final dialogue.[13] Schrader later provided an introduction to the Criterion Collection DVD of *Pickpocket*. Schrader re-visited many of the themes of *American Gigolo* in his 2007 film, *The Walker*,[14] and says the idea for that film came about while wondering what would have become of the Julian Kaye character.[15] Richard Gere's nude scenes marked the first time a major Hollywood actor was frontally nude in a film,[16][17] and the wardrobe used in the film put Armani on the fashion map.[18]

References

[1] Box Office Mojo. 2010. *American Gigolo (1980)*. [Online] IMDb.com, Inc. (Updated 2010) Available at: (http://www.boxofficemojo.com/movies/?id=americangigolo.htm) [Accessed 24 January 2010]. Archived at (http://www.webcitation.org/5n28WEaQl).

[2] Holden, S., 2007. Crimes of the Naïve, Superficial Heart. *The New York Times*, [internet] 7 December. Available at (http://movies.nytimes.com/2007/12/07/movies/07walk.html) [Accessed 28 January 2010].

[3] Jones, C. 2002. *Richard Gere: On guard*. [Online] BBC (Updated 27 Dec 2002) Available at: (http://news.bbc.co.uk/1/hi/in_depth/uk/2000/newsmakers/2591237.stm) [Accessed 25 January 2010]. Archived at (http://www.webcitation.org/5n2vlsIV6).

[4] Gilbey, R. 2009. *Who's next for a Mickey Rourke-style comeback?*. [Online] Guardian.co.uk (Updated 17 Feb 2009) Available at: (http://www.guardian.co.uk/film/filmblog/2009/feb/16/mickey-rourke-wrestler) [Accessed 25 January 2010]. Archived at (http://www.webcitation.org/5n2wXCKBR).

[5] Lawrence, W., 2007. Travolta as you've never seen him before. *Times Online*, [internet] 30 June. Available at (http://entertainment.timesonline.co.uk/tol/arts_and_entertainment/film/article1989219.ece) [Accessed 25 January 2010]. Archived at (http://www.webcitation.org/5n2wl0xoV).

[6] Holley, J., 2004. A Leading Man for Spinal Cord Research. *The Washington Post*, [internet] 12 October. Available at (http://www.washingtonpost.com/wp-dyn/articles/A23222-2004Oct11.html) [Accessed 25 January 2010]. Archived at (http://www.webcitation.org/5n3XvSoO5).

[7] Yahoo! Movies. 2010. *Julie Christie Biography*. [Online] Yahoo! (Updated 2010) Available at: (http://movies.yahoo.com/movie/contributor/1800020090/bio) [Accessed 26 January 2010]. Archived at (http://www.webcitation.org/5n4P3DZgY).

[8] Smurthwaite, N., 1984. *The Meryl Streep Story*. Beaufort Books. ISBN 978-0-8253-0229-9.

[9] Thompson, R.J., 1998. Pickpocket. *Senses of Cinema*, [online] 1998. Available at: (http://archive.sensesofcinema.com/contents/cteq/00/7/pickpocket.html) [Accessed 27 January 2010]. Archived at (http://www.webcitation.org/5n6kr6A2S).

[10] Auty, C. 2008. *Robert Bresson's Pickpocket*. [Online] Film Forum (Updated 4 Aug 2008) Available at: (http://www.filmforum.org/films/pickpocket.html) [Accessed 27 January 2010]. Archived at (http://www.webcitation.org/5n6lFFD91).

[11] Johnston, S., 2003. Film-makers on film: Paul Schrader. *Telegraph.co.uk*, [internet] 25 January. Available at (http://www.telegraph.co.uk/culture/film/3589003/Film-makers-on-film-Paul-Schrader.html) [Accessed 26 January 2010]. Archived at (http://www.webcitation.org/5n5CfRHMB).

[12] Dawson, T. 2005. *Pickpocket (2005)*. [Online] BBC (Updated 3 Apr 2005) Available at: (http://www.bbc.co.uk/films/2005/04/04/pickpocket_2005_review.shtml) [Accessed 26 January 2010]. Archived at (http://www.webcitation.org/5n5CyDtou).

[13] Sight & Sound. 2007. Robert Bresson: Alias Grace. *British Film Institute*, [internet] November 2007. Available at: (http://www.bfi.org.uk/sightandsound/feature/49407) [Accessed 26 January 2010]. Archived at (http://www.webcitation.org/5n5DP9fzc).

[14] Malcolm, D., 2007. American gigolo in the frame. *London Evening Standard*, [internet] 9 August. Available at (http://www.thisislondon.co.uk/film/review-23407689-american-gigolo-in-the-frame.do) [Accessed 27 January 2010]. Archived at (http://www.webcitation.org/5n65HEfVh).

[15] Schrader, P. 2007. *The Walker*. [Online] Landmark Theatres (Updated 2007) Available at: (http://www.landmarktheatres.com/mn/walker.html) [Accessed 27 January 2010]. Archived at (http://www.webcitation.org/5n65msC6g).

[16] Persall, S., 2009. Male movie stars' naughty bits are nothing new. *St. Petersburg Times*, [internet] 7 March. Available at (http://www.tampabay.com/features/movies/article981982.ece) [Accessed 24 January 2010]. Archived at (http://www.webcitation.org/5n26DnQUF).

[17] Dirks, T. 2009. *History of Sex in Cinema: The Greatest and Most Influential Sexual Films and Scenes*. [Online] Filmsite.org (Updated 2009) Available at: (http://www.filmsite.org/sexinfilms.html) (part 27) [Accessed 24 January 2010]. Archived at (http://www.webcitation.org/5n26j4TVJ).

[18] Allmovie. 2010. *American Gigolo: Overview*. [Online] Macrovision Corporation (Updated 2010) Available at: (http://www.allmovie.com/work/1969) [Accessed 24 January 2010]. Archived at (http://www.webcitation.org/5n27qN68m).

External links

- *American Gigolo* (http://www.imdb.com/title/tt0080365/) at the Internet Movie Database
- *American Gigolo* (http://www.allrovi.com/movies/movie/v1969) at AllRovi
- *American Gigolo* (http://www.rottentomatoes.com/m/american_gigolo/) at Rotten Tomatoes

An Officer and a Gentleman

An Officer and a Gentleman	
Original film poster	
Directed by	Taylor Hackford
Produced by	Martin Elfand Douglas Day Stewart
Written by	Douglas Day Stewart
Starring	Richard Gere Debra Winger Louis Gossett, Jr. David Keith Lisa Blount Robert Loggia Tony Plana
Music by	Jack Nitzsche
Cinematography	Donald E. Thorin
Editing by	Peter Zinner
Studio	Lorimar Film Entertainment
Distributed by	Paramount Pictures
Release date(s)	July 28, 1982
Running time	122 minutes
Country	United States
Language	English
Box office	$129,795,554 (United States)

An Officer and a Gentleman is a 1982 American drama film that tells the story of a U.S. Navy aviation officer candidate who comes into conflict with the Marine Corps Gunnery Sergeant[1] who trains him. It was written by Douglas Day Stewart and directed by Taylor Hackford. It starred Richard Gere, Debra Winger and Louis Gossett, Jr., and was produced by Lorimar Productions for Paramount Pictures. The film's title uses an old expression from the British Royal Navy and subsequently from the U.S. Uniform Code of Military Justice, as being charged with "conduct unbecoming an officer and a gentleman" (from 1860). *An Officer and a Gentleman* was commercially released in the U.S. on July 28, 1982.

Plot

Zachary "Zack" Mayo (Richard Gere) has been living with his father Byron (Robert Loggia), a U.S. Navy boatswain's mate, since early adolescence, after Zack's mother committed suicide. Hoping to put his life on a different path, Zack signs up for the Navy's Aviator Officer Candidate School.

Zack and his fellow OCs are "welcomed" by their head drill instructor, Marine Gunnery Sergeant Emil Foley (Louis Gossett, Jr.). Foley makes it clear that the program is designed to eliminate as many cadets as possible, and that only the best will earn their "prize", a commission in the Navy and a $1,000,000 flight education. Zack hits it off with fellow recruit Sid Worley (David Keith) and female recruit Casey Seeger (Lisa Eilbacher).

Zack and Sid meet two local girls at a Navy-hosted dance - factory workers Paula Pokrifki (Debra Winger) and Lynette Pomeroy (Lisa Blount), with whom each begins a romantic relationship.

Foley rides Zack mercilessly, believing that he could be an outstanding officer but lacks motivation and self discipline. When Zack's side business of selling preshined shoes and belt buckles is discovered, Foley hazes him for an entire weekend in an attempt to make him DOR (drop on request), but Zack refuses to give in. Foley then tells Zack that he will simply have him thrown out; Zack finally breaks down, telling Foley that he has nowhere else to go and has nothing else in his life. Satisfied that Zack has come to a crucial self-realization, Foley lets up on him.

While Zack and Paula spend the next weekend together, she takes him home to meet and have dinner with her family. After dinner, she shows Zack an old picture of her real father. He was an Officer Candidate who had refused to marry her mother when she became pregnant with her.

Later, Zack has a chance to break the record time for negotiating the obstacle course; meanwhile, Seeger will be disqualified if she can't negotiate the Wall that's been giving her so much trouble. Zack abandons his attempt to break the course record in order to coach Seeger over the wall, and she makes it.

Following dinner with Sid and his parents in town, Zack learns that Sid has a long-time girlfriend back home, whom he plans to marry after being commissioned. Meanwhile, Lynette has been dropping hints to Sid that she may be pregnant. During a high-altitude simulation in a pressure chamber, Sid has a sudden anxiety attack. Realizing that he joined up out of a sense of obligation to his family, Sid DORs. Sid then leaves the base without saying goodbye, and Zack and Paula go out to look for him.

Sid goes to Lynette's house and proposes marriage to her. She turns him down, but not before confessing she wasn't pregnant. She wanted him to graduate in order to fulfill her dream of marrying a Naval aviator, and all but curses him for dropping out. She is later cursed by both Zack and Paula when they come to see her about Sid's whereabouts. Despondent over Lynette's rejection, Sid checks into a motel and commits suicide. Zack decides to DOR himself but Foley won't let him go so close to graduation. He and Zack clash in an unofficial martial arts bout with the platoon looking on. Although Zack dominates for most of the fight (mostly fueled by his anger at Foley, who he believed played a part in Sid's suicide by not stopping him from leaving), Foley manages to win by kicking Zack in the groin. Foley tells him he can quit if he wants to.

Zack does show up for graduation, and is sworn into the Navy with his class. Following Naval tradition, he seeks out and receives his first salute from Foley in exchange for a US silver dollar. While tradition calls for the drill instructor to place the coin in his left shirt pocket, Foley places the coin in his right pocket and gives Zack a picture-perfect salute, acknowledging that Zack was a special candidate. Zack tells him he will never forget him and that he never would have made it through without his guidance.

Zack, now Ensign Mayo, seeks out Paula at the factory where she works. He picks her up and walks out with her in his arms to the applause and cheers of her co-workers.

Cast

- Richard Gere as Officer Candidate/Ensign Zack Mayo
- Debra Winger as Paula Pokrifki
- Louis Gossett, Jr. as Gunnery Sergeant Emil Foley
- David Keith as Officer Candidate Sid Worley
- Lisa Blount as Lynette Pomeroy
- Lisa Eilbacher as Officer Candidate/Ensign Casey Seeger
- Tony Plana as Officer Candidate/Ensign Emiliano Della Serra
- Harold Sylvester as Officer Candidate/Ensign Lionel Perryman
- David Caruso as Officer Candidate Topper Daniels
- Robert Loggia as Boatswain's Mate 1st Class Byron Mayo (Zack's father)

- Victor French as Joe Pokrifki (Paula's stepfather)
- Grace Zabriskie as Esther Pokrifki (Paula's mother)
- Ron Hayes as Midshipman
- Tommy Petersen as Young Zack
- Ed Begley Jr. as Voice of Altitude Chamber Instructor
- John Laughlin as Troy (townie who picks a fight with Zack)

Production

Locations

The film was shot in late 1981 on the Olympic Peninsula of Washington state, at Port Townsend and Fort Worden. The U.S. Navy did not permit filming at NAS Pensacola in western Florida, the traditional site of the Aviation Officer Candidate School. Port Townsend stood in for the real NAS (Naval Air Station) in the Puget Sound area, Whidbey Island, which is still an operating NAS today.

A real motel, The Tides Inn, located in Port Townsend was used for the film. Today, there is a plaque outside the room commemorating this. Some early scenes of the film were filmed in Bremerton, with ships of the Puget Sound Naval Shipyard in the background.

The "Dilbert Dunker" scenes were filmed in the swimming pool at what is now Mountain View Elementary School (Mountain View Middle School during filming). According to the director's commentary on the DVD, the dunking machine was constructed specifically for the film and was an exact duplicate of the actual one used by the Navy. As of 2010, Mountain View Elementary is closed; and is now home to the Mountain View Commons, which holds the police station, food bank and YMCA which holds the pool.

The filming location of Paula Pokrifiki's house was 1003 Tremont in Port Townsend. As of 2009, the house is shrouded by a large hedge and the front porch has been remodeled. The neighboring homes and landscape look identical to their appearance in the film, including the 'crooked oak tree' across the street from the Pokrifiki home. This oak tree is visible in the scene near the end of the film in which Richard Gere returns to the home to request Paula's help in finding his friend Sid. In the film, the plot has Paula living a ferry ride away from the naval base. In reality, Paula's home is located approximately 8 blocks from Fort Worden.

Lynette Pomeroy's house was located on Mill Road, just west of the main entrance of the Port Townsend Paper Corp. mill. The house no longer exists, but the concrete driveway pad is still visible.

The interior of the USO building at Fort Worden State Park was used for the reception scene near the beginning of the film.

The concrete structure used during the famous Richard Gere line "I got no place else to go!" is the Battery Kinzie located at Fort Worden State Park. The scene was filmed on the southwest corner of the upper level of the battery. The 'obstacle course' was constructed specifically for the film and was located in the grassy areas just south and southeast of Battery Kinzie.

The decompression chamber was one of the only sets constructed for the film and as of 2009, it is still intact in the basement of building number 225 of the Fort Worden State Park. It can be seen through the windows of the building's basement.

Building 204 of Fort Worden State Park was used as the dormitory and its porch was used for the film's closing 'silver dollar' scene.

The blimp hangar used for the famous fight scene between Louis Gossett Jr. and Richard Gere is located at Fort Worden State Park and as of 2009 is still intact, but has been converted into a 1200 seat performing arts center called the McCurdy Pavilion.

The filming location for the exterior of 'TJ's Restaurant' is located at the Point Hudson marina in Port Townsend. The space is now occupied by a company that makes sails.

Casting

Originally, Country music singer John Denver was signed to play Zack Mayo. But a casting process eventually involved Jeff Bridges, Christopher Reeve, and Richard Gere. Gere eventually beat out all the other actors for the part. John Travolta turned down the role as he did with American Gigolo (another Richard Gere hit).

The role of Paula was originally given to Sigourney Weaver, then to Anjelica Huston and later to Jennifer Jason Leigh, who dropped out to do *Fast Times at Ridgemont High* instead. Eventually, Debra Winger replaced Leigh for the role of Paula. Rebecca de Mornay, Meg Ryan, and Geena Davis, all virtually unknowns at the time, auditioned for the role of Paula before losing out to Winger.

The role of GySgt Foley was difficult to cast. Jack Nicholson turned down the part, and no one else the producers were interested in was available. Screenwriter Stewart then visited the Pensacola area to do research and found out all of the top drill instructors there were African-American, which inspired them to cast Gossett in the role. When cast, Taylor Hackford kept him in separate living quarters from the other actors during *An Officer and a Gentleman* so he could intimidate them more during his scenes as a drill instructor.[2] In addition, Gossett was advised by U.S. Marine Corps Gunnery Sergeant Buck Welcher & Gunnery Sergeant R. Lee Ermey.

Lisa Eilbacher, who played Officer Candidate Casey Seeger, is an avid bodybuilder/fitness buff and said that pretending to be out of shape for the character was the most difficult part about acting in the film.

Props

Richard Gere rides a 750cc T140E Triumph Bonneville introduced halfway in the 1978 selling season. Two T140E Bonnevilles were supplied by Dewey's Cycle Shop in Seattle. One had Receipt no.16787 dated April 8, 1981, as sold to Paramount Pictures. In the United Kingdom, Paramount successfully linked with Triumph Motorcycles (Meriden) Limited to do a mutual promotion. From Triumph's then-chairman, John Rosamond, in his book *Save The Triumph Bonneville !* (Veloce 2009), cinemas showing the film would be promoted at their local Triumph dealer and T140E Triumph Bonnevilles supplied by the dealer would be displayed in cinema foyers.

Ending

Richard Gere balked at shooting the ending of the film, in which Zack arrives at Paula's factory wearing his naval dress whites and carries her off the factory floor. Gere thought the ending wouldn't work because it was too sentimental. Director Taylor Hackford agreed with Gere until, during a rehearsal, the extras playing the workers began to cheer and cry. When Gere saw the scene later, with the music underneath it ("Up Where We Belong") at the right tempo, he said it gave him chills. Gere is now convinced Hackford made the right decision.[3] Screenwriter Michael Hauge, in his book *Writing Screenplays That Sell*, echoed this opinion: "I don't believe that those who criticized this Cinderella-style ending were paying very close attention to who exactly is rescuing whom."

Release

Two versions of the film exist. The original, uncensored R-rated cut and an edited for broadcast television cut (which first aired on NBC in 1986) are nearly identical. The main difference is that a majority of the foul language is edited out when the film airs on regular television. However, the group marching song near the beginning of the film and Mayo's solo marching song are not voiceover edits; they are reshoots of those scenes for television. Also, the sex scene between Mayo and Paula is cut in half, and the scene where Mayo finds Sid's body is also edited.

Reaction

Box office

An Officer and a Gentleman was an enormous box office success and went on to become the third highest grossing film of 1982.[4] It grossed $3,304,679 in its opening weekend[5] and $129,795,554 overall at the domestic box office.[6]

Reception

An Officer and a Gentleman was well received by critics and is widely considered one of the best films of 1982.[7][8][9] The film holds a very high 94% "Fresh" rating on the review aggregate website Rotten Tomatoes.[10] It received rave reviews from critics, most notably from Roger Ebert who gave it four stars. Ebert described *An Officer and a Gentleman* as "a wonderful movie precisely because it's so willing to deal with matters of the heart".[11]

Rex Reed gave a glowing review where he commented: "This movie will make you feel ten feet tall!" The British film critic Mark Kermode, an admirer of Taylor Hackford observed, "It's a much tougher film than people remember it being; it's not a romantic movie, it's actually a movie about blue-collar, down-trodden people."

The film also received recognition from the American Film Institute. It is ranked number 29 on AFI's *100 Years...100 Passions*, a list of America's greatest love stories.[12] *An Officer and a Gentleman* was also named the 68th most inspiring movie on *100 Years...100 Cheers*.[13] The song "Up Where We Belong" was also ranked number 75 on AFI's *100 Years...100 Songs*.[14]

Awards

Award wins:

- Academy Award for Best Supporting Actor - Louis Gossett, Jr.
- Best Music, Original Song - "Up Where We Belong", Jack Nitzsche and Buffy Sainte-Marie (music), Will Jennings (lyrics). Producer Don Simpson complained, "The song is no good. It isn't a hit," and unsuccessfully demanded it be cut from the film. "Up Where We Belong" later became the number one song on the Billboard charts.
- BAFTA Film Award for Best Original Song - "Up Where We Belong", Jack Nitzsche and Buffy Sainte-Marie (music), Will Jennings (lyrics)
- Award of the Japanese Academy for Best Foreign Language Film

Award nominations:

- Best Actress - Debra Winger
- Best Music, Original Score
- Best Film Editing
- Best Writing, Screenplay Written Directly for the Screen.

In popular culture

- The film's final scene has been widely imitated and parodied. The television series *Friends*, *Miranda*, *Killinaskully*, *Sabrina, the Teenage Witch*, Psych, *Reba*, *The Simpsons*, *Spin City*, *Scrubs*, *Spaced*, *South Park*, *The Office*, *Coronation Street*, *Chuck* and the motion picture *Diary of a Mad Black Woman* are among the productions that have paid tribute to this scene.
- *The Simpsons* also satirized the training sequence in "The Springfield Connection" with Marge having trouble climbing over the wall just as Casey Seegar did.
- In the *Family Guy* episode "Emission Impossible", Stewie and Bertram make Peter cry by playing "Up Where We Belong" and says "I love you, Lou Gossett Jr."

Soundtrack

Song	Lyrics by	Performed by
"Up Where We Belong"	Will Jennings	Joe Cocker and Jennifer Warnes
"Treat Me Right"	D. Lubahn and Pat Benatar	Pat Benatar
"Hungry for Your Love"	Van Morrison	Van Morrison
"Be Real"	D. Sahm	The Sir Douglas Quintet
"Tush"	B. Gibbons, D. Hill and F. Beard	ZZ Top
"Tunnel of Love"	M. Knopfler	Dire Straits
"Feelings"	Morris Albert	Morris Albert
"Tie a Yellow Ribbon Round the Ole Oak Tree"	Irwin Levine and L. Russell Brown	
"Anchors Aweigh"	Charles A. Zimmerman, George D. Lottman and Alfred H. Miles	
"Moon River"	Henry Mancini and Johnny Mercer	
"Big Money Dollars"	John Thomas Lenox	
"Gamelan Gong: Barong Dance"	David Lewiston	
"The Plains of Mindanao"	Bayanihan 7	
"Galan Kangin"	Gong Kebyar, Sebatu	

Adaptions

- Takarazuka Revue adapted the movie as a musical in 2010 in Japan (Takarazuka Grand Theater; Tokyo Takarazuka Theater). The production was performed by Star Troupe and the cast included Reon Yuzuki as Zack Mayo, Nene Yumesaki as Paula Pokrifki and Kaname Ouki as Gunnery Sergeant Emil Foley.[15]

References

[1] *Washington Post* (http://www.washingtonpost.com/wp-dyn/articles/A45559-2005Feb22.html)
[2] http://www.nctimes.com/articles/2007/07/03/entertainment/television/030307124750.txt
[3] "Gere begged director not to shoot romantic scene" (http://www.pr-inside.com/gere-begged-director-not-to-shoot-r108124.htm). PR Inside. 2007-04-29. .
[4] "1982 Domestic Grosses" (http://boxofficemojo.com/yearly/chart/?yr=1982&view=releasedate&view2=domestic&sort=gross&order=DESC&&p=.htm). Box Office Mojo.com. . Retrieved June 20, 2010.

[5] "Box Office and Business Information for *An Officer and a Gentleman*" (http://www.imdb.com/title/tt0084434/business). IMDb.com. . Retrieved June 20, 2010.
[6] "Box Office Information for *An Officer and a Gentleman*" (http://boxofficemojo.com/movies/?id=officerandagentleman.htm). Box Office Mojo.com. . Retrieved June 20, 2010.
[7] "The Greatest Films of 1982" (http://www.filmsite.org/1982.html). AMC Filmsite.org. . Retrieved June 20, 2010.
[8] "The Best Movies of 1982 by Rank" (http://www.films101.com/y1982r.htm). Films101.com. . Retrieved June 20, 2010.
[9] "Most Popular Feature Films Released in 1982" (http://www.imdb.com/search/title?year=1982,1982&title_type=feature&sort=moviemeter,asc). IMDb.com. . Retrieved June 20, 2010.
[10] "*An Officer and a Gentleman* Movie Reviews, Pictures" (http://www.rottentomatoes.com/m/officer_and_a_gentleman/). Rotten Tomatoes. . Retrieved June 20, 2010.
[11] "*An Officer and a Gentleman* Movie Review" (http://rogerebert.suntimes.com/apps/pbcs.dll/article?AID=/19820101/REVIEWS/201010336/1023). Chicago Sun-Times. . Retrieved June 20, 2010.
[12] "AFI's 100 Years... 100 Passions" (http://connect.afi.com/site/DocServer/passions100.pdf?docID=248). AFI.com. . Retrieved June 20, 2010.
[13] "AFI's 100 Years... 100 Cheers" (http://connect.afi.com/site/DocServer/cheers100.pdf?docID=202). AFI.com. . Retrieved June 20, 2010.
[14] "AFI's 100 Years... 100 Songs" (http://connect.afi.com/site/DocServer/songs100.pdf?docID=244). AFI.com. . Retrieved June 20, 2010.
[15] http://kageki.hankyu.co.jp/revue/backnumber/10/star_takarazuka_tabidachi/index.html

External links

- *An Officer and a Gentleman* (http://www.imdb.com/title/tt0084434/) at the Internet Movie Database
- *An Officer and a Gentleman* (http://tcmdb.com/title/title.jsp?stid=4742) at the TCM Movie Database
- *An Officer and a Gentleman* (http://www.allrovi.com/movies/movie/v36015) at AllRovi
- *An Officer and a Gentleman* (http://www.rottentomatoes.com/m/officer_and_a_gentleman/) at Rotten Tomatoes

The Honorary Consul (film)

The Honorary Consul	
Directed by	John Mackenzie
Written by	Graham Greene (novel) Christopher Hampton (screenplay)
Starring	Michael Caine Richard Gere Bob Hoskins
Music by	Paul McCartney
Cinematography	Phil Meheux
Editing by	Stuart Baird
Distributed by	Paramount Pictures
Release date(s)	30 September 1983
Running time	104 mins
Country	United Kingdom
Language	English

The Honorary Consul is a 1983 British drama film directed by John Mackenzie and starring Michael Caine, Richard Gere, Bob Hoskins and Elpidia Carrillo. It is based on the novel The Honorary Consul by Graham Greene. [1] [2] It was also released under the title ***Beyond the Limit***.

Cast

- Michael Caine - Charley Fortnum, Consul
- Richard Gere - Eduardo Plarr
- Bob Hoskins - Colonel Perez
- Elpidia Carrillo - Clara
- Joaquim de Almeida - Leon
- Geoffrey Palmer - British Ambassador

References

[1] *The Honorary Consul (film)* (http://www.imdb.com/title/tt0085236/) at the Internet Movie Database
[2] http://ftvdb.bfi.org.uk/sift/title/235999

Breathless (1983 film)

Breathless	
Theatrical release poster	
Directed by	Jim McBride
Produced by	Martin Erlichman
Written by	**Original screenplay** François Truffaut Jean-Luc Godard **Screenplay** L. M. Kit Carson Jim McBride
Starring	Richard Gere Valérie Kaprisky
Music by	Jack Nitzsche
Cinematography	Richard H. Kline
Editing by	Robert Estrin Rachel Igel
Distributed by	Orion Pictures Metro-Goldwyn-Mayer (video and DVD)
Release date(s)	May 13, 1983
Running time	97 min.
Country	United States
Language	English
Box office	$19,910,002

Breathless is a 1983 American drama film starring Richard Gere and Valérie Kaprisky. It is a remake of the 1960 French film *À bout de souffle* (known as *Breathless* in English) and was released in France under the title ***A Bout de Souffle Made in USA***. The original film is about an American girl and a French criminal in Paris. The remake is about a French girl and an American criminal in Los Angeles.

The film was directed by Jim McBride and written by McBride and L. M. Kit Carson.

Plot

Jesse Lujack (Richard Gere) is a drifter in Las Vegas, obsessed with Marvel *Silver Surfer* comic books, the rock and roll music of Jerry Lee Lewis and Monica Poiccard (Valérie Kaprisky), a UCLA architecture undergraduate whom he knows only from a weekend fling in Vegas. As the film opens, Jesse steals a car, intending to drive to Los Angeles. As he speeds down the highway and looks through the owner's possessions, he discovers an automatic handgun in the vehicle's glovebox. Seeing his reckless driving, a policeman gives chase and Jesse is forced off the road and becomes stuck. When the policeman orders him to step away from the car, Jesse impulsively grabs the gun and shoots the officer. Fleeing to Los Angeles, Jesse finds his picture splashed all over the newspaper and TV news as the "cop killer."

On the run, he moves in with Monica. She is captivated by this reckless American and resumes her affair with him. However, she is a star student with big plans and Jesse is jealous of the powerful, successful men in her life.

After Jesse's photograph appears in the newspaper, he is recognized on the street right after dropping Monica off at an architecture-school outing downtown. The police find her and question her on the street. She seems increasingly ambivalent about Jesse, repelled by his instability but drawn to his sense of risk and danger; she does not turn him in. When the police start following her right before Jesse comes back to pick her up, she impulsively accepts his offer to flee to Mexico together.

On the way to Mexico, Monica finds that her picture is on the front page of the national newspaper alongside Jesse's. Realizing the impossibility of her romantic fantasy, she phones the police, but then returns to tell him she did so and plead with him. The police corner them on the street, and he sings Jerry Lee Lewis' "Breathless" to her before grabbing a gun from the ground at his feet as she runs towards him. The film ends in a freeze-frame of Jesse turning to face the police with the gun.

Cast

- Richard Gere as Jesse Lujack
- Valérie Kaprisky as Monica Poiccard
- Art Metrano as Birnbaum
- John P. Ryan as Lt. Parmental
- Robert Dunn as Sgt. Enright
- Lisa Persky as Salesgirl
- James Hong as Grocer
- Miguel Pinero as Carlito

Soundtrack

There is no official soundtrack released. Along with the incidental music for the movie, provided by Jack Nitzsche, these are the songs that are featured in the film:

1. Bad Boy - Mink DeVille
2. High School Confidential - Jerry Lee Lewis
3. Breathless - Jerry Lee Lewis
4. Final Sunset - Brian Eno
5. Wonderful World - Sam Cooke
6. Opening - Philip Glass
7. No Me Hagas Sufrir - Ismael Quintana / Eddie Palmieri
8. Suspicious Minds - Elvis Presley
9. Wind on Wind - Brian Eno
10. Wind on Water - Brian Eno and Robert Fripp
11. Jack the Ripper - Link Wray
12. 365 is my Number / The Message - King Sunny Ade
13. Celtic Soul Brothers - Dexy's Midnight Runners
14. Message of Love - The Pretenders
15. Caca de Vaca - Joe "King" Carrasco
16. Breathless - X

Reception

The film grossed $19,910,002 in the United States.[1] It received mixed reviews; most critics questioned the wisdom of casting Valerie Kaprisky, a real-life, French UCLA student who had had very limited acting experience.

The film has since gained minor cult status. American director Quentin Tarantino cited it as one of the "coolest" movies, commenting: "Here's a movie that indulges completely all my obsessions - comic books, rockabilly music and movies."[2] The Silver Surfer poster in Freddy Newandyke's apartment seen in Reservoir Dogs is an homage to Jesse's Silver Surfer-obsession.[3]

References

[1] "Business details for *Breathless* at the Internet Movie Database" (http://www.imdb.com/title/tt0085276/business). . Retrieved 2007-04-11.
[2] "Tarantino's favorite films at Tarantino.info" (http://www.tarantino.info/wiki/index.php/Tarantino's_favorite_films). . Retrieved 2009-11-24.
[3] "Reservoir Dogs movie connections at imdb.com" (http://www.imdb.com/title/tt0105236/movieconnections). . Retrieved 2009-11-24.

External links

- *Breathless* (http://www.imdb.com/title/tt0085276/) at the Internet Movie Database
- *Breathless* (http://www.allrovi.com/movies/movie/v7055) at AllRovi
- *Breathless* (http://www.boxofficemojo.com/movies/?id=breathless.htm) at Box Office Mojo
- *Breathless* (http://www.rottentomatoes.com/m/1003066/) at Rotten Tomatoes

The Cotton Club (film)

The Cotton Club	
Theatrical release poster	
Directed by	Francis Ford Coppola
Produced by	Robert Evans
Written by	William Kennedy Francis Ford Coppola Mario Puzo Jim Haskins
Starring	Richard Gere Gregory Hines Diane Lane Lonette McKee James Remar Bob Hoskins Fred Gwynne Allen Garfield Nicolas Cage
Music by	John Barry
Cinematography	Stephen Goldblatt
Editing by	Robert Q. Lovett Barry Malkin
Studio	American Zoetrope
Distributed by	Orion Pictures (Theatrical) Metro-Goldwyn-Mayer (DVD)
Release date(s)	December 14, 1984
Running time	128 mins
Country	USA
Language	English
Budget	$58 million
Box office	$25,928,721

The Cotton Club is a 1984 crime-drama, centered on a famed Harlem jazz club of the 1930s, the Cotton Club.

The movie was co-written (with William Kennedy) and directed by Francis Ford Coppola, choreographed by Henry LeTang, and starred Richard Gere, Diane Lane, and Gregory Hines. The cast included Nicolas Cage, Bob Hoskins, Lonette McKee, Laurence Fishburne, Fred Gwynne, Maurice Hines, James Remar, Allen Garfield and Gwen Verdon.

Despite performing poorly at the box office, the film was nominated for several awards, including Golden Globes for Best Director and Best Picture (Drama) and Oscars for best Best Art Direction (Richard Sylbert, George Gaines) and Film Editing.[1] The film, however, also earned a Razzie Award nomination for Diane Lane as Worst Supporting Actress (also for *Streets of Fire*).

The Cotton Club was the first privately financed major motion picture, paid for almost entirely by brothers Fred and Ed Doumani of Las Vegas. The movie was not successful, making only $25,928,721 on a budget of over $50 million.

Plot

A musician named Dixie Dwyer begins working with mobsters to advance his career but falls in love with the girlfriend of gangland kingpin Dutch Schultz.

A dancer from Dixie's neighborhood, Sandman Williams, is hired with his brother by the Cotton Club, a jazz club where most of the performers are black and the customers white. Owney Madden, a mobster, owns the club and runs it with his right-hand man, Frenchy.

Dixie becomes a Hollywood film star, thanks to the help of Madden and the mob but angering Schultz. He also continues to see Schultz's moll, Vera Cicero, whose new nightclub has been financed by the jealous gangster.

In the meantime, Dixie's ambitious younger brother Vincent becomes a gangster in Schultz's mob and eventually a public enemy, holding Frenchy as a hostage.

Sandman alienates his brother Clay at the Cotton Club by agreeing to perform a solo number there. While the club's management interferes with Sandman's romantic interest in Lila, a singer, its cruel treatment of the performers leads to an intervention by Harlem criminal "Bumpy" Rhodes on their behalf.

Dutch Schultz is violently dealt with by Madden's men while Dixie and Sandman perform on the Cotton Club's stage.

Cast

- Richard Gere as Dixie Dwyer
- Gregory Hines as Sandman Williams
- Diane Lane as Vera Cicero
- Lonette McKee as Lila Rose Oliver
- Bob Hoskins as Owney Madden
- James Remar as Dutch Schultz
- Nicolas Cage as Vincent Dwyer
- Allen Garfield as Abbadabba Berman
- Fred Gwynne as Frenchy Demange
- Gwen Verdon as Tish Dwyer
- Lisa Jane Persky as Frances Flegenheimer
- Maurice Hines as Clay Williams
- Julian Beck as Sol Weinstein
- Laurence Fishburne as Bumpy Rhodes
- Tom Waits as Irving Starck
- Glenn Withrow as Ed Popke
- Jennifer Grey as Patsy Dwyer
- Woody Strode as Holmes
- Diane Venora as Gloria Swanson
- Tucker Smallwood as Kid Griffin
- Bill Cobbs as Big Joe Ison
- Rosalind Harris as Fanny Brice
- Sofia Coppola as Kid in Street
- Mario Van Peebles as Dancer
- Larry Marshall as Cab Calloway
- Kim Chan as Ling

Production

Inspired to make *The Cotton Club* by a picture-book history of the famous nightclub by Jim Haskin, Robert Evans was the film's original producer and wanted also to direct.[2] Evans eventually decided that he did not want to direct the film and asked Coppola at the last minute.[3] Richard Sylbert claimed that he told Evans not to hire Coppola because "he resents being in the commercial, narrative, Hollywood movie business".[4] Coppola claimed that he had letters from Sylbert that ask him to work on the film because Evans was crazy. The director also said that "Evans set the tone for the level of extravagance long before I got there".[4] Coppola accepted the job because he needed the money — he was deeply in debt from making *One From the Heart* with his own money.[5] By the time Evans decided not to direct and brought in Coppola, at least $13 million had already been committed.[4] Las Vegas casino owners Edward and Fred Doumani put $30 million into the film. Other financial backers included Arab arms dealer Adnan Khashoggi, and vaudeville promoter Roy Radin, who was eventually murdered. According to William Kennedy in an interview with *Vanity Fair*, the budget of the film was $47 million. However, Francis Ford Coppola told the head of Gaumont, Europe's largest distribution and production company, that he thought the film might cost $65 million.[2]

Author Mario Puzo was the original screenwriter and was eventually replaced by William Kennedy[5] who wrote a rehearsal script in eight days which the cast used for three weeks prior to shooting. According to actor Gregory Hines, a three-hour film was shot during rehearsals.[2]

Over 600 people built sets, created costumes and arranged music at a reported $250,000 a day.[2]

From July 15 to August 22, 1983, 12 scripts were produced, including five during one 48-hour non-stop weekend. Kennedy estimates that between 30-40 scripts were turned out.[2]

On June 7, 1984, Victor L. Sayyah filed a lawsuit against the Doumani brothers, their lawyer David Hurwitz, Evans and Orion Pictures for fraud and breach of contract.[3] Sayyah invested $5 million and claimed that he had little chance of recouping his money because the budget escalated from $25 to $58 million. He accused the Doumanis of forcing out Evans and that an Orion loan to the film of $15 million unnecessarily increased the budget. Evans, in turn, sued Edward Doumani to keep from acting as general partner on the film.[3]

Reaction

The Cotton Club was released on December 14, 1984 and grossed $2.9 million on its opening weekend, fourth place behind *Beverly Hills Cop*, *Dune*, and *2010*.[6] Robert Evans took the blame for hiring Coppola while the director responded that if he had not been hired, the film would have never been made. Evans claimed that Coppola made the budget escalate dramatically by rejecting the script, hiring his own crew, and falling behind schedule.[6]

This film appeared on both Siskel and Ebert's best of 1984.[7] It currently holds a 78% "Fresh" rating on Rotten Tomatoes.

References

[1] "NY Times: The Cotton Club" (http://movies.nytimes.com/movie/11102/The-Cotton-Club/awards). *NY Times*. . Retrieved 2009-01-01.
[2] Scott, Jay (November 12, 1984). "Making of *Cotton Club*: A Legend of its Own". *Globe and Mail*.
[3] Harmetz, Aljean (June 10, 1984). "*Cotton Club* Investor Sues Partners in Film". *New York Times*.
[4] Kroll, Jack (December 24, 1984). "Harlem on My Mind". *Newsweek*.
[5] Gussow, Michael (March 22, 1984). "Parting Film Shots: Coppola and Dutch". *New York Times*.
[6] Salmans, Sandra (December 20, 1984). "Cotton Club is Neither a Smash Nor a Disaster". *The New York Times*.
[7] (http://www.innermind.com/misc/s_e_top.htm#SE1984)

Further reading

- Parish, James Robert (2006). *Fiasco - A History of Hollywood's Iconic Flops*. Hoboken, New Jersey: John Wiley & Sons. pp. 359 pages.. ISBN 978-0-471-69159-4.

External links

- *The Cotton Club* (http://www.imdb.com/title/tt0087089/) at the Internet Movie Database
- *The Cotton Club* (http://www.allrovi.com/movies/movie/v11102) at AllRovi
- *The Cotton Club* (http://www.rottentomatoes.com/m/the_cotton_club/) at Rotten Tomatoes
- Roger Ebert review (http://rogerebert.suntimes.com/apps/pbcs.dll/article?AID=/19840101/REVIEWS/401010327/1023)

King David (film)

King David	
Original film poster	
Directed by	Bruce Beresford
Produced by	Martin Elfand
Written by	Andrew Birkin James Costigan
Starring	Richard Gere Edward Woodward Alice Krige Luigi Montefiori Niall Buggy Jack Klaff
Music by	Carl Davis
Cinematography	Donald McAlpine
Editing by	William M. Anderson
Distributed by	Paramount Pictures
Release date(s)	March 29, 1985
Running time	115 minutes
Country	United Kingdom United States
Language	English
Budget	$21 million
Box office	$5,111,099

King David is a 1985 film about the second king of Israel, David. It was filmed in 1984 in Matera and Craco, Italy. It was directed by Bruce Beresford and starred Richard Gere in the title role.

Cast

- Richard Gere as "David"
- Edward Woodward as "Saul"
- Alice Krige as "Bathsheba"
- Denis Quilley as "Samuel"
- Niall Buggy as "Nathan"
- Cherie Lunghi as "Michal"
- Hurd Hatfield as "Ahimelech"
- Jack Klaff as "Jonathan"
- John Castle as "Abner"
- Tim Woodward as "Joab"
- David de Keyser as "Ahitophel"
- Ian Sears as "Young David"
- Simon Dutton as "Eliab"

- Jean-Marc Barr as "Absalom"
- Arthur Whybrow as "Jesse"
- Christopher Malcolm as "Doeg the Edomite"
- Valentine Pelka as "Shammah"
- Ned Vukovic as "Malchishua"
- Gina Bellman as "Tamar"
- James Coombes as "Amnon"

Reception

The film was not well received by the critics, with the New York Times calling it "...not a good film..." [1]. Rotten Tomatoes gives *King David* a 14% rating. Gere's performance in the film earned him a Golden Raspberry Award nomination for Worst Actor.

External links

- *King David* [2] at the Internet Movie Database
- Rotten Tomatoes [3]

References

[1] http://movies.nytimes.com/movie/review?res=9407E7D91438F93AA15750C0A963948260
[2] http://www.imdb.com/title/tt0089420/
[3] http://www.rottentomatoes.com/m/king_david/

No Mercy (film)

No Mercy	
Theatrical release poster	
Directed by	Richard Pearce
Produced by	D. Constantine Conte
Written by	James Carabatsos
Starring	Richard Gere Kim Basinger
Music by	Alan Silvestri
Cinematography	Michel Brault
Editing by	Gerald B. Greenberg Bill Yahraus
Distributed by	TriStar Pictures
Release date(s)	December 19, 1986
Running time	106 minutes
Country	United States
Language	English
Box office	$12,303,904

No Mercy is a 1986 film starring Richard Gere and Kim Basinger about a cop who accepts an offer to kill a Cajun gangster.

Plot

Eddie Jilette is a Chicago cop on the vengeance trail as he follows his partner's killers to New Orleans to settle his own personal score. Eddie and a Cajun sexpot, Michele, flee through the Louisiana bayous from a murderous crime lord who wants his baby doll back and to destroy the Chicago detective who would avenge his partner's murder. The sexy swamp girl finds herself falling for Eddie, although they clash repeatedly while handcuffed together as they attempt to elude the brutal underworld figure and his henchmen.

Cast

- Richard Gere - Eddie Jillette
- Kim Basinger - Michel Duval
- Jeroen Krabbé - Losado
- George Dzundza - Captain Stemkowski
- Gary Basaraba - Joe Collins
- William Atherton - Allan Deveneux
- Terry Kinney - Paul Deveneux
- Ely Pouget - Julia Fischer
- Bruce McGill - Lieutenant Hall
- Ray Sharkey - Angles Ryan
- Kim Chan - Old Asian Man

External links

- *No Mercy* [1] at the Internet Movie Database

References

[1] http://www.imdb.com/title/tt0091637/

Power (1986 film)

Power	
	Theatrical release poster
Directed by	Sidney Lumet
Produced by	Reene Schisgal Mark Tarlov Kenneth Utt Wolfgang Glattes
Written by	David Himmelstein
Starring	Richard Gere Julie Christie Gene Hackman Kate Capshaw Denzel Washington E. G. Marshall Beatrice Straight
Music by	Cy Coleman
Cinematography	Andrzej Bartkowiak
Studio	Lorimar Productions
Distributed by	20th Century Fox (theatrical) Warner Bros. (DVD)
Release date(s)	January 31, 1986
Running time	111 minutes
Budget	$16 million
Box office	$3,800,000

Power is a 1986 American drama film directed by Sidney Lumet and starring Richard Gere. The original screenplay by David Himmelstein focuses on political corruption and how power affects both those who wield it and the people they try to control.

Denzel Washington's performance in the film as public relations expert Arnold Billing earned him the 1987 NAACP Image Award for Outstanding Supporting Actor in a Motion Picture. Beatrice Straight's performance as Claire Hastings, however, earned her a Golden Raspberry Award nomination for Worst Supporting Actress.

Plot summary

Pete St. John (Richard Gere), a ruthless and highly successful media consultant, is juggling a couple of other political candidates when asked to join the campaign of wealthy but little-known Ohio businessman Jerome Cade (J. T. Walsh), who hopes to win the Senate seat being vacated by St. John's friend Sam Hastings (E. G. Marshall).

He comes into conflict with Arnold Billing (Denzel Washington), a public relations expert whose firm Cade has hired. St. John's investigation into Cade's background prompts Billing to retaliate by bugging St. John's office phones, flooding the basement of his headquarters, tampering with his private jet, and interfering with his other clients.

These actions force St. John to take a hard look at himself and what he has become and to decide whether his ex-wife Ellen Freeman (Julie Christie) and his former partner Wilfred Buckley (Gene Hackman) are right in believing that his success is due primarily to the exploitation of others.

Cast

- Richard Gere ..... Pete St. John
- Julie Christie ..... Ellen Freeman
- Gene Hackman ..... Wilfred Buckley
- Kate Capshaw ..... Sydney Betterman
- Denzel Washington ..... Arnold Billing
- E. G. Marshall ..... Sam Hastings
- Beatrice Straight ..... Claire Hastings
- Fritz Weaver ..... Wallace Furman
- Michael Learned ..... Andrea Stannard
- J. T. Walsh ..... Jerome Cade
- Matt Salinger ..... Phillip Aarons

Production

- Film editing ..... Andrew Mondshein
- Original Music ..... Cy Coleman
- Cinematography ..... Andrzej Bartkowiak
- Production Design ..... Peter S. Larkin
- Art Direction ..... William Barclay
- Set Decoration ..... Thomas C. Tonery
- Costume Design ..... Anna Hill Johnstone

The 20th Century Fox release was filmed in Armonk, New York; the Kaufman Astoria Studios in Queens, New York City; Alburquerque and Santa Fe, New Mexico; Durango, Mexico; Seattle, Washington; Vasquez Rocks Natural Area Park in Agua Dulce, California; and Washington, D.C.

Poster

The poster for the film is primarily black in color, with a white bar on top that reads, in black letters:

"More seductive than sex...

"More addictive than any drug...

"More precious than gold.

"And one man can get it for you.

"For a price."

Below this is the film's title, in all-capital white letters. A small human silhouette is located at the base of the "W" in

"Power." On the black field below is written, in red letters against the black:
"Nothing else comes close."

Critical reception

In his review in the *New York Times*, Vincent Canby described the film as "a well-meaning, witless, insufferably smug movie that . . . suffers from the total lack of a comic imagination." [1]

In the *Chicago Sun-Times*, Roger Ebert observed, "It's smart, it's knowledgeable, sometimes it's funny, occasionally it is very touching, and I learned something from it . . . The movie builds up considerable momentum during its first hour. There's a sense of excitement, of identification with this man who is being driven by his own energy, ambition and cynicism . . . During the second half of the movie, however, a growing disappointment sets in. *Power* is too episodic. It doesn't really declare itself to be about any particular story, any single clear-cut issue . . . the movie itself seems to sense that it's going nowhere. The climax is a pointless, frustrating montage of images. It's a good montage, but it belongs somewhere in the middle of the movie; it states the problem, but not the solution or even the lack of a solution. The movie seems to be asking us to walk out of the theater shaking our heads in disillusionment, but I was more puzzled than disillusioned." [2]

References

[1] *New York Times* review (http://query.nytimes.com/gst/fullpage.html?res=9A0DE1DA113DF932A05752C0A960948260)

[2] *Chicago Sun-Times* review (http://rogerebert.suntimes.com/apps/pbcs.dll/article?AID=/19860131/REVIEWS/601310302/1023)

External links

- *Power* (http://www.imdb.com/title/tt0091786/) at the Internet Movie Database
- *Power* (http://uk.rottentomatoes.com/m/1016609-power/) at Rotten Tomatoes

Miles from Home

Miles from Home	
Theatrical release poster	
Directed by	Gary Sinise
Produced by	Paul Kurta
Written by	Chris Gerolmo
Starring	Brian Dennehy Jason Campbell Richard Gere Helen Hunt Laurie Metcalf
Music by	Robert Folk
Cinematography	Elliot Davis
Editing by	Jane Schwartz Jaffe
Distributed by	Cinecom Pictures
Release date(s)	September 12, 1988
Running time	108 minutes
Country	United States
Language	English

Miles From Home is a 1988 film starring Richard Gere. It is about two brothers who, after being forced off their farm in the debt stricken mid-west, become folk heroes when they begin robbing the banks that have been foreclosing on farmers. The movie was directed by Gary Sinise and written by Chris Gerolmo. The film uses many members of Chicago's Steppenwolf Theatre Company of which Sinise is a co-founder.

The film was filmed entirely on location throughout the state of Iowa, including Worthington, Iowa and Cedar Rapids, Iowa. It was entered into the 1988 Cannes Film Festival.[1]

Featured cast

- Richard Gere as Frank Roberts, Jr.
- Kevin Anderson as Terry Roberts
- Penelope Ann Miller as Sally
- Helen Hunt as Jennifer
- Terry Kinney as Mark
- Brian Dennehy as Frank Roberts, Sr.
- Laurie Metcalf as Exotic Dancer
- Francis Guinan as Tommy Malin
- Judith Ivey as Frances
- Dennis Blome as Sheriff
- John Malkovich as Barry Maxwell
- Laura San Giacomo as Sandy (uncredited)
- Larry Poling as Nikita Khrushchev
- Moira Harris as Frank's Girl (uncredited)

- Dick Stout as Random Fair Goer (uncredited)

References

[1] "Festival de Cannes: Miles from Home" (http://www.festival-cannes.com/en/archives/ficheFilm/id/319/year/1988.html). *festival-cannes.com.* . Retrieved 2009-07-27.

External links

- *Miles from Home* (http://www.imdb.com/title/tt0095640/) at the Internet Movie Database

Internal Affairs (film)

Internal Affairs	
Theatrical release poster	
Directed by	Mike Figgis
Produced by	Frank Mancuso Jr.
Written by	Henry Bean
Starring	Richard Gere Andy García Laurie Metcalf Nancy Travis William Baldwin
Music by	Brian Banks Mike Figgis Anthony Marinelli
Cinematography	John A. Alonzo
Editing by	Robert Estrin
Distributed by	Paramount Pictures
Release date(s)	January 12, 1990
Running time	114 minutes
Country	United States
Language	English
Box office	$27,734,391 (USA)

Internal Affairs is a 1990 American crime-thriller film set in Los Angeles about the police department's Internal Affairs Division.

Directed by Mike Figgis, the film stars Richard Gere as Dennis Peck, a suave womanizer, clever manipulator, and crooked cop who uses his fellow officers as pawns for his own nefarious purposes while showing a tender side as a devoted father. Andy García plays Raymond Avilla, the Internal Affairs agent who becomes obsessed with catching Peck when he suspects that Peck is not the poster boy police officer that the precinct has made him out to be.

Plot

At a night-time drug bust, patrolmen Dennis Peck and Van Stretch arrest a drug pusher and his girlfriend. The girlfriend resists and Stretch viciously assaults both of them. Outside, patrolman Dorian Fletcher sees a man running towards him; he orders the man to stop, then promptly shoots him. Peck discovers that the man had no weapon; Dorian is shocked and repentant, but Peck proceeds to take a knife out of his boot, clean off his prints, and place it in the dead man's hand. Dorian tries to stop Peck, who convinces him that cops watch each others' backs.

Los Angeles, 7 November 1989

Raymond Avila joins the Internal Affairs Division (IAD) of the Los Angeles Police Department (LAPD) and is partnered with Amy Wallace. They are initially assigned to investigate Van Stretch's conduct from the drug-bust. During a mandatory interrogation, it is discovered that Stretch has committed three code 181's for excessive force in less than ten months, has an uncontrollable substance abuse issue, and is a racist. After interviewing his wife Penny, who shows signs of domestic abuse, they start looking closely at his financial holdings, which suggest something suspicious.

Stretch's partner Dennis Peck, so called role model of the LAPD, seems to have no clue to his partner's private life. Yet, as Stretch comes under pressure from Avila to sort himself out, certain issues about Peck begin to surface. An altercation between Peck and Dorian over the arrest of a prostitute/informant is witnessed by several patrolmen, and other officers express their distaste for Peck and his techniques. Stretch is pressured to provide evidence against Peck in return for immunity from prosecution. While this fails, Avila finds a type of ally in Dorian, who shows disgust with the similarities between Avila and Peck but agrees to help. Peck also insinuates making advances on Kathleen, Raymond's wife, if Avila persists in his investigation. Raymond's marriage is starting to wilt due to his increased obsession with the case.

Stretch, pushed to the breaking point, calls his wife and tells her he intends to testify against Peck. Penny, who is having sex with Peck at the time, urges Van not to talk to anyone before she speaks with him first.

6 December 1989

Peck and Stretch are on patrol during the graveyard shift in Huntington Park. While heading through an industrial sector, they run across an abandoned blue van. Everything appears routine, until Stretch opens the sliding door and takes a shotgun blast point blank in the chest. As the shooter emerges from the vehicle, it is clear that this was a hit staged by Peck, who congratulates the killer, and then murders him. He requests assistance to a 187 on a peace officer when the blue van suddenly speeds away, indicating a witness to the crime. Van, amazingly still alive, begs for help. Dennis instead positions himself to strangle him, making it appear to the arriving ambulance crew as if Van died in his arms.

17 December 1989

After making efforts to track down the witness to Van Stretch's murder, a sting is set up to catch him. However, things get bloody after information of the sting is somehow leaked, and Avila and Wallace notice a sudden response from two LAPD SWAT tactical units, who shoot on sight. The witness panics, shooting and killing Dorian, before he is taken out by a police sniper. As he dies in Avila's arms, he identifies Peck as the man behind Stretch's murder.

7 January 1990

Peck meets with Kathleen, insinuating to be IAD himself, to ask about Raymond's behavior at home and other innocent, on-the-surface questions. The real intent is so Raymond, who is "covertly" following Dennis, sees him with Kathleen, thus establishing that Dennis can manipulate the game to his advantage. The episode puts Raymond "on tilt" as he goes back to the office, slams a chair down and is sent home. Entering the elevator he is confronted by Dennis, who beats him up and throws a pair of panties in his face, boasting that he bedded Raymond's wife earlier.

Raymond's rage boils over, and he goes looking for Kathleen, finding her at a restaurant with a client from the gallery where she works. Raymond proves he is totally off the hook when he repeatedly asks Kathleen "who did you have lunch with?" When she does not reply, he reveals that he knows. He then punches the client, slaps Kathleen to the floor and screams obscenities in Spanish at the other patrons as he storms out.

The two (forcefully) make up the following morning when Kathleen convinces Raymond that she would never sleep with Peck.

10 January 1990

Avila and Wallace's continued pressure on Peck's family bears fruit when Peck's wife reveals the name of one of his associates, Steven Arrocas, which also happens to be the last name of two recent homicide victims. (Earlier, Arrocas hired Peck to murder his parents for business purposes.) Wallace and Avila know this is far more than a coincidence.

Arrocas walks in on Peck making love to his (Arrocas') wife. Peck tries to goad Arrocas into killing her, but Arrocas accidentally shoots Peck in the foot instead. Avila and Wallace arrive; when they split up and clear the house, Avila finds the bodies of the Arrocases in the bedroom. Peck bursts out from behind some garbage cans in the garage and shoots Wallace in the flank, then flees. Wallace is rushed to the hospital; her fate is not revealed, though the doctor says she stands a chance. Avila, fearing for his wife's safety, returns home to find Peck about to rape her. Avila holds

Peck at gun-point; Peck pulls his knife out of his boot and lunges at Raymond, who shoots him dead, and then tries to comfort his terrorized wife.

Cast

- Richard Gere as Dennis Peck
- Andy García as Raymond Avila
- Laurie Metcalf as Amy Wallace
- Nancy Travis as Kathleen Avila
- William Baldwin as Van Stretch
- Annabella Sciorra as Heather Peck
- Elijah Wood as Sean Stretch
- Michael Beach as Dorian Fletcher
- Katherine Borowitz as Tova Arrocas
- Faye Grant as Penny Stretch
- John Kapelos as Steven Arrocas
- Hamlet Arman as Carlos

References

External links

- *Internal Affairs* (http://www.imdb.com/title/tt0099850/) at the Internet Movie Database

Pretty Woman

Pretty Woman	
Theatrical release poster	
Directed by	Garry Marshall
Produced by	Arnon Milchan Steven Reuther Gary W. Goldstein
Written by	J.F. Lawton
Starring	Richard Gere Julia Roberts
Music by	James Newton Howard
Cinematography	Charles Minsky
Editing by	Raja Gosnell Priscilla Nedd
Studio	Silver Screen Partners IV
Distributed by	Touchstone Pictures
Release date(s)	March 23, 1990
Running time	119 minutes
Country	United States

Language	English
Budget	$14 million
Box office	$463,407,268

Pretty Woman is a 1990 romantic comedy film set in Los Angeles, California. Written by J.F. Lawton and directed by Garry Marshall, this motion picture features Richard Gere and Julia Roberts, and also Hector Elizondo, Ralph Bellamy, and Jason Alexander in supporting roles. Roberts played the only important female character. The story of *Pretty Woman* centers on the down-on-her-luck Hollywood prostitute Vivian Ward who is hired by a wealthy businessman, Edward Lewis, to be his escort for several business and social functions, and their developing relationship over the course of Vivian's week-long stay with him.

Originally intended to be a dark drama about prostitution in New York City, this motion picture was reconceived as romantic comedy with a large budget. It was widely successful at the box office, and it became one of the highest moneymakers of 1990.

Today it is one of the most financially successful entries in the romantic comedy genre, with an estimated gross income of $463.4 million.[1] Boxofficemojo lists it as the #1 romantic comedy by the highest estimated domestic tickets sold at 42,176,400, slightly ahead of My Big Fat Greek Wedding at 41,419,500 tickets.

The film also received a moderate amount of critical praise, particularly for the performance of Roberts, for which she received a Golden Globe Award, and a nomination for the Academy Award for Best Actress. In addition, the screenwriter J.F. Lawton was nominated for a Writers Guild Award and a BAFTA Award. This movie was followed by a string of similar romantic comedies, including *Runaway Bride* (1999), which re-united Gere and Roberts under the direction of Garry Marshall once again.

Plot

Edward Lewis (Richard Gere), a successful businessman and "corporate raider", takes a detour on Hollywood Boulevard to ask for directions. Receiving little help, he encounters a beautiful prostitute named Vivian Ward (Julia Roberts) who is willing to assist him in getting to his destination.

The morning after, Edward hires Vivian to stay with him for a week as an escort for social events. Vivian advises him that it "will cost him," and he agrees to give her $3,000 and access to his credit cards. Vivian then goes shopping on Rodeo Drive, only to be snubbed by saleswomen who disdain her because of her immodest clothing. Initially, hotel manager Barnard Thompson (Hector Elizondo) is also somewhat taken aback. But he relents and decides to help her buy a dress, even coaching her on dinner etiquette. Edward returns and is visibly amazed by Vivian's transformation. The business dinner does not end well, Edward making clear his intention to dismantle Morse's corporation once it was bought, close down the shipyard which Morse spent 40 years building, and sell the land for real estate. Morse and his grandson leave angrily, and Edward remains preoccupied with the deal afterward. Back in the hotel Edward reveals that he had not spoken to his recently deceased father for 14 and half years.

The next morning, Vivian tells Edward about the snubbing that took place the day before. Edward takes Vivian on a shopping spree. Vivian returns to the same shop that had snubbed her, telling the salesgirls they had made a big mistake.

The following day, Edward takes Vivian to a polo match where he is interested in networking for his business deal. While Vivian chats with David Morse, the grandson of the man involved in Edward's latest deal, Philip Stuckey (Edward's attorney) wonders if she is a spy. Edward re-assures him by telling him how they met, and Philip (Jason Alexander) then approaches Vivian and offers to hire her once she is finished with Edward, inadvertently insulting her. When they return to the hotel, she is furious with Edward for telling Phillip about her. She plans to leave, but he apologizes and persuades her to see out the week. Edward leaves work early the next day and takes a breath-taking Vivian on a date to the opera in San Francisco in his private jet. She is clearly moved by the opera (which is *La traviata*, whose plot deals with a rich man tragically falling in love with a courtesan).

While playing chess with Edward after returning, Vivian convinces him to take the next day off. They spend the entire day together, and then make love, in a personal rather than professional way. Just before she falls asleep, Vivian admits that she's in love with Edward. Over breakfast, Edward offers to put Vivian up in an apartment so he can continue seeing her. She feels insulted and says this is not the "fairy tale" she wants. He then goes off to work without resolving the situation. Vivian's friend, Kit De Luca (Laura San Giacomo), comes to the hotel and realizes that Vivian is in love with Edward.

Edward meets with Mr. Morse, about to close the deal, and changes his mind at the last minute. His time with Vivian has shown him another way of living and working, taking time off and enjoying activities for which he initially had little time. As a result, his strong interest towards his business is put aside. He decides that he would rather help Morse than take over his company. Furious, Philip goes to the hotel to confront Edward, but only finds Vivian there. He blames her for changing Edward and tries to rape her. Edward arrives in time to stop Philip, angrily ordering him to leave the hotel room.

Edward tends to Vivian and tries to convince her to stay with him because she wants to, not because he's paying her. She refuses once again and returns to the apartment she shares with Kit, preparing to leave for San Francisco to earn a G.E.D. in the hopes of a better life. Edward gets into the car with the chauffeur that took her home. Instead of going to the airport, he goes to her apartment arriving accompanied by music from La Traviata. He climbs up the fire escape, despite his fear of heights, with a bouquet of roses clutched between his teeth, to woo her.

His leaping from the white limousine, and then climbing the outside ladder and steps, is a visual urban metaphor for the knight on white horse rescuing the "princess" from the tower, a childhood fantasy Vivian told him about. The film ends as the two of them kiss on the fire escape.

Cast

- Richard Gere as Edward Lewis, a rich, ruthless businessman who is alone on business for a week in Los Angeles. At the start of the film, he borrows a fancy car from his lawyer and winds up, lost, in the red-light district. While asking for directions back to the Beverly Wilshire Hotel he meets a hooker named Vivian.
- Julia Roberts as Vivian Ward, a beautiful, kind-hearted prostitute on Hollywood Boulevard, who is independent and assertive—refusing to have a pimp and fiercely reserving the right to choose her customers and what she would do and not do when with them. She runs into Edward, a wealthy businessman, when he asks her for directions to Beverly Hills. Edward hires Vivian for the night and offers her $3,000 to spend the week as his escort to business social engagements.
- Ralph Bellamy as James Morse, a businessman and owner of an underperforming company that Edward is interested in buying and breaking up. Edward later has a change of heart and offers to partner with Morse for a Navy shipbuilding contract that would effectively make his company strong again.
- Jason Alexander as Philip Stuckey, Edward's insensitive lawyer. Philip pesters Edward after he sees Vivian and David Morse getting along. After learning that Vivian is a prostitute, Philip propositions her (to her dismay). After a lucrative deal falls through because of Edward's feelings for Vivian, he angrily tries to force himself on her but is stopped by Edward.
- John David Carson as Mark Roth
- Laura San Giacomo as Kit De Luca, Vivian's wisecracking friend and roommate, who spent their rent money on drugs. After Vivian gives her rent money and a little more, while telling her that she has 'potential', an inspired Kit begins to plan for a life off the streets.
- Alex Hyde-White as David Morse, James Morse's grandson, who is smart and is being groomed to take over the Morse Company when his grandfather either dies or retires. He plays polo and might have feelings toward Vivian as he shows her his horse during the game that Edward and Vivian attend.

- Amy Yasbeck as Elizabeth Stuckey, Philip's wife, who likes to be the center of attention in everything. She is quite sarcastic to Vivian when they first meet at the polo game, although she does tell Edward that Vivian is sweet.
- Elinor Donahue as Bridget, a friend of Barney Thompson who works in a women's clothing store and is asked by Barney to help Vivian purchase a dress after Vivian has an encounter with two snobby women in another dress store.
- Hector Elizondo as Barnard "Barney" Thompson, the stuffy but golden-hearted manager of the hotel. At first, Barnard does not hide his disdain for Vivian, but he eventually befriends her, helps her buy a cocktail dress, and gives her lessons in table manners.
- Judith Baldwin as Susan, one of Edward's ex-girlfriends, with whom Edward reunites at the beginning of the film. She has gotten married and reveals to Edward that his secretary was one of her bridesmaids.
- Laurelle Brooks Mehus as the night desk clerk where among other scenes she shared the opening hotel scene with Vivian and Edward.

Production

Development

Pretty Woman was initially conceived to be a dark drama about prostitution in New York City in the late 1980s.[2] The relationship between Vivian and Edward also originally harboured controversial themes, including the concept of having Vivian addicted to drugs; part of the deal was that she had to stay off cocaine for a week, because she needed the money to go to Disneyland. Edward eventually throws her out of his car and drives off. The movie was scripted to end with Vivian and her prostitute friend on the bus to Disneyland.[2] These traits, considered by producer Laura Ziskin to be detrimental to the otherwise sympathetic portrayal of her, were removed or incorporated into the character of Vivian's friend, Kit. These "cut scenes" have been found in public view, and some were included on the DVD released on the film's 15th anniversary.[2] One such scene has Vivian offering Edward, "I could just pop ya good and be on my way", indicating a lack of interest in "pillow talk". In another, she is confronted by drug dealers outside The Blue Banana, and rescued by Edward and Darryl.

Pretty Woman bears striking resemblances to Pygmalion myths: particularly George Bernard Shaw's play of the same name, which also formed the basis for the Broadway musical *My Fair Lady*. It was then-Disney Studio President Jeffrey Katzenberg who insisted the film should be re-written as a modern-day fairy tale with qualities of a love story, as opposed to being the dark drama it was originally developed as. It was pitched to Touchstone Pictures and re-written as a romantic comedy. The original script was titled *$3,000*, however this title was changed because executives at Touchstone thought it sounded like a title for a Science Fiction film.[3] It also has unconfirmed references to *That Touch of Mink*, starring Doris Day and Cary Grant.

The opera scene in "Pretty Woman" is also similar to a chapter in one of A.J. Cronin's books ('The Judas Tree') in which a poor girl (not used to upper-class gentility) is taken up by a wealthy gentleman, who wooing her, buys her precious things (such as a beautiful dress and gem necklace) and takes her to the opera: "..while the haunting melody of the aria 'Un bel di' swelled, then faded from the darkening room, he took one swift glance at his companion. Tears were streaming down her cheeks." ('The Judas Tree, Book Club Edition, Page 240, 1961).

Casting

Casting of *Pretty Woman* was a rather lengthy process. Marshall had initially considered Christopher Reeve for the role of Lewis, and Al Pacino turned it down.[4] Pacino went as far as doing a casting reading with Roberts before turning the leading role down.[5] Gere agreed to the project. Reportedly, Gere started off much more active in his role, but Garry Marshall took him aside and said "No, no, no. Richard. In this movie, one of you moves and one of you does not. Guess which one you are?" Julia Roberts was not the first-choice for the role of Vivian, and was not wanted by Disney. Many other actresses were considered at the time. Marshall originally envisioned Karen Allen for the role. When she declined, it went to many better-known actresses of the time including Molly Ringwald, who turned it down because she felt uncomfortable with the content in the script, and did not like the idea of playing a prostitute. She has since stated in several interviews that she regrets turning the role down. Winona Ryder, a popular box-office draw at the time, was considered, and auditioned, but turned down because Marshall felt she was "too young". Jennifer Connelly was also dismissed for the same reason.[2]

Meg Ryan, who was a top choice of Marshall's, turned it down. According to a note written by Marshall, Mary Steenburgen was the first choice to play Vivian Ward. Michelle Pfeiffer turned the role down as well, because she did not like the "tone" of the script.[6] Daryl Hannah was also considered, but turned the role down because she believed it was "degrading to women".[6] Valeria Golino also turned it down as she did not think the movie could work with her thick Italian accent. Jennifer Jason Leigh had auditioned for the part, but later decided not to do the movie after she read the script because she felt it was sexist.[7] When all the other actresses turned down the role, 21-year-old Julia Roberts, who was relatively unknown at the time, with the exception of her Oscar nominated performance in the film *Steel Magnolias* (1989), won the role of Vivian. Her performance made Roberts a star.

Filming

Pretty Woman's budget was not limited, therefore producers could acquire as many locations as possible for shooting on the film's estimated budget of $14 million.[2] The majority of the film was shot on location in Los Angeles, California, specifically in Beverly Hills, and inside soundstages at Walt Disney Studios in Burbank. The escargot restaurant called "The Voltaire" was shot at the "Rex" restaurant), now called the "Cicada" restaurant. The filming of the Beverly Wilshire Hotel lobby was shot at the Ambassador Hotel in Los Angeles. Filming commenced on July 24, 1989, but was immediately plagued by countless problems, including issues with space and time. This included Ferrari and Porsche, who had declined the product placement opportunity of the car Edward drove, because the manufacturers did not want to be associated with soliciting prostitutes.[2] Lotus Cars saw the placement value with such a major feature film. This company supplied a Silver 1989.5 Esprit SE (which was later sold). This gamble paid off as the sales of the Lotus Esprit tripled during 1990-91.

The film's primary shooting commenced on July 24, 1989. Shooting was a generally pleasurable and easy-going experience for those involved, the films budget was broad and the shooting schedule was not tight.[2] While shooting the scene where Vivian is lying down on the floor of Edward's penthouse, watching re-runs of *I Love Lucy*, in order to achieve a genuine laughter, Garry Marshall had to tickle Roberts's feet (out of camera range) to get her to laugh so hysterically, which is featured in the film. Likewise the scene in which Gere playfully snaps the lid of a jewelry case on Roberts' fingers was improvised by Gere, and Roberts' surprised laugh was genuine. During the scene in which Roberts sings along to Prince in the bathtub sliding down and dunking her head under the bubbles, Roberts came up and opened her eyes and saw that everyone had left even the cameraman, who got the shot. In addition, during the love-making scene between Roberts and Gere, Roberts got so nervous that a vein visibly popped out on her forehead. She also developed a case of hives, and calamine lotion was given to clear them until shooting could resume.[2] The filming was completed on October 18.

Reception

Box office

In its opening weekend, *Pretty Woman* opened at #1 at the box office grossing $11,280,591 and averaging $8,513 per theater.[8] Despite the film dropping to number two in its second weekend, it grossed more in its second weekend, grossing $12,471,670.[8] It remained number one at the box office for four non-consecutive weeks and on the top ten for sixteen weeks.[8] The film has grossed $178,406,268 in the United States and $285,000,000 in other territories for a total worldwide gross of $463,406,268.[9] It was also the fourth highest-grossing film of the year in the United

States[10] and the third highest-grossing worldwide.[11]

Critical response

The film received mixed to positive reviews from critics. On Metacritic, *Pretty Woman* received an average score of 51 out of 100 from the 17 reviews it collected.[12] Owen Gleiberman of *Entertainment Weekly* gave the film a D, stating that the film "starts out as a neo-Pygmalion comedy" and with "its tough-hooker heroine, it can work as a feminist version of an upscale princess fantasy." Gleiberman also said that it "pretends to be about how love transcends money" and that it "is really obsessed with status symbols."[13] However, on the movie's twentieth anniversary, Gleiberman wrote another article explaining his review, and ultimately saying that he was wrong.[14] In contrast, Janet Maslin of *The New York Times* stated that "*Pretty Woman* manages to be giddy, lighthearted escapism much of the time" and that "Ms. Roberts... is a complete knockout, and this performance will make her a major star."[15]

Awards and honors

The film received four 1990 Golden Globe Awards nominations: Best Motion Picture, Best Actor for Richard Gere, Best Actress for Julia Roberts, and Best Supporting Actor for Hector Elizondo. The film also earned Roberts her second Academy Award nomination and her first nomination for Best Actress.

Win

- 48th Golden Globe Awards
  - Best Actress - Julia Roberts

Nominated

- British Academy Film Awards
  - BAFTA Award for Best Film (Lost to *Goodfellas*)
- 63rd Academy Awards
  - Best Actress - Julia Roberts (Lost to Kathy Bates)
- 48th Golden Globe Awards
  - Best Motion Picture (Lost to *Green Card*)
  - Best Actor - Richard Gere (Lost to Gérard Depardieu)
  - Best Supporting Actor - Hector Elizondo (Lost to Bruce Davison)
- Writers Guild of America Award for Best Drama Written Directly for the Screen - J.F. Lawton

American Film Institute recognition:

- AFI's 100 Years... 100 Laughs - Nominated[16]
- AFI's 100 Years...100 Movie Quotes:
  - "I want the fairy tale." - Nominated[17]

Music

Pretty Woman is noted for its musical selections and hugely successful soundtrack. The film features the song "Oh, Pretty Woman" by Roy Orbison, which inspired the movie's title. Roxette's "It Must Have Been Love" reached No. 1 on the *Billboard* Hot 100 in June 1990. The soundtrack also features "King of Wishful Thinking" by Go West, "Show Me Your Soul" by the Red Hot Chili Peppers, "No Explanation" by Peter Cetera, "Wild Women Do" by Natalie Cole and "Fallen" by Lauren Wood. The soundtrack went on to be certified three times platinum by the RIAA.[18]

The opera featured in the movie is *La Traviata*, which also served as inspiration for the plot of the movie. The highly dramatic aria fragment that is repeated in the movie is from the end of "*Dammi tu forza!*" ("Give me your strength!")

from the opera. The piano piece which Richard Gere's character plays in the hotel lobby was composed by and performed by Gere. Julia Roberts sings the song "Kiss" by Prince while Richard Gere's character is on the phone. Background music is composed by James Newton Howard. Entitled "He Sleeps/Love Theme", this piano composition is inspired by Bruce Springsteen's "Racing in the Street."

Soundtrack

Pretty Woman	
Soundtrack album by Various artists	
Released	February 14, 1990
Genre	Pop, Rock
Length	43:36
Label	Capitol

Professional ratings	
Review scores	
Source	**Rating**
Allmusic	★★★★★ link [19]

The soundtrack was released on February 14, 1990[20][21] and featured snapshot of up-and-coming acts of the 90s and power-pop.

Track listing

No.	Title	Length
1.	"Wild Women Do" (performed by Natalie Cole)	4:06
2.	"Fame '90" (performed by David Bowie)	3:36
3.	"King of Wishful Thinking" (performed by Go West)	4:00
4.	"Tangled" (performed by Jane Wiedlin)	4:18
5.	"It Must Have Been Love" (performed by Roxette)	4:17
6.	"Life in Detail" (performed by Robert Palmer)	4:07
7.	"No Explanation" (performed by Peter Cetera)	4:19
8.	"Real Wild Child (Wild One)" (performed by Christopher Otcasek)	3:39
9.	"Fallen" (performed by Lauren Wood)	3:59
10.	"Oh, Pretty Woman" (performed by Roy Orbison)	2:55
11.	"Show Me Your Soul" (performed by Red Hot Chili Peppers)	4:20
Total length:		**43:36**

References

[1] "[[Box Office Mojo (http://www.boxofficemojo.com/movies/?id=prettywoman.htm)]"]. . Retrieved 2007-07-12.
[2] (DVD) *Pretty Woman: 15th anniversary*. Buena Vista Home Entertainment, Touchstone. 2005.
[3] Stewart, James B (2005). DisneyWar. New York: Simon & Schuster. p. 110. ISBN 978-0-7432-6709-0.
[4] *Pretty Woman* casting information and trivia at IMDB (http://www.imdb.com/title/tt0100405/trivia); accessed May 17, 2007.
[5] "Al Pacino interview by Larry King transcript" (http://transcripts.cnn.com/TRANSCRIPTS/0706/15/lkl.01.html). *CNN*. .
[6] "Darly Hannah pleased to decline Pretty Woman" (http://www.contactmusic.com/news.nsf/article/hannah pleased to decline pretty woman offer_1023365). .
[7] Boris Kachka (December 4, 2005). "Lone Star. Jennifer Jason Leigh plays an extroverted striver in Abigail's Party. Now, that's a stretch." (http://nymag.com/nymetro/arts/theater/15247/). *New York Magazine* (New York Media Holdings, LLC.): 2. .
[8] "Pretty Woman (1990) - Weekend Box Office" (http://www.boxofficemojo.com/movies/?page=weekend&id=prettywoman.htm). *Box Office Mojo* (Amazon.com). . Retrieved 2009-09-29.
[9] "Pretty Woman (1990)" (http://www.boxofficemojo.com/movies/?id=prettywoman.htm). *Box Office Mojo* (Amazon.com). . Retrieved 2009-09-29.
[10] "1990 Yearly Box Office Results" (http://www.boxofficemojo.com/yearly/chart/?yr=1990&p=.htm). *Box Office Mojo* (Amazon.com). . Retrieved 2009-09-29.
[11] "1990 Yearly Box Office Results" (http://www.boxofficemojo.com/yearly/chart/?view2=worldwide&yr=1990&p=.htm). *Box Office Mojo* (Amazon.com). . Retrieved 2009-09-29.
[12] "Pretty Woman reviews at Metacritic.com" (http://www.metacritic.com/movie/pretty-woman). Metacritic. . Retrieved 2009-09-29.
[13] Owen Gleiberman (1990-03-23). *Pretty Woman* (http://www.ew.com/ew/article/0,,316998,00.html). Entertainment Weekly. . Retrieved 2009-09-29.
[14] Gleiberman, Owen. "'Pretty Woman': 20 years after my most infamous review (yes, I gave it a D), here's my mea culpa -- and also my defense" (http://insidemovies.ew.com/2010/03/24/pretty-woman-my-most-infamous-review/). *Entertainment Weekly*. Entertainment Weekly. . Retrieved 15 July 2011.
[15] Janet Maslin (1990-03-23). *Movie Review - Pretty Woman - Review* (http://movies.nytimes.com/movie/review?res=9C0CE2DD143EF930A15750C0A966958260). The New York Times. . Retrieved 2009-09-29.
[16] AFI's 100 Years...100 Laughs Nominees (http://www.afi.com/Docs/100Years/laughs500.pdf)
[17] AFI's 100 Years...100 Movie Quotes Nominees (http://www.afi.com/Docs/100Years/quotes400.pdf)
[18] "Pretty Woman's soundtrack RIAA multi platinum award" (http://www.riaa.com/goldandplatinumdata.php?resultpage=1&table=SEARCH_RESULTS&action=&title=pretty woman&perPage=25). www.riaa.com. . Retrieved 2009-10-12.
[19] http://www.allmusic.com/album/r117951
[20] "Pretty Woman Original Soundtrack" (http://www.amazon.com/Pretty-Woman-1990-Various-Artists/dp/B000002UW2/ref=pd_sim_sbs_m_1). Amazon.com. . Retrieved 21 February 2011.
[21] "Pretty Woman Original Soundtrack" (http://www.allmusic.com/album/pretty-woman-r117951). Allmusic.com. . Retrieved 21 February 2011.

External links

- *Pretty Woman* (http://www.imdb.com/title/tt0100405/) at the Internet Movie Database
- *Pretty Woman* (http://www.allrovi.com/movies/movie/v39093) at AllRovi
- *Pretty Woman* (http://www.rottentomatoes.com/m/pretty_woman/) at Rotten Tomatoes
- *Pretty Woman* (http://www.boxofficemojo.com/movies/?id=prettywoman.htm) at Box Office Mojo

http://www.filmpinari.com http://www.ek-gelir-kariyer.net http://www.dizimizizle.com

Rhapsody in August

Rhapsody in August	
Directed by	Akira Kurosawa
Produced by	Hisao Kurosawa
Written by	Akira Kurosawa
Starring	Sachiko Murase Richard Gere
Music by	Shinichirô Ikebe
Distributed by	Shochiku Films Ltd.
Release date(s)	May 25, 1991
Running time	98 minutes
Country	Japan
Language	Japanese and English

Rhapsody in August (八月の狂詩曲 *Hachigatsu no rapusodī*, aka *Hachigatsu no kyōshikyoku*) is a 1991 Japanese film by Akira Kurosawa. The story centers on an elderly hibakusha, who lost her husband in the 1945 atomic bombing of Nagasaki, caring for her four grandchildren over the summer. She learns of a long-lost brother, Suzujiro, living in Hawaii who wants her to visit him before he dies. American film star Richard Gere appears as Suzujiro's son Clark.

Plot

Rhapsody in August is a tale of three generations and their responses to the atomic bombing of Japan. Kane is an elderly woman whose husband was killed in the bombing of Nagasaki. Next, come her two children and their spouses, all of whom grew up in postwar Japan, as well as their Nisei cousin Clark (played by Richard Gere) who grew up in America. Finally, there are Kane's four grandchildren, who were born after the Japanese economic miracle and provide most of the dialogue in the film.

Kane's grandchildren come to visit her at her rural home on Kyūshū one summer while their parents visit a man who may or may not be Kane's brother in Hawaii. Like most children, they are bored out of their minds, find her cooking to be disgusting, and escape to the urban environment of Nagasaki the first chance they get. While in Nagasaki the children visit the spot where their grandfather was killed in 1945 and become aware of the atomic bombing for the first time in their lives. They slowly come to have more respect for their grandmother and also grow to question the United States for dropping the Bomb.

In the meantime they receive a telegram from their American cousins, who turn out to be rich and offer the parents a job managing their pineapple fields in Hawaii. Matters are complicated when, in their response, the grandchildren mention the attack, which infuriates their parents. To smooth things over, one of the Japanese-Americans (Clark) travels to Japan to be with Kane for the anniversary. While there, Kane and the grandchildren reconcile with Clark over the bombing.

Cast

- Sachiko Murase as Kane (The Grandmother)
- Hisashi Igawa as Tadao (Kane's Son)
- Narumi Kayashima as Machiko (Tadao's Wife)
- Tomoko Otakara as Tami (Tadao's Daughter)
- Mitsunori Isaki as Shinjiro (Tadao's Son)
- Toshie Negishi as Yoshie (Kane's Daughter)
- Hidetaka Yoshioka as Tateo (Yoshie's Son)
- Choichiro Kawarazaki as Noboru (Yoshie's Husband)
- Mieko Suzuki as Minako (Yoshie's Daughter)
- Richard Gere as Clark (Kane's Nephew)

Reception

Rhapsody in August received mixed reviews on its release in 1991.

Some critics made much of the fact that the film centered on the film's depiction of the atomic bombing as a war crime while omitting details of Japanese war crimes in the Pacific War. When *Rhapsody* premiered at the 1991 Cannes Film Festival,[1] one journalist cried out at a press conference, "Why was the bomb dropped in the first place?" At the Tokyo Film Festival, critics of Japanese militarism said Kurosawa had ignored the historical facts leading up to the bomb. Japanese cultural critic Inuhiko Yomota commented:

"Many critics, myself included, thought Kurosawa chauvinistic in his portrayal of the Japanese as victims of the war, while ignoring the brutal actions of the Japanese and whitewashing them with cheap humanist sentiment."[2]

Kurosawa's response was that wars are between governments, not people, and denied any anti-American agenda.[3]

About the Japanese title

The Japanese title (八月の狂詩曲 *Hachigatsu no rapusodī*) is also known as *Hachigatsu no kyōshikyoku*.[4] "八月" means August, and "狂詩曲" means rhapsody. Both are Japanese kanji words. "狂詩曲" is usually pronounced "kyōshikyoku." When this film released in Japan, 1991, Kurosawa added furigana "ラプソディー rapusodī" to the word "狂詩曲" contrary to the standard usage of Japanese.[5][6][7] So the correct romanization of the official Japanese title is *Hachigatsu no rapusodī*. But, often, the Japanese title has been cited without the furigana in various media. This is the reason why the misreading *Hachigatsu no kyōshikyoku* has become more widely known than the correct pronunciation.

References

[1] "Festival de Cannes: Rhapsody in August" (http://www.festival-cannes.com/en/archives/ficheFilm/id/84/year/1991.html). *festival-cannes.com*. . Retrieved 2009-08-12.
[2] Hibakusha Cinema:Intro (http://wwwmcc.murdoch.edu.au/~mickbrod/postmodm/m/text/hibakeds.html#foot 27)
[3] "Rhapsody In August" (http://rogerebert.suntimes.com/apps/pbcs.dll/article?AID=/19920221/REVIEWS/202210302/1023). *Chicago Sun-Times*. .
[4] The Internet Movie Database (http://www.imdb.com/title/tt0101991/)
[5] Shochiku official web site (Japanese) (http://www.shochiku.co.jp/video/japanese/ha/dvd/da0721.html)
[6] Akira Kurosawa, Masato Harada. (1995). *Akira Kurosawa Talks* (□澤明語る Kurosawa Akira kataru). Benesse Corporation (Japanese)
[7] Kazuko Kurosawa. (2004). *Papa, Akira Kurosawa* (パパ、□澤明 Papa, Kurosawa Akira), page 306. Bungei Shunjū. (Japanese)

External links

- *Rhapsody in August* (http://www.imdb.com/title/tt0101991/) at the Internet Movie Database
- *Rhapsody in August* (http://www.jmdb.ne.jp/1991/do001040.htm) (**Japanese**) at the Japanese Movie Database

Final Analysis

Final Analysis	
Theatrical release poster	
Directed by	Phil Joanou
Produced by	**Executive Producers:** Richard Gere Maggie Wilde **Producers:** Paul Junger Witt Charles Roven Tony Thomas
Screenplay by	Wesley Strick
Story by	Robert H. Berger Wesley Strick
Starring	Richard Gere Kim Basinger Uma Thurman Eric Roberts Keith David
Music by	George Fenton
Cinematography	Jordan Cronenweth
Editing by	Thom Noble
Distributed by	Warner Bros.
Release date(s)	February 7, 1992 (United States)
Running time	124 minutes
Country	United States
Language	English
Budget	$43 million
Box office	$28,590,665

Final Analysis (1992) is an American neo-noir drama directed by Phil Joanou and written by Wesley Strick. It stars Richard Gere, Kim Basinger and Uma Thurman. The executive producers were Gere and Maggie Wilde.[1]

The neo-noir style of *Final Analysis* imitates Hitchcockian thrillers like *Vertigo*.

Plot

Isaac Barr (Richard Gere) is a top-notch San Francisco Freudian psychiatrist, who has Diana Baylor (Uma Thurman) on the patient's couch. He is treating her for frightening and horrific childhood memories, which include images of her drunken father and his death in a fire for which she wasn't blamed.

One night, Heather Evans (Kim Basinger) enters Barr's office and says she is Baylor's sister. She asks Barr for information about her sister's case. It is implied, as part of the treatment, that Isaac speak to Heather to find out more about her sister's past experiences and determine if she might provide information Diana has forgotten.

Not long after, Heather seduces Isaac, and a steamy affair follows. The problem: Heather is married to Jimmy Evans (Eric Roberts), a violent and wealthy gangster. She also has a way of embarrassing Jimmy in public by taking a sip of wine and then flipping into an attack of "pathological intoxication," which can end with the restaurant in shambles.

It turns out Heather is trying to involve unsuspecting Isaac in a diabolical plan to murder Jimmy and collect a $4 million double indemnity life insurance policy on him. She's also using Diana as bait and wants Isaac framed for the murder.

Cast

- Richard Gere as Dr. Isaac Barr
- Kim Basinger as Heather Evans
- Uma Thurman as Diana Baylor
- Eric Roberts as Jimmy Evans
- Paul Guilfoyle as Mike O'Brien
- Keith David as Detective Huggins
- Robert Harper as Alan Lowenthal
- Agustin Rodriguez as Pepe Carrero
- Rita Zohar as Dr. Grusin
- George Murdock as Judge Costello
- Shirley Prestia as Dist. Atty. Kaufman
- Tony Genaro as Hector
- Katherine Cortez as Woman Speaker
- Wood Moy as Dr. Lee
- Corey Fischer as Forensic Doctor
- Jack Shearer as Insurance Consultant Doctor
- Lee Anthony as Judge
- Derick Alexander as Ambulance Attendant
- Abigail Van Alyn as Night Nurse

Filming

Filming locations included City Hall in Downtown Los Angeles, California.

Reception

Critical response

Film critic Roger Ebert liked the screenplay and thought director Alfred Hitchcock, known for these types of thrillers, would have liked it as well. He wrote, "I'm a sucker for movies that look and feel like this. I like the pounding romantic music, the tempestuous sex scenes, the crafty ways that neurotic meddlers destroy the lives of their victims, and of course the handcrafted climax..."[2]

Vincent Canby, film critic for *The New York Times,* was pleased with the work of the actors in the film and wrote, "Mr. Gere and Ms. Basinger are attractive as the furious lovers, but Mr. Roberts is the film's electrical force whenever he is on screen. Ms. Thurman does well as a sort of up scale slavey."[3]

The staff at *Variety* magazine gave the film a positive film review, writing, "Final Analysis is a crackling good psychological melodrama [from a screen story by Robert Berger and Wesley Strick] in which star power and slick surfaces are used to potent advantage. Tantalizing double-crosses mount right up to the eerie final scene."[4]

However, many reviews were negative. Critic Kathleen Maher wrote, "Joanou, with his puppy dog devotion to *noir* thrillers and Hitchcock, is hoping to get it all right by painting by the numbers. He's mixed parts of *Double Indemnity, The Big Sleep,* and *Vertigo,* but the result doesn't even live up to *Dead Again...*" Maher also says she's seen Gere's acting like this before, and added: "[B]ut Gere reverts to that shell-shocked acting style he adopts when lost at sea."[5] Rita Kempley, writing in *The Washington Post*, called the film "an implausible psycho thriller" and said director Joanou "doesn't have any of his own ideas."[6]

Currently, the film has a 52% "Rotten" rating at Rotten Tomatoes, based on 23 reviews.[7]

Awards

Nominations

- MTV Movie Awards
  - Most Desirable Female, Kim Basinger; 1992.
- Golden Raspberry Awards
  - Worst Actress - Kim Basinger (also for *Cool World*)
  - Worst Picture - Charles Roven, Paul Junger Witt, and Tony Thomas
  - Worst Screenplay - Wesley Strick (also story) and Robert Berger (story)

Distribution

The producers used the following tagline to market the film:

> *A psychiatrist and two beautiful sisters playing the ultimate mind game.*

The film opened in wide release on February 7, 1992.

Box office

The box-office receipts were considered poor given the talent of Gere and Basinger, and the well regarded director. The first week's gross was $6,411,441 and the total receipts for the film's run were $28,590,665.

In its widest release the film was featured in 1,599 theaters across the United States.[8]

References

[1] *Final Analysis* (http://www.imdb.com/title/tt0104265/) at the Internet Movie Database.
[2] Ebert, Roger (http://rogerebert.suntimes.com/apps/pbcs.dll/article?AID=/19920207/REVIEWS/202070301/1023). *Chicago Sun-Times,* film review, February 7, 1992. Last accessed: January 18, 2008.
[3] Canby, Vincent (http://movies2.nytimes.com/mem/movies/review.html?_r=1&title1=FINAL ANALYSIS (MOVIE)&title2=&reviewer=Vincent Canby&pdate=19920207&v_id=&oref=slogin). *The New York Times,* film review, February 7, 1992.
[4] *Variety* (http://www.variety.com/review/VE1117790901.html?categoryid=31&cs=1&p=0). Film review, February 7, 1992. Last accessed: January 18, 2008.
[5] Maher, Kathleen (http://www.austinchronicle.com/gyrobase/Calendar/Film?Film=oid:139193). *The Austin Chronicle,* February 14, 1992.
[6] Kempley, Rita (http://www.washingtonpost.com/wp-srv/style/longterm/movies/videos/finalanalysisrkempley_a0a298.htm). *The Washington Post,* "*Final Analysis,* an implausible psycho thriller," February 7, 1992.
[7] *Final Analysis* (http://www.rottentomatoes.com/m/final_analysis/) at Rotten Tomatoes. Last accessed: November 3, 2011.
[8] The Numbers (http://www.the-numbers.com/movies/1992/0FASS.php) box office data. Last accessed: November 30, 2007.

External links

- *Final Analysis* (http://www.imdb.com/title/tt0104265/) at the Internet Movie Database

Mr. Jones (film)

Mr. Jones	
Theatrical release poster	
Directed by	Mike Figgis
Produced by	Debra Greenfield Alan Greisman
Written by	Eric Roth Michael Cristofer
Starring	Richard Gere Lena Olin Anne Bancroft Tom Irwin Delroy Lindo Lauren Tom
Music by	Maurice Jarre
Cinematography	Juan Ruiz Anchía
Editing by	Tom Rolf
Distributed by	TriStar Pictures
Release date(s)	October 8, 1993
Running time	114 min.
Budget	$25 million
Box office	$8,345,845

Mr. Jones is a 1993 romantic drama film starring Richard Gere, Lena Olin, Anne Bancroft, Tom Irwin and Delroy Lindo, and directed by Mike Figgis.

Plot

Mr. Jones (Gere) is a man suffering from bipolar disorder, a disease that affords him periods of intense emotional pleasure and expansiveness but which also results in periods of suicidal depression. Libbie (Olin), a doctor at a psychiatric hospital, takes an interest in his condition, and also in him.

Reception

The film was released to mixed reviews; movie historian Leonard Maltin remarked that "Gere is fine, but his onscreen behavior turns this into *The Jester of Tides*." Indeed, Gere received praise for his performance as the troubled title character. Many critics noted that the film would've been better if the romance plot was left out, since it appeared forced and contrived.

Production

To prepare for the film, Richard Gere, Mike Figgis and Eric Roth did a tremendous amount of research and studying on bipolar disorder. Gere met with several people who have the disorder to gain insight and knowledge on what to accurately portray. There is a a shorter director's cut that Figgis presented at the Munich film festival in 2006.

Michelle Pfeiffer gave up the female lead to take on the part of Catwoman in *Batman Returns*.

Props

As in his earlier hit film, *An Officer and a Gentleman*, Richard Gere's character rides a Triumph Bonneville motorcycle.

External links

- *Mr. Jones* [1] at the Internet Movie Database
- *Mr. Jones* [2] at Rotten Tomatoes
- *Mr. Jones* [3] at Box Office Mojo

References

[1] http://www.imdb.com/title/tt0107611/
[2] http://www.rottentomatoes.com/m/mr_jones/
[3] http://www.boxofficemojo.com/movies/?id=mrjones.htm

Sommersby

Sommersby	
Sommersby Promotional Movie Poster	
Directed by	Jon Amiel
Produced by	Arnon Milchan Steven Reuther
Written by	**1982 screenplay:** Daniel Vigne Jean-Claude Carrière Natalie Zemon Davis **Story:** Nicholas Meyer Anthony Shaffer **Screenplay:** Nicholas Meyer Sarah Kernochan
Starring	Richard Gere Jodie Foster Bill Pullman James Earl Jones
Music by	Danny Elfman
Cinematography	Philippe Rousselot
Editing by	Peter Boyle
Studio	Le Studio Canal+ Regency Enterprises Alcor Films
Distributed by	Warner Bros.
Release date(s)	February 5, 1993
Running time	114 minutes
Country	United States
Language	English
Budget	$30 million
Box office	$140,081,992

Sommersby is a 1993 romantic drama film directed by Jon Amiel and starring Richard Gere, Jodie Foster, Bill Pullman and James Earl Jones.

Set in the Reconstruction period following the U.S. Civil War, the story is adapted from the historical account of 16th century French peasant Martin Guerre (previously filmed by Daniel Vigne as *The Return of Martin Guerre* in 1982).

Plot

John "Jack" Sommersby left his farm to fight in the American Civil War but has not returned home afterward, and is presumed dead. Despite the hardship of working their farm without him, his apparent widow Laurel (played by Foster) is quite content in his absence, as Jack was an unpleasant and abusive husband. She even makes remarriage plans with one of her neighbors, Orin Meacham (Pullman), who despite his own hardships (such as a wooden foot, which he wears to replace one that was lost in the war) has been helping her and her young son with the farmwork.

One day, Jack (Gere) seemingly returns with a complete change of heart. He is now kind and loving to Laurel and their young son. In the evenings, he reads to them from Homer's *Iliad*, which the old Jack never would have done. He claims that the book was given to him by a man he met in prison, and that "War changes you; makes you appreciate things". Jack and Laurel rekindle their intimacy and Laurel soon becomes pregnant.

Displaced from his courtship of Laurel, Meacham immediately suspects this "new" Sommersby as an impostor. The town shoemaker also finds that this man's foot is two sizes smaller than the shoe template which had been made for Sommersby before the war.

In order to revive the local economy, Sommersby suggests Burley tobacco as a cash crop. He raises the seed money by selling parts of his own farm to people who will then work the land to grow tobacco. This raises further doubts in his old neighbors who believe that the "old" Jack would not be so hasty to give away his beloved father's land, as well as resentment among Confederate veterans about the inclusion of former slaves.

One black freedman living on Sommersby's land is brutally attacked and dropped at Sommersby's door, by men proclaiming themselves the Knights of the White Camellia (one of them is Meacham, distinguished by his wooden foot). Jack is threatened in an attempt to force him to exclude Black people from the landowning but he refuses, saying that they can "own what they pay for".

Upon taking the townspeople's money, he sets off to buy the tobacco seed claiming that the crops will raise enough funds to rebuild the town church. Great suspicion and skepticism falls upon him (and by association, Laurel and their son) when he does not return at the expected time. He does, however, return. All those that bought in on the deal set to work, transforming the dull and lifeless plantation into a breeding ground of promise and prosperity. Laurel gives birth to a daughter, Rachel.

Shortly after Rachel's baptism, two U.S. Marshals appear in town to arrest Jack Sommersby. He is charged with murder, which carries the death penalty if convicted. Once the trial begins, Laurel's attempts to save her husband quickly focus on the question of his identity: whether this "Jack" is who he claims to be, or a look-a-like who met the real Sommersby whilst in prison for deserting the Confederate Army.

Laurel and Jack's lawyer agree to argue that her husband is an impostor, not the same man who left Laurel to fight in the war. This would save her husband (or supposed husband) from hanging for murder, although he would still be imprisoned for several years for fraud and desertion. Meacham devises this plan in exchange for Laurel promising to marry him upon "Sommersby's" imprisonment.

Jack fires the lawyer and sets about re-establishing himself as the real Sommersby. Several witnesses are brought up to discredit this Sommersby as a fraud, who state that he is one Horace Townsend, an English teacher from Virginia.

One witness says that the man currently posing as Jack defrauded his township of several thousand dollars after claiming he wanted to help rebuild the schoolhouse there. Sommersby quickly discredits the man's testimony by identifying him as one of the Klansmen who had threatened him earlier. Jack also points out that Orin Meacham was another of those men, and that this is all a set-up to try to rob the new black farmers of the land they have bought. When the black judge confronts the witness on this charge, the witness snaps, "When the Yankees have all gone you'll be back in the field where you belong!" The judge silences him and sentences him to 30 days for contempt, increased to 60 days upon the man's protest.

As the drama unfolds, Jack asks Laurel to give the reason she knows he is not the "real" Jack Sommersby; she replies (after some berating) "…because I never loved him the way I love you!" With this her charade ends and she says that she believes the Jack before her to be her real husband.

The judge calls Jack to his bench to ask whether he wishes to be tried as Jack Sommersby even if it will certainly mean death by hanging. Jack glances at the freed blacks who have been farming his land, and then he glances at his wife and his daughter, who would be respectively condemned as an adulteress and a bastard child if he claimed the identity of Horace Townsend. He calmly states that he wants to be tried as John "Jack" Sommersby.

Jack is convicted of first degree murder and is sentenced to death by hanging. While awaiting death, he is asked by Laurel to tell the truth. She asks, "Are you John Sommersby?" Laurel mentions the book on Homer's works that he holds. Jack tells her the story of how a man had to share a cell with another man, who looked so much a like they could have been brothers. After sharing a cell for four years, they got to know everything about each other. Upon his release, Jack Sommersby killed another man, then died from a wound he got during the fight. Horace Townsend then buries Jack Sommersby, which is seen in the opening scene of the film. When Laurel asks him "You mean you buried Jack," he answers "I buried Horace." Horace Townsend decided to take Jack Sommerby's place, and no longer be the man he was. Jack concludes by saying he can't admit to the judge that he is Horace Townsend, because then they would have no money and no house.

As Jack is taken to the gallows, he asks Laurel to be amongst the crowds as he cannot "hang alone". But as Jack Sommersby is about to be hanged, Laurel makes her way to the front of the crowd. Jack calls for her, claiming to the executioner that he "isn't ready". She calls back and the two see each other. Then he is executed.

The closing scenes show Laurel walking up a hill with flowers. She then kneels by the grave of "Jack Sommersby" and lays the flowers down for him. It is revealed that work is being done on the steeple of the village church, as Jack had wished.

Cast

- Richard Gere - John "Jack" Sommersby
- Jodie Foster - Laurel Sommersby
- Brett Kelley - Rob Sommersby, son
- Bill Pullman - Orin Meecham
- James Earl Jones - Judge Barry Conrad Isaacs
- Lanny Flaherty - Buck
- William Windom - Reverend Powell
- Wendell Wellman - Travis
- Clarice Taylor - Esther
- Frankie Faison - Joseph
- R. Lee Ermey - Dick Mead
- Caileb Ryder/Caitlen Ryder - Baby Rachel

Reaction

The film got a 61% on Rotten Tomatoes, marking it a close "Fresh."[1] Critics praised the acting of the two leads Richard Gere and Jodie Foster, but panned the vague redemption of the imposter. [2]

References

Footnotes

[1] Rotten Tomatoes - Sommersby (http://www.rottentomatoes.com/m/sommersby/?critic=columns) Retrieved 1 April 2007.
[2] "Foster, Gere Rob `Sommersby' Of Credibility" (http://articles.courant.com/1993-02-05/features/0000106286_1_laurel-sommersby-martin-guerre-confederate-soldier). *Courant*. . Retrieved 2010-11-12.

External links

- *Sommersby* (http://www.imdb.com/title/tt0108185/) at the Internet Movie Database
- *Sommersby* (http://www.allrovi.com/movies/movie/v1:45600~T0) at AllRovi
- *Sommersby* (http://www.rottentomatoes.com/m/sommersby/) at Rotten Tomatoes
- *Sommersby* (http://www.boxofficemojo.com/movies/?id=sommersby.htm) at Box Office Mojo

And the Band Played On (film)

And the Band Played On	
Promotional poster	
Distributed by	HBO
Creator	Randy Shilts (book)
Directed by	Roger Spottiswoode
Produced by	Sarah Pillsbury Midge Sanford
Written by	Arnold Schulman
Starring	Matthew Modine Alan Alda
Music by	Carter Burwell
Cinematography	Paul Elliott
Editing by	Lois Freeman-Fox
Budget	$8 million
Country	United States
Language	English
Release date	September 11, 1993
Running time	141 minutes

And the Band Played On is a 1993 American television film docudrama directed by Roger Spottiswoode. The teleplay by Arnold Schulman is based on the best-selling 1987 non-fiction book *And the Band Played On: Politics, People, and the AIDS Epidemic* by Randy Shilts.

The film premiered at the Montreal Film Festival before being broadcast by HBO on September 11, 1993. It later was released theatrically in the United Kingdom, Canada, Spain, Germany, Argentina, Austria, Italy, Sweden, the Netherlands, France, Denmark, New Zealand and Australia.

Plot

In a prologue set in 1976, American epidemiologist Don Francis arrives in a village on the banks of the Ebola River in Zaire and discovers many of the residents and the doctor working with them have died from a mysterious illness later identified as Ebola hemorrhagic fever. It is his first exposure to such an epidemic, and the images of the dead he helps cremate will haunt him when he later becomes involved with HIV and AIDS research at the Centers for Disease Control and Prevention.

In 1981, Francis becomes aware of a growing number of deaths from unexplained sources among gay men in Los Angeles, New York City and San Francisco, and is prompted to begin an in-depth investigation of the possible causes. Working with no money, limited space, and outdated equipment, he comes in contact with politicians and numerous members of the medical community, many of whom resent his involvement because of their personal agendas, and gay leaders. Of the latter, some—such as Bill Kraus—support him, while others express resentment at what they see as unwanted interference in their lifestyles, especially his attempts to close the local bathhouses. While Francis pursues his theory that AIDS is caused by a sexually transmitted virus on the model of feline leukemia, he finds his efforts are stonewalled by, among others, the CDC, which is loath to prove the disease is transmitted through blood, and competing French and American scientists, particularly Dr. Robert Gallo, who squabble about who should receive credit for discovering the virus. Meanwhile, the death toll climbs rapidly.

Principal cast

- Matthew Modine ..... Dr. Don Francis
- Alan Alda ..... Dr. Robert Gallo
- Ian McKellen ..... Bill Kraus
- Glenne Headly ..... Dr. Mary Guinan
- Richard Masur ..... William Darrow
- Saul Rubinek ..... Dr. Jim Curran
- Lily Tomlin ..... Dr. Selma Dritz
- Jeffrey Nordling ..... Gaëtan Dugas
- Donal Logue ..... Bobbi Campbell
- B.D. Wong ..... Kico Govantes
- Patrick Bauchau ..... Dr. Luc Montagnier
- Nathalie Baye ..... Dr. Françoise Barre
- Phil Collins ..... Eddie Papasano
- Steve Martin ..... Brother of AIDS patient
- Richard Gere ..... Choreographer
- David Marshall Grant ..... Dennis Seeley
- Ronald Guttman ..... Dr. Jean-Claude Chermann
- Anjelica Huston ..... Dr. Betsy Reisz
- Ken Jenkins ..... Dr. Dennis Donohue
- Richard Jenkins ..... Dr. Marc Conant
- Tchéky Karyo ..... Dr. Willy Rozenbaum
- Peter McRobbie ..... Dr. Max Essex
- Charles Martin Smith ..... Dr. Harold Jaffe
- David Clennon ..... Mr. Johnstone
- Swoosie Kurtz ..... Mrs. Johnstone
- Lawrence Monoson ..... Chip

Closing montage

The film closes with footage of a candlelight vigil and march in San Francisco, followed by a montage of images of persons with HIV, accompanied by Elton John singing his "The Last Song." The montage includes:

- Bobbi Campbell
- Ryan White
- Michael Jackson
- Rock Hudson
- Anthony Perkins
- Tina Chow
- Rudolf Nureyev
- Arthur Ashe
- Michael Bennett
- Liberace
- Freddie Mercury
- Elizabeth Glaser
- Magic Johnson
- Larry Kramer
- Alison Gertz
- Max Robinson
- Halston
- Willi Smith
- Perry Ellis
- Peter Allen
- Steve Rubell
- Keith Haring
- Stewart McKinney
- Denholm Elliot
- Brad Davis
- Amanda Blake
- Robert Reed
- Michel Foucault
- Tom Waddell

Critical reception

Most reviewers agreed that the filmmakers had a daunting task in adapting Shilts' massive, fact-filled text into a dramatically coherent film. Many critics praised the results. Film review website Rotten Tomatoes gives the film a 100% "Fresh" rating based on eight reviews.[1]

In his review in *Variety*, Tony Scott said, "If there are lapses, director Spottiswoode's engrossing, powerful work still accomplishes its mission: Shilts' book, with all its shock, sorrow and anger, has been transferred decisively to the screen."[2] John O'Connor of *The New York Times* agreed that the adaptation "adds up to tough and uncommonly courageous television. Excessive tinkering has left the pacing of the film sluggish in spots, but the story is never less than compelling."[3] And *Time* magazine said that "Shilts' prodigiously researched 600-page book has been boiled down to a fact-filled, dramatically coherent, occasionally moving 2 hours and 20 minutes. At a time when most made-for-TV movies have gone tabloid crazy, here is a rare one that tackles a big subject, raises the right issues, fights the good fight."[4]

Ken Tucker of *Entertainment Weekly* graded the film B+ and called it an "intriguing, sometimes awkward, always earnest combination of docudrama, medical melodrama, and mystery story ... The stars lend warmth to a movie necessarily preoccupied with cold research and politics, and they lend prestige: The movie must be important, since actors of this stature agreed to appear. The result of the stars' generosity, however, works against the movie by halting the flow of the drama every time a familiar face pops up on screen ... The emotions and agony involved in this subject give *Band* an irresistible power, yet the movie's rhythm is choppy and the dialogue frequently stiff and clichéd. The best compliment one can pay this TV movie is to say that unlike so many fact-based films, it does not exploit or diminish the tragedy of its subject."[5]

Time Out New York says, "So keen were the makers of this adaptation of Randy Shilts' best-seller to bombard us with the facts and figures of the history of AIDS that they forgot to offer a properly dramatic human framework to make us care fully about the characters." The review also says that the multiple issues the film attempts to cover "make for a disjointed, clichéd narrative."[6] Channel 4 says the film "is stifled by good intentions and a distractingly generous cast of stars in leads and cameos."[7]

Awards and nominations

Emmy Awards

- Outstanding Made for Television Movie (**winner**)
- Outstanding Individual Achievement in Casting (**winner**)
- Outstanding Individual Achievement in Editing for a Miniseries or a Special - Single Camera Production (**winner**)
- Outstanding Individual Achievement in Directing for a Miniseries or a Special (nominee)
- Outstanding Individual Achievement in Writing in a Miniseries or a Special (nominee)
- Outstanding Lead Actor in a Miniseries or a Special (Matthew Modine, nominee)
- Outstanding Supporting Actor in a Miniseries or a Special (Alan Alda, nominee)
- Outstanding Supporting Actor in a Miniseries or a Special (Richard Gere, nominee)
- Outstanding Supporting Actor in a Miniseries or a Special (Ian McKellen, nominee)
- Outstanding Supporting Actress in a Miniseries or a Special (Swoosie Kurtz, nominee)
- Outstanding Supporting Actress in a Miniseries or a Special (Lily Tomlin, nominee)
- Outstanding Individual Achievement in Art Direction for a Miniseries or a Special (nominee)
- Outstanding Individual Achievement in Hairstyling for a Miniseries or a Special (nominee)
- Outstanding Individual Achievement in Makeup for a Miniseries or a Special (nominee)

Golden Globe Awards

- Best Mini-Series Or Motion Picture Made for Television (nominee)

- Best Performance by an Actor in a Mini-Series or Motion Picture Made for Television (Matthew Modine, nominee)

CableACE Awards

- Best Supporting Actor in a Movie or Miniseries (Ian McKellen, **winner**)
- Best Movie or Miniseries (nominee)
- Best Supporting Actor in a Movie or Miniseries (Richard Gere, nominee)
- Best Supporting Actor in a Movie or Miniseries (Lawrence Monoson, nominee)
- Best Supporting Actress in a Movie or Miniseries (Swoosie Kurtz, nominee)
- Best Supporting Actress in a Movie or Miniseries (Lily Tomlin, nominee)
- Best Make-Up (nominee)

Additional awards

- GLAAD Media Award for Outstanding TV Movie (**winner**)
- Casting Society of America Artios Award for Best Casting for TV Movie of the Week (**winner**)
- American Cinema Editors Eddie Award for Best Edited Motion Picture for Non-Commercial Television (**winner**)
- Humanitas Prize (Arnold Schulman, **winner**)
- Montréal World Film Festival Special Grand Prize of the Jury (Roger Spottiswoode, **winner**)

References

[1] *And the Band Played On* at RottenTomatoes.com (http://www.rottentomatoes.com/m/and_the_band_played_on/)
[2] *Variety* review (http://www.variety.com/review/VE1117901186.html?categoryid=32&cs=1&p=0)
[3] O'Connor, John J. "Beyond the Re-editing, Rage Over AIDS." (http://www.nytimes.com/1993/09/10/arts/tv-weekend-beyond-the-re-editing-rage-over-aids.html) *New York Times*. September 10, 1993.
[4] Zoglin, Richard. "Fighting The Good Fight." (http://www.time.com/time/magazine/article/0,9171,979190-1,00.html) *Time*. September 13, 1993.
[5] *Entertainment Weekly* review (http://www.ew.com/ew/article/0,,307958,00.html)
[6] *Time Out New York* review (http://www.timeout.com/film/newyork/reviews/77950/And_the_Band_Played_On.html)
[7] Channel 4 review (http://www.channel4.com/film/reviews/film.jsp?id=100467)

External links

- *And the Band Played On* (http://www.imdb.com/title/tt0106273/) at the Internet Movie Database
- *And the Band Played On* (http://www.allrovi.com/movies/movie/v2221) at AllRovi

Intersection (film)

Intersection	
Directed by	Mark Rydell
Produced by	Mark Rydell Bud Yorkin
Written by	David Rayfiel Marshall Brickman
Starring	Richard Gere Sharon Stone Lolita Davidovich Martin Landau Jennifer Morrison
Music by	James Newton Howard
Cinematography	Vilmos Zsigmond
Editing by	Mark Warner
Distributed by	Paramount Pictures
Release date(s)	January 21, 1994
Running time	98 minutes
Language	English
Budget	$35 million
Box office	$21,355,893

Intersection is a 1994 film, directed by Mark Rydell and starring Richard Gere, Sharon Stone, and Lolita Davidovich.

A remake of the French film *Les choses de la vie* (1970) by Claude Sautet, the story — set in Vancouver, British Columbia — concerns an architect (played by Gere) who, as his classic Mercedes 280SL roadster hurtles into a collision at an intersection, flashes through key moments in his life, including his marriage to a beautiful but chilly heiress (Stone) and his subsequent affair with a younger woman (Davidovich).

Reception

The film received poor reviews from critics, with Rotten Tomatoes holding this film an 8% rating. It also won Sharon Stone a Razzie Award for her performance (also for *The Specialist*).

External links

- *Intersection* [1] at the Internet Movie Database
- *Intersection* [2] at Rotten Tomatoes
- *Intersection* [3] at Box Office Mojo

References

[1] http://www.imdb.com/title/tt0110146/
[2] http://www.rottentomatoes.com/m/intersection/
[3] http://www.boxofficemojo.com/movies/?id=intersection.htm

First Knight

First Knight	
Theatrical release poster	
Directed by	Jerry Zucker
Produced by	Hunt Lowry Jerry Zucker
Screenplay by	William Nicholson
Story by	Lorne Cameron David Hoselton William Nicholson
Starring	Sean Connery Richard Gere Julia Ormond
Music by	Jerry Goldsmith
Cinematography	Adam Greenberg
Editing by	Walter Murch
Studio	Zucker Brothers Entertainment
Distributed by	Columbia Pictures
Release date(s)	July 7, 1995
Running time	134 minutes
Country	United States
Language	English
Budget	$55 million
Box office	$127,600,435

First Knight is a 1995 American medieval film based on Arthurian legend, directed by Jerry Zucker. It stars Richard Gere as Lancelot, Julia Ormond as Guinevere, Sean Connery as King Arthur and Ben Cross as Malagant.

The film follows the rogue Lancelot's romance with Lady Guinevere of Leonesse, who is to marry King Arthur of Camelot, while the land is threatened by the renegade knight Malagant. The film is noteworthy within Arthurian cinema for its absence of magical elements, its drawing on the material of Chrétien de Troyes for plot elements and the substantial age difference between Arthur and Guinevere.[1]

Plot

The film's opening text establishes that King Arthur (Sean Connery) of Camelot, victorious from his wars, has dedicated his reign to promoting justice and peace and now wishes to marry. However, Malagant (Ben Cross), a Knight of the Round Table, desires the throne for himself and rebels.[1]

The film opens with Lancelot (Richard Gere), a vagabond and skilled swordsman, dueling in small villages for money. Lancelot attributes his skill to his lack of concern whether he lives or dies. Guinevere (Julia Ormond), the ruler of Leonesse, decides to marry Arthur partly out of admiration and partly for security against Malagant, who is shown raiding a village. While traveling, Lancelot chances by Guinevere's carriage on the way to Camelot, and helps spoil Malagant's ambush meant to kidnap her. He falls in love with Guinevere, who refuses his advances. Though Lancelot urges her to follow her heart, Guinevere remains bound by her duty. She is subsequently reunited with her escort.[1]

Later, Lancelot arrives in Camelot and successfully navigates an obstacle course on the prospect of a kiss from Guinevere, though he instead kisses her hand. He also wins an audience with her husband-to-be, Arthur. Impressed by Lancelot's courage and struck by his recklessness and freewheeling, Arthur shows him the Round Table which symbolizes a life of service and brotherhood. Guinevere is subsequently kidnapped by Malagant's followers and imprisoned in an oubliette. Lancelot poses as a messenger to Malagant only to escape with Guinevere and return her to Camelot. Once again, Lancelot tries to win her heart, but is unsuccessful. On the return journey, it is revealed that Lancelot was orphaned and rendered homeless after bandits attacked his village, and has been wandering ever since.[1]

In gratitude, Arthur offers Lancelot a higher calling in life as a Knight of the Round Table. Amidst the protests of the other Knights (who are suspicious of his station), and of Guinevere (who struggles with her feelings for him), Lancelot accepts and takes Malagant's place at the Table, saying he has found something to care about. Arthur and Guinevere are subsequently wedded. However, a messenger from Leonesse arrives, with news that Malagant has invaded. Arthur leads his troops to Leonesse and successfully defeats Malagant's forces. Lancelot wins the respect of the other Knights with his prowess in battle. He also learns to embrace Arthur's philosophy, moved by the plight of villagers.[1]

Lancelot feels guilty about his feelings for the queen and in private announces his departure to her. She cannot bear the thought of him leaving and asks him for a kiss, which turns into a passionate embrace, just in time for the king to interrupt. Though Guinevere claims to love both Arthur and Lancelot – albeit in different ways – the two are charged with treason. The open trial in the great square of Camelot is interrupted by a surprise invasion by Malagant, ready to burn Camelot and kill Arthur if he does not swear fealty. Instead Arthur commands his subjects to fight, and Malagant's men shoot him with crossbows. A battle between Malagant's men and Camelot's soldiers and citizens ensues, and Lancelot and Malagant face off. Disarmed, Lancelot seizes Arthur's fallen sword and kills Malagant. The people of Camelot win the battle, but Arthur dies of his wounds. On his deathbed, he asks Lancelot to "*take care of her for me*" – a double entendre referring to both Camelot and Guinevere. The film closes with a funeral raft carrying Arthur's body floating out to sea, which is set aflame.[1]

Cast

- Richard Gere as Lancelot
- Julia Ormond as Guinevere
- Sean Connery as King Arthur
- Ben Cross as Prince Malagant
- John Gielgud as Oswald
- Liam Cunningham as Sir Agravaine
- Christopher Villiers as Sir Kay
- Valentine Pelka as Sir Patrise
- Colin McCormack as Sir Mador
- Alexis Denisof as Sir Gaheris
- Ralph Ineson as Ralf
- Stuart Bunce as Peter
- Angus Wright as The Marauder

Production

Director Jerry Zucker, who also co-produced with Hunt Lowry, made *First Knight* as a follow-up to his Academy Award-nominated 1990 hit *Ghost*. Previously, he was primarily known for teaming with his brother David Zucker and with Jim Abrahams to create comedies such as *Airplane!* and *The Naked Gun*.

The script was written by William Nicholson. Adam Greenberg was in charge of cinematography, while production design was under John Box. The score was composed by Jerry Goldsmith. The film was edited and mixed by Walter Murch.

Locations

Filming was shot on location in Great Britain. Exteriors were done in Gwynedd, North Wales and in England around Hertfordshire and Buckinghamshire. Interiors were completed at Pinewood Studios.

Music

The critically acclaimed orchestral score for *First Knight* was composed and conducted by veteran composer Jerry Goldsmith. Goldsmith was hired as a last-minute replacement to other noteworthy film score veteran Maurice Jarre, whose score was rejected by the producers. As a result, Goldsmith had limited time to compose original music and was left with only three and a half days to record the entire score. A soundtrack was released 4 July 1995 through Epic Soundtrax and features ten tracks of score at a running time of forty minutes. Due to the shortness of the original release, bootleg versions began to appear in 2000. However, a 5000 copy limited edition 2-disk soundtrack was released 12 April 2011 through La-La Land Records and features the complete score plus the original album tracks and addition alternate recordings.[2]

Box office and reception

The film managed to earn a domestic gross of $37,600,435 and $90,000,000 in foreign markets; overall, earning a combined take of $127,600,435 worldwide.

Critical reaction to the film has been mixed. Based on 41 reviews, *First Knight* is rated at 44% on Rotten Tomatoes' Tomatometer.[3]

References

[1] Aronstein, Susan (September 2005). *Arthurian Cinema and the Politics of Nostalgia*. Palgrave Macmillan. ISBN 978-1403966490.
[2] Clemmenson, Christian. "*First Knight* soundtrack review" (http://www.filmtracks.com/titles/first_knight.html). Filmtracks.com. . Retrieved June 6, 2011.
[3] "*First Knight* (1995)" (http://www.rottentomatoes.com/m/first_knight/). Rotten Tomatoes. . Retrieved August 30, 2011.

External links

- *First Knight* (http://www.imdb.com/title/tt0113071/) at the Internet Movie Database
- *First Knight* (http://www.allrovi.com/movies/movie/v134964) at AllRovi
- *First Knight* (http://www.boxofficemojo.com/movies/?id=firstknight.htm) at Box Office Mojo
- *First Knight* (http://www.rottentomatoes.com/m/first_knight/) at Rotten Tomatoes
- Movie stills (http://film.virtual-history.com/film.php?filmid=8734)

Primal Fear (film)

Primal Fear	
Theatrical release poster	
Directed by	Gregory Hoblit
Produced by	Gary Lucchesi Howard W. Koch, Jr.
Screenplay by	Steve Shagan Ann Biderman
Based on	*Primal Fear* by William Diehl
Starring	Richard Gere Laura Linney John Mahoney Alfre Woodard Frances McDormand Edward Norton
Music by	James Newton Howard
Cinematography	Michael Chapman
Editing by	David Rosenbloom
Distributed by	Paramount Pictures Buena Vista International (Europe) Gaumont (France)
Release date(s)	April 3, 1996
Running time	130 minutes
Country	United States
Language	English
Budget	$30 million
Box office	$102,616,183[1]

Primal Fear is a 1996 American crime drama thriller film directed by Gregory Hoblit and starring Richard Gere and Edward Norton. The film tells the story of a defense attorney, Martin Vail (Gere), who defends an altar boy, Aaron Stampler (Norton), charged with the murder of a Catholic archbishop. The movie is an adaptation of William Diehl's 1993 novel of the same name. Norton's role in the film received multiple accolades, including a nomination for an Academy Award for Best Supporting Actor.

Plot

Martin Vail is a prominent defense attorney in Chicago who jumps at the chance to represent Aaron Stampler, a young, stuttering altar boy accused of murdering the Archbishop. At first interested primarily in the publicity that the case will bring, Vail comes to believe that his client is truly innocent, much to the chagrin of the prosecutor (and Vail's former lover), Janet Venable.

Vail discovers that powerful civic leaders, including the District Attorney, have lost millions in real estate investments due to a decision by the Archbishop not to develop certain church lands. The archbishop received numerous death threats as a result. He also learns that the archbishop had been sexually abusing altar boys, including Stampler.

Introducing this evidence, while it would make Stampler more sympathetic to the jury, would also give his client a motive for murder, something the prosecution otherwise has lacked.

The trial does not proceed well for the defense, as there is considerable evidence against Stampler and public opinion holds him almost certainly guilty. When Vail confronts his client and accuses him of having lied, Aaron breaks down and transforms into a new persona, a violent sociopath who calls himself "Roy." He confesses to the murder of the archbishop and throws Vail against the wall, injuring him.

When this incident is over, Aaron appears to have no recollection of it. Molly Arrington, the psychiatrist examining Aaron, is convinced he suffers from multiple personality disorder due to childhood abuse by his own father.[2] However, Vail cannot enter an insanity plea during an ongoing trial.

Vail sets up a confrontation in court. After Venable questions him harshly, Aaron turns into Roy and charges at her, threatening to snap her neck if anyone comes near him. Aaron is subdued by courthouse marshals and is rushed back to his cell. In light of Aaron's apparent insanity, the judge dismisses the jury in favor of a bench trial and then finds Aaron not guilty by reason of mental insanity, and remands him to a mental hospital.

Vail visits to tell him this news. Aaron says he recalls nothing of what happened in the courtroom, having again "lost time." However, just as Vail is leaving, Aaron asks him to "tell Ms. Venable I hope her neck is okay," which is not something that Aaron should have been able to remember if he had "lost time." Vail points this out, whereupon Stampler grins slyly and reveals that he has been pretending to be insane the whole time. But he didn't make up the identity of Roy, he made up Aaron.

Stampler now admits to having murdered the archbishop, as well as his girlfriend, Linda, whom the cleric also had molested. Stunned and disillusioned, Vail walks away, with Roy taunting him from the cell.

Cast

- Richard Gere as Martin Vail
- Laura Linney as Janet Venable
- John Mahoney as John Shaughnessy
- Alfre Woodard as Judge Shoat
- Frances McDormand as Dr. Molly Arrington
- Edward Norton as Aaron Stampler
- Terry O'Quinn as Bud Yancy
- Andre Braugher as Tommy Goodman
- Steven Bauer as Joey Pinero
- Joe Spano as Abel Stenner
- Tony Plana as Martinez
- Stanley Anderson as Archbishop Rushman
- Maura Tierney as Naomi Chance
- Jon Seda as Alex

Reception

Primal Fear garnered positive reviews from critics, earning a 72% "Fresh" rating on Rotten Tomatoes.[3] According to Janet Maslin, Hoblit "has had a substantial Emmy-winning television career ... and sticks to a television style for his first feature. If that means glossy storytelling and one-note insights into character, it also means a good deal of surface charm. Mr. Hoblit also turns the film's closing revelation into one of its better selling points." And in spite of the film's two hour, 10 minute length, the novel on which the film was based is "pared down to a farfetched plot and paper-thin motives, [while] the story relies on an overload of tangential subplots to keep it looking busy."[4]

The film spent three weekends at the top of the U.S. box office.

Primal Fear inspired the 2002 Bollywood movie *Deewangee*.

Accolades

Edward Norton's depiction of Aaron Stampler garnered him multiple awards and nominations. Norton won:

- Los Angeles Film Critics Association Award for Best Supporting Actor (won for *Primal Fear* as well as his roles in *Everyone Says I Love You* and *The People vs. Larry Flynt*)
- Boston Society of Film Critics Awards for Best Supporting Actor (won for *Primal Fear* as well as his roles in *Everyone Says I Love You* and *The People vs. Larry Flynt*)
- Chicago Film Critics Association Award for Most Promising Actor (but lost to Cuba Gooding, Jr. for Best Supporting Actor)
- Kansas City Film Critics Circle Award for Best Supporting Actor

Norton was nominated for

- Academy Award for Best Supporting Actor Edward Norton (lost to Cuba Gooding, Jr., who won for his role in *Jerry Maguire*)
- British Academy Film Award for Best Actor in a Supporting Role (lost to Paul Scofield depiction of Judge Thomas Danforth in *The Crucible*)
- National Society of Film Critics Award for Best Supporting Actor (lost to co-winners Martin Donovan and Tony Shalhoub, for their roles in in *The Portrait of a Lady* and *Big Night*, respectively)
- MTV Movie Award for Best Villain (lost to Jim Carrey's portrayal of the title character in *The Cable Guy*)

American Film Institute recognition:

- AFI's 100 Years...100 Heroes and Villains:
    - Aaron Stampler - Nominated Villain[5]

References

[1] Primal Fear (1996) (http://boxofficemojo.com/movies/?id=primalfear.htm). *Box Office Mojo*. Retrieved 2011-01-16.
[2] Psychologist Richard Gartner reports that as of 1999, *Primal Fear* was one of only two feature films to feature male-male incest as a theme (the other film was the 1998 Danish drama *The Celebration*). See Gartner, Richard. 1999. Cinematic Depictions of Boyhood Sexual Victimization (Page four, Cinematic Depictions) (http://www.richardgartner.com/fcinematic4Z.html). *Gender and Psychoanalysis* (1999), Volume 4:253-28.
[3] Primal Fear Movie Reviews, Pictures (http://www.rottentomatoes.com/m/1070992-primal_fear). *Rotten Tomatoes*. Retrieved 2011-01-16.
[4] Janet Maslin (April 3, 1996). "A Murdered Archbishop, Lawyers In Armani" (http://movies.nytimes.com/movie/review?res=940DEED81239F930A35757C0A960958260). The New York Times. . Retrieved 2011-10-24.
[5] AFI's 100 Years...100 Heroes and Villains Nominees (http://connect.afi.com/site/DocServer/handv400.pdf?docID=245)

External links

- *Primal Fear* (http://www.imdb.com/title/tt0117381/) at the Internet Movie Database
- *Primal Fear* (http://www.rottentomatoes.com/m/1070992/) at Rotten Tomatoes
- *Primal Fear* (http://www.metacritic.com/movie/primalfear) at Metacritic
- *Primal Fear* (http://www.boxofficemojo.com/movies/?id=primalfear.htm) at Box Office Mojo

The Jackal (1997 film)

The Jackal	
Theatrical release poster	
Directed by	Michael Caton-Jones
Produced by	James Jacks Sean Daniel Michael Caton-Jones Kevin Jarre
Written by	Chuck Pfarrer
Based on	screenplay *The Day of the Jackal* by Kenneth Ross
Starring	Bruce Willis Richard Gere Sidney Poitier Diane Venora
Music by	Carter Burwell
Cinematography	Karl Walter Lindenlaub
Editing by	Jim Clark
Distributed by	Universal Pictures
Release date(s)	November 14, 1997
Running time	124 min.
Language	English Russian
Budget	$60 million[1]
Box office	$159,330,280[1]

The Jackal is a 1997 suspense film directed by Michael Caton-Jones and starring Bruce Willis, Richard Gere, and Sidney Poitier. It is a loose remake of the 1973 film *The Day of the Jackal*, although the director of that film, Fred Zinnemann, fought with the studio to ensure that this remake did not share the first film's title, and Frederick Forsyth, the author of the novel that the first film was based on, asked for his name to be removed from the credits of this film.[2]

Plot

A joint mission of the American FBI and the Russian MVD leads to the death of the younger brother of an Azerbaijani mobster (David Hayman). In retaliation, the mobster hires an enigmatic assassin known only by the pseudonym "The Jackal" (Willis) to kill an unseen target. Meanwhile, the MVD capture one of the mobster's henchmen. During interrogation by torture, the henchman reveals the name "Jackal." This coupled with the documents recovered from the henchman's briefcase lead the FBI and MVD to assume the target for the retaliatory hit is FBI Director Donald Brown (John Cunningham).

As the Jackal begins his preparations for the assassination — utilising a series of disguises and stolen IDs in the process — the FBI learns of one person who can identify him. FBI Deputy Director Carter Preston (Poitier) and

Russian Police Major Valentina Koslova (Diane Venora) turn to a former Irish Republican Army sniper named Declan Mulqueen (Gere), who had a relationship with a Basque woman named Isabella Zanconia (Mathilda May), who they believe can identify The Jackal. Mulqueen eventually agrees to help in exchange for their best efforts to get him released from prison.

It becomes apparent that Mulqueen has a personal motive for hunting the Jackal: the assassin wounded Zanconia while she was pregnant with Mulqueen's child, causing a miscarriage. Zanconia provides information that can help identify the Jackal, including the fact that he is American and that he had acquired military training in El Salvador. Meanwhile, the Jackal hires gunsmith Ian Lamont (Jack Black) to design and build a mount for the weapon he intends to use for the assassination. Underestimating the danger posed by the Jackal, Lamont demands more money in exchange for keeping quiet; The Jackal responds by brutally murdering Lamont using the very equipment Lamont built. The FBI discovers Lamont's body and, with the help of Mulqueen, deduce that the Jackal intends to utilise a long-range heavy machine gun for the assassination. With the help of a Russian mole in the FBI, the Jackal realizes he is being tracked by Mulqueen with assistance from Zanconia, he infiltrates Zanconia's house after receiving an FBI access code from his insider. Instead of Zanconia, however, he finds Koslova and Agent Witherspoon (J.K. Simmons), promptly killing Witherspoon and mortally wounding Koslova. The Jackal gives Koslova a taunting message, "He can't protect his women", which she delivers moments before her death.

As the Jackal makes his final preparations, Mulqueen realizes that his target is not the now heavily protected and isolated FBI Director, but instead the First Lady (Tess Harper), who is due to give a major public speech. Arriving just in time, Mulqueen successfully disables the Jackal's weapon, while Preston saves the First Lady from a volley of gunfire. The Jackal attempts to escape into the subway, eventually having Mulqueen at his mercy; unbeknownst to the Jackal, however, Mulqueen has summoned Zanconia, who along with Mulqueen shoots the assassin dead.

A few days later, Preston and Mulqueen stand as the only witnesses to the Jackal's burial in an unmarked grave. Preston reveals that he is going back to Russia to pursue the mobsters who hired the Jackal. It is revealed that Mulqueen's request to be released was denied, but that he will likely be moved to a less secure prison. Preston's heroics in saving the First Lady have made him a golden boy in the FBI: he can now "screw everything else up for the rest of his life and still be untouchable," which he credits Mulqueen for. After exchanging a farewell, and knowing his current clout will prevent any real backlash against him, Preston turns his back on Mulqueen, allowing him to go free.

Cast

- Bruce Willis as The Jackal
- Richard Gere as Declan Mulqueen
- Sidney Poitier as Preston
- Diane Venora as Valentina Koslova
- Mathilda May as Isabella
- J. K. Simmons as Witherspoon
- Richard Lineback as McMurphy
- John Cunningham as Donald Brown
- Jack Black as Lamont
- Tess Harper as The First Lady
- Leslie Phillips as Woolburton
- Stephen Spinella as Douglas
- David Hayman as Terek Murad

Production

Fred Zinnemann, director of *The Day of the Jackal*, fought with Universal Pictures to change the title of the movie so it wouldn't share the original's name. Frederick Forsyth, who wrote the novel the first film was based on, also publicly distanced himself from the remake. As a result, the title of the film was shortened and Forsyth's name was removed from the credits; it is instead credited as being "based on the motion picture screenplay *The Day of the Jackal* by Kenneth Ross."[2]

Reception

Critical response

The film received mostly negative reviews from critics. Roger Ebert of the *Chicago Sun-Times* called it a "glum, curiously flat thriller";[3] Ruthe Stein of the *San Francisco Chronicle* called it "more preposterous than thrilling";[4] and Russell Smith of the *Austin Chronicle* called it "1997's most tedious movie".[5] *The Jackal* currently holds a 12% rating on Rotten Tomatoes.

Box office

The Jackal premièred on November 14, 1997 with an opening weekend totaling $15,164,595.[1] It would go on to gross $159,330,280 worldwide. Against its $60m budget, the movie was a financial success.

References

[1] "Box Office Mojo: The Jackal" (http://www.boxofficemojo.com/movies/?id=jackal.html). . Retrieved 2009-03-01
[2] IMDb: Trivia about "The Jackal" (http://www.imdb.com/title/tt0119395/trivia) Retrieved 2011-08-30
[3] "The Jackal" (http://rogerebert.suntimes.com/apps/pbcs.dll/article?AID=/19971114/REVIEWS/711140302/1023). *Chicago Sun-Times*. .
[4] Stein, Ruthe (November 14, 1997). "'Jackal' Can't Hide From Absurd Plot / Willis alters look in mishmash thriller" (http://www.sfgate.com/cgi-bin/article.cgi?f=/c/a/1997/11/14/DD16221.DTL). *The San Francisco Chronicle*. .
[5] The Austin Chronicle: Film Listings (http://www.austinchronicle.com/gyrobase/Calendar/Film?Film=oid:140948).

External links

- *The Jackal* (http://www.imdb.com/title/tt0119395/) at the Internet Movie Database
- *The Jackal* (http://www.boxofficemojo.com/movies/?id=jackal.htm) at Box Office Mojo
- *The Jackal* (http://www.rottentomatoes.com/m/jackal/) at Rotten Tomatoes

Red Corner

Red Corner	
Theatrical release poster	
Directed by	Jon Avnet
Produced by	Jon Avnet Jordan Kerner Charles Mulvehill Rosalie Swedlin **Executive:** Wolfgang Petersen
Written by	Robert King
Starring	Richard Gere Bai Ling Bradley Whitford
Music by	Thomas Newman
Cinematography	Karl Walter Lindenlaub
Editing by	Peter E. Berger
Distributed by	Metro-Goldwyn-Mayer
Release date(s)	October 31, 1997[1]
Running time	122 minutes
Box office	$22,415,440 (USA)

Red Corner is a drama film produced in 1997, directed by Jon Avnet and written by Robert King.

Plot

It tells the story of a wealthy American businessman named Jack Moore (played by Richard Gere) working in China and attempting to put together a satellite communications deal as part of a joint venture with the Chinese government. Before the deal goes through, he is framed for the murder of a powerful Chinese general's daughter, and the satellite contract is awarded to Moore's competitor, Gerhardt Hoffman. Moore's court-appointed lawyer Shen Yuelin, (played by Bai Ling), initially does not believe his claims of innocence, but the pair gradually unearths further evidence that not only vindicates Moore but also implicates powerful figures within the Chinese central government administration, exposing undeniavle conspiracy and corruption.

Filming

Red Corner was shot in Los Angeles using elaborate sets and CGI rendering of 3,500 still shots and two minutes of footage from China. In order to establish the film's verisimility, several Beijing actors were brought to the United States on visas for filming. The judicial and penitentiary scenes were recreated from descriptions given by attorneys and judges practicing in China and the video segment showing the execution of Chinese prisoners was an actual execution. The individuals providing the video and the descriptions to Avnet and his staff took on a significant risk by providing it.[2]

Reception

The film received generally negative reviews when it was released in the United States. The movie review aggregator website Rotten Tomatoes found that 33% of the film critics gave the movie positive reviews, while only 20% of top critics reviewed it positively.[3]

Cynthia Langston of *Film Journal International* responded to the film: "So unrealistic, so contrived and so blatantly "Hollywood" that Gere can't possibly imagine he's opening any eyes to the problem, or any doors to its solution, for that matter".[4] The *Los Angeles Times* described *Red Corner* as a "sluggish and uninteresting melodrama that is further hampered by the delusion that it is saying something significant. But its one-man-against-the-system story is hackneyed and the points it thinks it's making about the state of justice in China are hampered by an attitude that verges on the xenophobic."[5] *Salon* film critic Andrew O'Hehir noted "...more the movie's subtext swallows its story, until all that is left is Gere's superior virtue, intermixed with his superior virility – both of which are greatly appreciated by the evidently underserviced Chinese female population..." O'Hehir also noted that the film reinforces the infamous Western stereotypes of Asian female sexuality (as in those of *The World of Suzie Wong*) as well as the hoariest stereotyping.[6]

Rating

The film is rated "R" in the USA for violence and sexuality.[1] It is banned in the People's Republic of China for political reasons.[7]

For various countries, the film's ratings are: [8]
Iceland:14 / Iceland:16 (video rating) / South Korea:18 / Argentina:13 / Australia:M / Belgium:KT / Chile:14 / Finland:K-16 / France:U / Germany:12 (w) / India:A / Mexico:B / Peru:14 / Portugal:M/12 / Singapore:NC-16 / Spain:13 / Sweden:15 / Switzerland:12 (canton of Geneva) / Switzerland:12 (canton of Vaud) / UK:15 / USA:R

Cast

- Richard Gere — *Jack Moore*
- Bai Ling — *Shen Yuelin (Lawyer)*
- Bradley Whitford — *Bob Ghery*
- Byron Mann — *Lin Dan*
- Peter Donat — *David McAndrews*
- Robert Stanton — *Ed Pratt*
- Tsai Chin — *Chairman Xu*
- James Hong — *Lin Shou*
- Tzi Ma — *Li Cheng*
- Ulrich Matschoss — *Gerhardt Hoffman*
- Richard Venture — *Ambassador Reed*
- Jessey Meng — *Hong Ling*
- Roger Yuan — *Huan Minglu*
- Chi Yu Li — *General Hong*
- Henry O — Procurator General Yang
- Kent Faulcon — Marine Guard

References

[1] "Red Corner" (http://www.mgm.com/title_title.php?title_star=REDCORNR). Metro-Goldwyn-Mayer. .
[2] See director's cometary on DVD.
[3] "Red Corner Movie Reviews" (http://www.rottentomatoes.com/m/red_corner/). Rottentomatoes. .
[4] Red Corner. *Film Journal International*. (http://www.filmjournal.com/filmjournal/search/article_display.jsp?vnu_content_id=1000698469)
[5] Red Corner: A Heavy-Handed Battle With Justice in China. *Los Angeles Times*. (http://www.calendarlive.com/movies/reviews/cl-movie971111-19,0,7979115.story)
[6] Red Corner. *Salon* (http://www.salon.com/ent/movies/1997/10/31red.html)
[7] Total Film – Red Corner – Film Review (http://www.totalfilm.com/cinema_reviews/red_corner)
[8] Cf. Internet Movie Database article/parentalguide (http://www.imdb.com/title/tt0119994/parentalguide)

External links

- *Red Corner* (http://www.imdb.com/title/tt0119994/) at the Internet Movie Database

Runaway Bride (1999 film)

Runaway Bride	
Directed by	Garry Marshall
Produced by	Ted Field Tom Rosenberg Scott Kroopf Robert W. Cort
Written by	Josann McGibbon Sara Parriott Audrey Wells
Starring	Julia Roberts Richard Gere Joan Cusack
Music by	James Newton Howard
Cinematography	Stuart Dryburgh
Editing by	Bruce Green
Studio	Lakeshore Entertainment Interscope Communications
Distributed by	**USA/Canada** Paramount Pictures **International** Touchstone Pictures
Release date(s)	July 30, 1999
Running time	116 minutes
Country	United States
Language	English
Budget	$70 million
Box office	$309,457,509

Runaway Bride is a 1999 American romantic comedy film starring Julia Roberts and Richard Gere and directed by Garry Marshall. The screenplay was written by Josann McGibbon, Audrey Wells and Sara Parriott.

Plot

Maggie Carpenter (Julia Roberts) is a spirited and attractive young woman who has had a number of unsuccessful relationships. Maggie, nervous of being married, has left a trail of fiances. It seems, she's left three men waiting for her at the altar on their wedding day (all of which are caught on tape), receiving tabloid fame and the dubious nickname "The Runaway Bride".

Meanwhile, in New York, reporter Homer Eisenhower Graham or "Ike" (Richard Gere), writes a column about her that contains several factual errors, supplied to him by one of Maggie's jilted exes for revenge. He's fired for not verifying his source and then decides to write an in-depth article about Maggie in a bid to get his job back. He travels to Hale, Maryland, where he finds her living with her family and on her fourth attempt to become married. The fourth groom-to-be, Bob Kelly (Christopher Meloni), a football coach at the local high school who treats Maggie like one of the players on his sports team. He constantly makes references to Maggie "focusing" on the goal-line.

While doing research for his story, Ike's realizations are forcing Maggie to face her fears, and eventually the two find themselves becoming more and more attracted to each other. In the meantime, Maggie is still set to marry Bob. In the midst of the wedding rehearsal, Bob helps walk Maggie down the aisle, and asks Ike to stand in his place as the groom. This proves to be a mistake, when Ike and Maggie "practice" the kiss right in front of Bob, finally admitting their feelings for one another. As a result, Bob punches Ike in the face before storming out of the church. Soon after, Ike and Maggie agree to marry since the wedding is already set to take place. But on the day of the wedding, Maggie gets cold feet, and leaves Ike, too, standing at the altar. As she rides away on a FedEx truck, Ike runs after her, but can't catch up.

Later, we see Ike living in New York and Maggie trying to discover herself, trying different types of eggs, and putting her lighting designs up for sale in New York. She shows up unexpectedly at Ike's apartment one night where he finds her making friends with his cat, Italics. Maggie then explains that she's been running because every other guy she was engaged to was only engaged to the idea she had created for them rather than the real her- and when she was marrying Ike she was simply freaked out at the crowd-, and "turns in" her running shoes just before proposing to Ike. The two are married in a private ceremony outside, on a hill, avoiding the big ceremonies that drove Maggie away in the past. In the end, they are shown riding away on horseback while everyone celebrates the fact that Maggie *finally* got married.

Cast

- Julia Roberts as Maggie Carpenter- A woman who has run away from 3 weddings but is hoping not to do so on her fourth wedding attempt
- Richard Gere as Ike Graham- a New York City news reporter who writes an article about Maggie and later falls in love with her. His real name is Homer
- Joan Cusack as Peggy Flemming - *"not the ice skater"*; this is a running gag in the film
- Héctor Elizondo as Fisher
- Christopher Meloni as Bob Kelly
- Paul Dooley as Walter Carpenter
- Rita Wilson as Ellie Graham
- Lisa Roberts Gillan as Elaine from Manhattan
- Donal Logue as Priest Brian Norris
- Reg Rogers as George "Bug Guy" Swilling
- Yul Vazquez as Dead Head Gill Chavez
- Kathleen Marshall as Cousin Cindy
- Sela Ward as Pretty woman in bar
- Garry Marshall (*uncredited*) as First softball baseman
- Laurie Metcalf (*uncredited*) as Betty Trout
- Larry Miller (*uncredited*) as NY bartender Kevin
- Emily Eby ("uncredited") as reporter

Production history

The film was in development for over a decade. Actors attached at various times: Anjelica Huston, Mary Steenburgen, Lorraine Bracco, Geena Davis, Demi Moore, Sandra Bullock, Ellen DeGeneres, Téa Leoni (for the role of Maggie); Christopher Walken, Harrison Ford, Mel Gibson, Michael Douglas (for the role of Ike) and Ben Affleck (for the role of Bob). Director Michael Hoffman was attached. Writers Elaine May and Leslie Dixon did unused rewrites.

The theme song is titled "Before I Fall in Love" and is sung by Coco Lee

Release

Box office

The film opened on July 30, 1999 with $12,000,000 on its opening day.[1] In its opening weekend, *Runaway Bride* peaked at #1 with $35,055,556.[2]

By the end of its run, the film had grossed $152,257,509 domestically and an international $157,200,000, altogether making $309,457,509 worldwide.[3]

Critical reception

The film earned positive to mixed reviews. While Richard Gere and Julia Roberts were liked in their second film since *Pretty Woman*, viewers and critics felt the film was not as good as it could have been. Originally, Marshall was going to do a *Pretty Woman* sequel, but he let the sequel sit on the back burner and did this movie instead.

References

[1] http://www.boxofficemojo.com/movies/?page=daily&id=runawaybride.htm
[2] http://www.boxofficemojo.com/weekend/chart/?yr=1999&wknd=31&p=.htm
[3] http://www.boxofficemojo.com/movies/?id=runawaybride.htm

External links

- *Runaway Bride (1999 film)* (http://www.imdb.com/title/tt0163187/) at the Internet Movie Database
- *Runaway Bride (1999 film)* (http://tcmdb.com/title/title.jsp?stid=333458) at the TCM Movie Database
- *Runaway Bride (1999 film)* (http://www.allrovi.com/movies/movie/v1:180254) at AllRovi
- *Runaway Bride (1999 film)* (http://www.boxofficemojo.com/movies/?id=runawaybride.htm) at Box Office Mojo
- Movie stills (http://film.virtual-history.com/film.php?filmid=7836)

Dr. T & the Women

Dr. T & the Women	
Theatrical release poster	
Directed by	Robert Altman
Produced by	Robert Altman Cindy Cowan
Written by	Anne Rapp
Starring	Richard Gere Helen Hunt Farrah Fawcett Laura Dern Shelley Long Kate Hudson Liv Tyler Tara Reid
Music by	Lyle Lovett
Cinematography	Jan Kiesser
Editing by	Geraldine Peroni
Distributed by	Artisan Entertainment
Release date(s)	October 13, 2000
Running time	122 minutes
Country	United States Germany
Language	English German Spanish
Budget	$12 million
Box office	$22,844,291

Dr. T & the Women is a 2000 American romantic comedy film directed by Robert Altman. It stars Richard Gere as wealthy gynecologist Dr. Sullivan Travis ("Dr. T") and Helen Hunt, Farrah Fawcett, Laura Dern, Shelley Long, Tara Reid, Kate Hudson and Liv Tyler as the various "women" that encompass his everyday life. The movie was primarily filmed in Dallas, Texas, and was released in US theaters on October 13, 2000. The film's music was composed by alternative country singer Lyle Lovett, who released an album of his score in September 2000.

Plot

Dr. Sullivan Travis (aka "Dr. T.") (Richard Gere) is a wealthy Dallas gynecologist for some of the wealthiest women in Texas who finds his life beginning to fall apart starting when his wife, Kate (Farrah Fawcett), suffers a nervous breakdown and is committed to the state mental hospital. Dr. T's eldest daughter, Dee Dee (Kate Hudson), is planning to go through with her approaching wedding despite the secret that she is romantically involved with Marilyn (Liv Tyler), the maid of honor. Dr. T's youngest daughter, Connie (Tara Reid), is a spunky conspiracy theorist who has her own agenda, while Dr. T's loyal secretary, Carolyn (Shelley Long), has romantic feelings for him, which are not mutual. Dr. T's sister-in-law, Peggy (Laura Dern), meddles in every situation she stumbles into, while one woman, Bree (Helen Hunt), a golf instructor, offers him comfort.

Cast

- Richard Gere as Dr. Sullivan Travis (Dr. T)
- Helen Hunt as Bree Davis
- Farrah Fawcett as Kate Travis
- Laura Dern as Peggy
- Shelley Long as Carolyn
- Kate Hudson as Dee Dee Travis
- Liv Tyler as Marilyn
- Tara Reid as Connie Travis
- Robert Hays as Harlan
- Matt Malloy as Bill
- Andy Richter as Eli
- Lee Grant as Dr. Harper
- Janine Turner as Dorothy Chambliss
- Sarah Shahi as Cheerleader (*uncredited*)

Release and critical reception

Dr. T & the Women was released in US cinemas on October 13, 2000, and earned $5,012,867 in its opening weekend on 1,489 screens, ranking #7 in the weekend of October 13, 2000[1] ultimately grossing $13,113,041 in the United States. It was later released in the United Kingdom on July 6, 2001, and went on to gross $9,731,250 in foreign profits.

The film received mixed reviews from critics. Critic Roger Ebert gave the film three stars, stating "When you hear that Dr. T is a gynecologist played by Richard Gere, you assume he is a love machine mowing down his patients. Nothing could be further from the truth".[2] The review aggregator Rotten Tomatoes reported that the film received 58% positive reviews, based on 102 reviews.[3] Metacritic reported the film had an average score of 64 out of 100, based on 35 reviews.[4]

References

[1] Box Office Mojo (http://www.boxofficemojo.com/movies/?id=drtandthewomen.htm)
[2] Roger Ebert (http://rogerebert.suntimes.com/apps/pbcs.dll/article?AID=/20001013/REVIEWS/10130304/1023)
[3] "Dr. T and the Women - Movie Reviews, Trailers, Pictures - Rotten Tomatoes" (http://www.rottentomatoes.com/m/dr_t_and_the_women/). Rotten Tomatoes. . Retrieved 2008-02-16.
[4] "Dr. T and the Women (2000): Reviews" (http://www.metacritic.com/film/titles/drtandthewomen). Metacritic. . Retrieved 2008-02-16.

External links

- *Dr. T & the Women* (http://www.imdb.com/title/tt0205271/) at the Internet Movie Database
- *Dr. T & the Women* (http://www.allrovi.com/movies/movie/v212176) at AllRovi
- *Dr. T & the Women* (http://www.boxofficemojo.com/movies/?id=drtandthewomen.htm) at Box Office Mojo
- *Dr. T & the Women* (http://www.rottentomatoes.com/m/dr_t_and_the_women/) at Rotten Tomatoes
- *Dr. T & the Women* (http://www.metacritic.com/movie/drtandthewomen) at Metacritic

Autumn in New York (film)

Autumn in New York	
Directed by	Joan Chen
Produced by	Gary Lucchesi Amy Robinson Tom Rosenberg
Written by	Allison Burnett
Starring	Winona Ryder Richard Gere Anthony LaPaglia Elaine Stritch Vera Farmiga
Music by	Gabriel Yared
Cinematography	Gu Changwei
Editing by	Ruby Yang
Distributed by	Metro-Goldwyn-Mayer
Release date(s)	August 11, 2000
Running time	103 minutes
Country	United States
Language	English
Budget	$65 million
Box office	$90,726,668[1]

Autumn in New York is a 2000 romantic drama film directed by Joan Chen and starring Richard Gere, Winona Ryder, and Anthony LaPaglia.

The movie focuses on Will Keane (Gere) who falls in love with Charlotte Fielding (Ryder), a sweet, but terminally ill young woman.

Plot

Will Keane, a 48-year old restaurant owner, has a persistent case of commitment-phobia. When he meets Charlotte Fielding, a free-spirited woman half his age, he expects another quick and easy romance. But nothing about their relationship is quick or easy. Instead their encounters are rife with intergenerational clashes, differing philosophies and an urgent sense of sensuality and connection.

Just when Will is tempted to bail out with his usual line about "not promising forever," Charlotte responds with reasons of her own about why she feels this relationship can't last forever: she's dying because she has a heart neuroblastoma.

Although Charlotte's grandma, Dolly is not too keen on their budding relationship, she doesn't express any fears in front of her. But she warns Will to leave her alone on account of the fact that she is "really sick". Her fears though have another dimension to them. She doesn't want her granddaughter to be hurt the same way her daughter was and more so by the same man. When Charlotte comes home one evening soaked in tears, after learning that Will has slept with someone else, Dolly divulges the details of the past about her mom and Will that she had kept from her so far. Charlotte gets angry with her for not trying to "protect" her especially being the only family that she had in the world. Will visits Charlotte seeking forgiveness. Charlotte though angry, forgives Will and they go on to have a short sweet affair.

In the end, she dies and Will is left alone, but later is shown to have a relationship with both Lisa, his estranged daughter, and newborn grandson.

Cast

- Richard Gere - Will Keane
- Winona Ryder - Charlotte Fielding
- Anthony LaPaglia - John Volpe
- Elaine Stritch - Dolores "Dolly" Talbot
- Vera Farmiga - Lisa Tyler
- Sherry Stringfield - Sarah Volpe
- Jill Hennessy - Lynn McCale
- J.K. Simmons - Dr. Tom Grandy
- Sam Trammell - Simon
- Mary Beth Hurt - Dr. Paul Sibley
- Kali Rocha - Shannon
- Steven Randazzo - Alberto
- George Spielvogel III - Netto
- Ranjit Chowdhry - Fakir
- Audrey Quock - Eriko
- Tawny Cypress - Melissa
- Daniella van Graas - Model at Bar
- Rachel Nichols - Model at Bar

Reception

The film opened at #4 at the North American box office making $10,987,006 in its opening weekend, behind The Replacements, Space Cowboys and Hollow Man. The film received overwhelmingly negative reviews. It was also a flop at the box office, grossing $37 million domestically from its $65 million budget. The film was nominated for one Razzie Award, Worst Screen Couple (Richard Gere and Winona Ryder).

References

[1] "Autumn in New York" (http://boxofficemojo.com/movies/?id=autumninnewyork.htm). *Box Office Mojo*. . Retrieved 2010-06-01.

External links

- *Autumn in New York* (http://www.imdb.com/title/tt0174480/) at the Internet Movie Database
- *Autumn in New York* (http://www.rottentomatoes.com/m/autumn_in_new_york/) at Rotten Tomatoes
- Movie stills (http://film.virtual-history.com/film.php?filmid=17866)
- Yahoo movie review (http://movies.yahoo.com/movie/1800421189/details)

Chicago (2002 film)

Chicago	
Theatrical release poster	
Directed by	Rob Marshall
Produced by	- Bob Weinstein - Harvey Weinstein - Craig Zadan - Martin Richards
Written by	- Maurine Dallas Watkins - Bob Fosse - Fred Ebb - Bill Condon
Starring	- Renée Zellweger - Catherine Zeta-Jones - Richard Gere - Queen Latifah - John C. Reilly - Christine Baranski - Taye Diggs - Lucy Liu
Cinematography	Dion Beebe
Editing by	Martin Walsh
Distributed by	Miramax Films
Release date(s)	December 27, 2002
Running time	113 minutes
Country	United States
Language	English
Budget	$45,000,000
Box office	$306,776,732[1]

Chicago is a 2002 musical film adapted from the satirical stage musical of the same name, exploring the themes of celebrity, scandal, and corruption in Jazz-age Chicago.[2]

Directed and choreographed by Rob Marshall, and adapted by screenwriter Bill Condon, *Chicago* won six Academy Awards in 2003, including Best Picture. The film was the first musical to win Best Picture since *Oliver!* in 1969.

Chicago centers on Roxie Hart and Velma Kelly, two murderesses who find themselves on death row together in 1920s Chicago. Velma, a vaudevillian, and Roxie, a housewife, fight for the fame that will keep them from the gallows. The film stars Renée Zellweger, Richard Gere, and Catherine Zeta-Jones also featuring Queen Latifah, John C. Reilly, Christine Baranski, Lucy Liu, Taye Diggs, Colm Feore, and Mýa Harrison.

Plot

Chicago, circa 1924. Naïve Roxie Hart (Renée Zellweger) visits a nightclub, where star Velma Kelly (Catherine Zeta-Jones) performs ("*All That Jazz*"), with Fred Casely (Dominic West), a lover she hopes will get her a vaudeville gig. After the show, Velma is arrested for killing her husband and sister, Veronica, after finding them in bed together. Later, Fred reveals to Roxie that he lied about his connections in order to sleep with her, at which point Roxie, in a fit of rage, shoots Fred three times, killing him. Roxie convinces her husband, Amos (John C. Reilly), to take the blame, telling him it was a burglar and that he needn't worry, he'll get off. When the officer points out that the victim is Fred Casely, who sold the Harts furniture, Amos abandons his lie and says Casely was dead when he got home ("*Funny Honey*"). Roxie is sent to Cook County Jail.

Upon her arrival, she is sent to Murderess' Row to await trial — under the care of the corrupt Matron "Mama" Morton (Queen Latifah), who takes bribes and supplies her prisoners with cigarettes and contraband ("*When You're Good to Mama*"). Roxie meets Velma, and learns the backstories of the other women in Murderess' Row ("*Cell Block Tango*"). Roxie decides that she wants to engage Velma's lawyer, Billy Flynn (Richard Gere) ("*All I Care About*"), and convinces her husband to talk to him. Flynn and Roxie manipulate the press at a press conference, reinventing Roxie's identity to make Chicago fall in love with her ("*We Both Reached for the Gun*"). Roxie becomes the new infamous celebrity of the Cook County Jail ("*Roxie*"), much to Velma's disgust and Mama's delight. Velma, desperate to get back into the limelight, tries to talk Roxie into opening a vaudeville act with her once they get out of jail ("*I Can't Do It Alone*"). Seeking revenge for an earlier mocking, Roxie haughtily refuses, and Roxie and Velma become locked in a rivalry to outshine each other.

After an heiress (Lucy Liu) is arrested for a triple homicide (she killed her husband and the two women in bed with him), Roxie finds herself ignored by the paparazzi and neglected by Flynn. After being told by Velma that her name isn't in the paper, Roxie manages to steal back the limelight by claiming to be pregnant, which is confirmed by a doctor, whom it is implied she seduced. As paparazzi chase Roxie, Amos remains ignored ("*Mister Cellophane*"). Roxie witnesses the execution by hanging of another inmate (who was falsely accused) after losing her last appeal, which fuels Roxie's desire to be free. Roxie and Billy design their scheme to prove her innocence, by using her star power and sympathy vote. Her trial becomes a media spectacle ("*Razzle Dazzle*"), fed on the sensationalist reports of newspaper reporter and radio personality, Mary Sunshine (Christine Baranski). Meanwhile, Mama gives Velma Roxie's diary, as she hopes this will get Velma off the hook. In court next day, Velma is called by the prosecutor Harrison (Colm Feore) as a surprise rebuttal witness. During her testimony, she reads pages from Roxie's diary that state that she deliberately shot Fred Casely and would do it again. Now faced with a seemingly damning testimony, Billy cross-examines Velma and makes her admit that Harrison got her testimony in exchange for dropping all charges against her. Billy then suggests that Harrison concocted the phony diary pages to falsely convict Roxie. The jury quickly find Roxie not guilty. However, Roxie's publicity is short-lived: as soon as the trial concludes, the public's attention turns quickly to a new murderess. Roxie leaves the courthouse after discovering that Billy arranged for the diary testimony so that Velma also gets off death row. Roxie reveals to Amos she faked her pregnancy for the fame. It is implied, but never stated, that Amos leaves her at this point.

With nothing left, Roxie once more sets off to find a stage career, with little success ("*Nowadays*"). However, she is soon approached by Velma, also down on her luck, who is willing to revive a two-person act with Roxie. Roxie refuses at first, still not over the hate they shared for each other while in prison, but relents when Velma points out that "there's only one business in the world where that's not a problem at all" - show business. The two murderesses, no longer facing jail time, finally become the enormous successes they have been longing to be ("*Nowadays/Hot Honey Rag*"). The film concludes with Roxie and Velma receiving a standing ovation from an enthusiastic audience that includes Mama and Billy.

Cast

- Renée Zellweger as Roxanne "Roxie" Hart, a housewife who aspires to be a vaudevillian.
- Catherine Zeta-Jones as Velma Kelly, a showgirl who is arrested for the murders of her husband and her sister.
- Richard Gere as Billy Flynn, a treacherous, smooth-talking lawyer who turns his clients into celebrities to gain public support for them.
- Queen Latifah as Matron "Mama" Morton, the corrupt matron of the Cook County Jail.
- John C. Reilly as Amos Hart, Roxie's naïve, simple-minded, but devoted husband.
- Christine Baranski as Mary Sunshine, an overtrusting reporter who only highlights the good in people (a role originally intended to be played by a man in drag).
- Taye Diggs as The Bandleader, a shadowy, mystical master of ceremonies who introduces each song.
- Lucy Liu as Kitty Baxter, a millionaire heiress who briefly outshines Velma and Roxie when she kills her husband and his two mistresses.
- Dominic West as Frederick "Fred" Casely, Roxie's deceitful lover and murder victim.
- Colm Feore as Harrison, the prosecutor in both Roxie and Velma's court cases.
- Jayne Eastwood as Mrs. Borusewicz, the Harts neighbor from across the hall.
- Chita Rivera as Nicky
- Susan Misner, Denise Faye, Deidre Goodwin, Ekaterina Chtchelkanova, and Mýa Harrison as The Merry Murderesses (Liz, Annie, June, the Hunyak, and Mona)
- Ken Ard as Wilbur, one of the murdered husbands.

Musical numbers

1. "Overture/All That Jazz" – Velma, Company
2. "Funny Honey" – Roxie
3. "When You're Good to Mama" – Mama
4. "Cell Block Tango" – Velma, Cell Block Girls
5. "All I Care About" – Billy, Chorus Girls
6. "We Both Reached For The Gun" – Billy, Roxie, Mary, Reporters
7. "Roxie" – Roxie, Chorus Boys
8. "I Can't Do It Alone" – Velma
9. "Mister Cellophane" – Amos
10. "Razzle Dazzle" – Billy, Company
11. "Class" – Velma and Mama (This song, performed by Queen Latifah and Catherine Zeta-Jones, was filmed, but it was cut from the film. The scene was later included on the DVD release and the film's broadcast television premiere on NBC in 2005, and the song was included on the soundtrack album.)
12. "Nowadays" – Roxie
13. "Nowadays/Hot Honey Rag" – Roxie, Velma
14. "I Move On" – Roxie and Velma (over the end credits)
15. "All That Jazz (reprise)" - Velma, Company
16. "Exit Music" - Instrumental

History

The film is based on the 1975 Kander and Ebb Broadway musical of the same name, which in turn was based on the Maurine Watkins play, *Chicago*. That original play was in turn based on the stories of two real-life Jazz-era killers, Beulah Annan and Belva Gaertner. The same story was adapted into William Wellman's 1942 film *Roxie Hart*, starring Ginger Rogers as Roxie and Adolphe Menjou as Billy.

The original 1975 Broadway production was not well-received by audiences, primarily due to the show's cynical tone. However, the minimalist 1996 revival was much more successful, still running on Broadway in 2011, and the influences of both productions can be seen in the film version. The original production's musical numbers were staged as vaudeville acts; the film respects this but presents them in a cutaway form, while scenes that take place in "real life" have a hard-edged realism.

A film version of *Chicago* was to have been the next project for legendary stage and film choreographer and director Bob Fosse, who directed and choreographed the original 1975 Broadway production. Though he died before this film was made, his distinctive jazz choreography style is evident throughout. In particular, the parallels to *Cabaret* (1972) are numerous and distinct. He is thanked in the film's credits.

Chicago was produced by American companies Miramax Films and The Producers Circle in association with the German company Kallis Productions. *Chicago* was filmed in Toronto, Ontario, Canada. The courthouse scene was shot in Osgoode Hall. Other scenes were filmed at Queen's Park, former Gooderham and Worts Distillery, Casa Loma, the Elgin Theatre, Union Station, the Canada Life Building, the Danforth Music Hall, and at the Old City Hall. All vocal coaching for the film was led by Toronto-based Elaine Overholt, whom Richard Gere thanked personally during his Golden Globe acceptance speech.

Release and reception

Chicago was received with very positive reviews and universal acclaim. On the review aggregate website Rotten Tomatoes, the film currently holds an 88% approval rating;[3] Roger Ebert called it "Big, brassy fun".[4] On Metacritic, the film averaged a critical score of 82 (indicating "universal acclaim").[5]

This musical-turned-film received widespread attention from overseas and was even labeled as "The best screen musical for 30 years," by Tim Robey, writer for the *Telegraph* in the United Kingdom. He also states that it has taken a "three-step tango for us to welcome back the movie musical as a form." Rob Marshall's film has also been labeled as one of the most enjoyable pictures of its kind since Fosse`s *Cabaret* of 1972. This particular *Chicago* makes the most prolific use it possibly can out of one specific advantage the cinema has over the stage when it comes to song and dance: "it's a sustained celebration of parallel montage." [6]

Other reviews claimed that there were issues with the film being too streamlined, and minor complaints were made toward Marshall's directing influences. AMC Filmcritic Sean O'Connell explains in his review of the film that "All That Jazz", "Funny Honey", and "Cell Block Tango" play out much like you'd expect them to on stage, with little enhancement (or subsequent interference) from the camera. But by the time "Razzle Dazzle" comes around, all of these concerns are diminished.[7]

Box office

The film grossed $170,687,518 in the United States and Canada, as well $136,089,214 in other territories. Combined, the film grossed $306,403,013 worldwide, which was, at the time, the highest gross of any film never to reach #1 or #2 in the weekly box office charts in the North American markets (Canada and United States—where it peaked at #3). This record has since been outdone by *Alvin and the Chipmunks: The Squeakquel*.[8]

Home release

Chicago was released on DVD in Region 1 (USA, Canada, and US territories) on August 19, 2003. It was released in Full Screen and Widescreen. In addition to this release, a two-disc "Razzle Dazzle" Edition was released over two years later on December 20, 2005, and later, on Blu-ray format, in January 2007 and, in an updated release, in May 2011. Miramax was the label responsible for the production of the DVDs and the discs themselves provide a feature-length audio commentary track with director Rob Marshall and screenwriter Bill Condon. There's also a deleted musical number called "Class," performed by Catherine Zeta-Jones and Queen Latifah.

Awards and nominations

Category	Nominee	Result
Academy Awards[9][10]		
Best Picture	Martin Richards	Won
Best Actress	Renee Zellweger	Nominated
Best Supporting Actor	John C. Reilly	Nominated
Best Supporting Actress	Catherine Zeta-Jones	Won
Best Supporting Actress	Queen Latifah	Nominated
Best Director	Rob Marshall	Nominated
Best Adapted Screenplay	Bill Condon	Nominated
Best Cinematography	Dion Beebe	Nominated
Best Art Direction	John Myhre	Won
Best Costume Design	Colleen Atwood	Won
Best Film Editing	Martin Walsh	Won
Best Sound Mixing	Michael Minkler, Dominick Tavella and David Lee	Won
Best Original Song	John Kander (for "I Move On")	Nominated
BAFTA Awards[11]		
Best Film		Nominated
Best Actress	Renee Zellweger	Nominated
Best Supporting Actress	Catherine Zeta-Jones	Won
Best Supporting Actress	Queen Latifah	Nominated
David Lean Award for Direction	Rob Marshall	Nominated
Best Cinematography	Dion Beebe	Nominated
Best Production Design	John Myhre	Nominated
Best Costume Design	Colleen Atwood	Nominated
Best Make Up and Hair	Judi Cooper-Sealy	Nominated

Best Editing	Martin Walsh	Nominated
Best Sound	Michael Minkler, David Lee, and Dominick Tavella	Won
Anthony Asquith Award for Film Music	Danny Elfman	Nominated
Golden Globes[12]		
Best Motion Picture - Musical or Comedy		Won
Best Actor - Musical or Comedy	Richard Gere	Won
Best Actress - Musical or Comedy	Renee Zellweger	Won
Best Actress - Musical or Comedy	Catherine Zeta-Jones	Nominated
Best Supporting Actor	John C. Reilly	Nominated
Best Supporting Actress	Queen Latifah	Nominated
Best Director	Rob Marshall	Nominated
Best Screenplay	Bill Condon	Nominated
Broadcast Film Critics Association Awards[13]		
Best Picture		Won
Best Supporting Actress	Catherine Zeta-Jones	Won
Best Acting Ensemble		Won
Chicago Film Critics Association Award		
Best Actress	Renee Zellweger	Nominated
Dallas-Fort Worth Film Critics Association Award		
Best Picture		Won
Directors Guild of America Awards		
Outstanding Directing	Rob Marshall	Won
Evening Standard British Film Awards		
Best Actress	Catherine Zeta-Jones	Won
Florida Film Critics Circle		
Best Song	"Cell Block Tango"	Won
National Board of Review of Motion Pictures		
Best Directorial Debut	Rob Marshall	Won
Online Film Critics Society Awards[14]		
Best Supporting Actress	Catherine Zeta-Jones	Nominated
Best Ensemble		Nominated
Best Breakthrough Filmmaker	Rob Marshall	Nominated
Best Costume Design	Colleen Atwood	Nominated
Best Editing	Martin Walsh	Nominated
Phoenix Film Critics Society		
Best Picture		Nominated
Best Actress	Renee Zellweger	Nominated
Best Supporting Actress	Catherine Zeta-Jones	Won
Best Acting Ensemble		Nominated

Best Director	Rob Marshall	Nominated
Best Cinematography	Dion Beebe	Nominated
Best Costume Design	Colleen Atwood	Won
Best Film Editing	Martin Walsh	Won
Best Newcomer	Rob Marshall	Nominated
Screen Actors Guild Awards[15]		
Best Actress	Renee Zellweger	Won
Best Actor	Richard Gere	Nominated
Best Supporting Actress	Catherine Zeta-Jones	Won
Best Supporting Actress	Queen Latifah	Nominated
Best Acting Ensemble		Won
Writers Guild of America Award		
Best Adapted Screenplay	Bill Condon	Nominated

References

[1] *Chicago* (http://www.boxofficemojo.com/movies/?id=chicago.htm) at Box Office Mojo

[2] New York Times (http://movies.nytimes.com/movie/review?res=9B0DE0DC113CF934A15751C1A9649C8B63)

[3] "Chicago Movie Reviews, Pictures" (http://www.rottentomatoes.com/m/chicago/). *Rotten Tomatoes*. . Retrieved June 5, 2009.

[4] "Chicago (2002) - Cream of the Crops" (http://www.rottentomatoes.com/m/chicago/?critic=creamcrop). Rotten Tomatoes. . Retrieved June 5, 2009.

[5] "Chicago reviews" (http://www.metacritic.com/video/titles/chicago). *Metacritic*. . Retrieved August 13, 2009.

[6] Robey, Tim (Decembery 27, 2002). "This Jailhouse Rocks" (http://www.telegraph.co.uk/culture/4729504/This-jailhouse-rocks.html). *The Telegraph* (London). . Retrieved November 17, 2009.

[7] O'Connell, Sean (January 21, 2003). "Chicago" (http://www.filmcritic.com/misc/emporium.nsf/reviews/Chicago). *Filmcritic.com*. . Retrieved November 18, 2009.

[8] "Top Grossing Movies That Never Hit #1 at the Box Office" (http://www.boxofficemojo.com/alltime/domestic/never1.htm). Box Office Mojo. . Retrieved July 18, 2010.

[9] "The 75th Academy Awards (2003) Nominees and Winners" (http://www.oscars.org/awards/academyawards/legacy/ceremony/75th-winners.html). oscars.org. . Retrieved 2011-11-20.

[10] "The 2003 Oscar Winners" (http://www.ropeofsilicon.com/award_show/oscars/2003). *Ropeofsilicon.com*. . Retrieved August 10, 2009.

[11] "Awards Database - The BAFTA site" (http://www.bafta.org/awards-database.html?year=2002&category=Film&award=false). *Bafta.org*. . Retrieved August 10, 2009.

[12] "The 2003 Golden Globe Award Winners" (http://www.ropeofsilicon.com/award_show/golden_globe_awards/2003). *Ropeofsilicon.com*. . Retrieved August 10, 2009.

[13] "The BFCA Critics' Choice Awards :: 2002" (http://www.bfca.org/ccawards/2002.php). *Bfca.org*. . Retrieved August 10, 2009.

[14] "O.F.C.S.: The Online Film Critics Society" (http://ofcs.rottentomatoes.com/pages/awards/2002nominees). *Rotten Tomatoes*. January 6, 2003. . Retrieved August 10, 2009.

[15] "The 2003 Screen Actors Guild Award Winners" (http://www.ropeofsilicon.com/award_show/screen_actors_guild_awards/2003). *Ropeofsilicon.com*. . Retrieved August 10, 2009.

External links

- *Chicago (2002 film)* - (2011 blu-ray) (http://www.blu-ray.com/movies/Chicago-Blu-ray/22132/)
- *Chicago (2002 film)* - (2007 blu-ray) (http://www.blu-ray.com/movies/Chicago-Blu-ray/257/)
- *Chicago (2002 film)* (http://www.imdb.com/title/tt0299658/) at the Internet Movie Database
- *Chicago* (http://tcmdb.com/title/title.jsp?stid=439832) at the TCM Movie Database
- *Chicago* (http://www.boxofficemojo.com/movies/?id=chicago.htm) at Box Office Mojo
- *Chicago* (http://www.rottentomatoes.com/m/chicago/) at Rotten Tomatoes

Unfaithful (2002 film)

Unfaithful	
Theatrical release poster	
Directed by	Adrian Lyne
Produced by	Adrian Lyne Arnon Milchan G. Mac Brown
Written by	**1968 screenplay:** Claude Chabrol **Screenplay:** Alvin Sargent William Broyles Jr.
Starring	Richard Gere Diane Lane Olivier Martinez Erik Per Sullivan
Music by	Jan A. P. Kaczmarek
Cinematography	Peter Biziou
Editing by	Anne V. Coates
Studio	Regency Enterprises
Distributed by	20th Century Fox
Release date(s)	May 10, 2002
Running time	124 minutes
Country	United States
Language	English
Budget	$50 million
Box office	$119,137,784

Unfaithful is a 2002 American erotic drama film directed by Adrian Lyne and starring Richard Gere, Diane Lane and Olivier Martinez. It was adapted by Alvin Sargent and William Broyles Jr. from the French film *The Unfaithful Wife* (1968) (*La Femme infidèle*) by the noted director Claude Chabrol. It tells about a couple living in suburban New York City whose marriage goes dangerously awry when the wife indulges in an adulterous fling with a stranger she encounters by chance in Manhattan.

The production was unusual for its demanding and extended sex scenes shot through smoke. Lyne shot a total of five endings, based on his experience with the controversial content of *Fatal Attraction*.

Unfaithful grossed $52 million in North America and a total of $119 million worldwide. Despite mixed to negative reviews overall, Lane received much praise for her performance. She won awards for best actress from the National Society of Film Critics and New York Film Critics, and was nominated for a Golden Globe and an Academy Award for Best Actress.

Plot

Connie Sumner (Lane) and Edward Sumner (Gere) are a couple who live in suburban New York City. Their marriage is solid and loving but lacking passion. One day, Connie journeys into the city, where she is caught in a windstorm. As she seeks a taxi, she bumps into a stranger (Martinez). They both fall and Connie scrapes her knees. The stranger offers to let her use his apartment to clean up. At that moment, an empty cab goes by, but Connie accepts the offer instead of heading back to the train station. The stranger introduces himself as Paul Martel, a Frenchman who buys and sells used books. When Martel makes small advances toward her, Connie becomes uncomfortable and decides to leave . He lets her go but gives her a book of Persian poetry, *Rubaiyat of Omar Khayyam* as a gift.

Later that night, Connie mentions the incident to her husband. The next morning, after Edward and their son Charlie (Sullivan) leave, she picks up the poetry book. Paul's business card falls out. She takes the train into the city again and calls him from Grand Central Station. He invites her over for coffee. He makes her coffee and shows her how to read a book in braille. But when Paul begins caressing her hands, Connie decides to leave. Later that night, Connie seems distracted, obviously thinking about Paul. The next morning she shows up at his door. When Connie enters Paul's apartment, he asks her to dance. She obliges and they begin flirting with each other. As the record they are dancing to begins to skip, she decides that what they are doing is a mistake. Paul tells her, "There is no such thing as a mistake. There is what you do and what you don't do." Connie replies, "I can't do this," and starts to leave the building. But when she has to come back into the apartment for her coat, Paul grabs her and kisses her and then they engage in intercourse.

Connie and Paul begin a passionate sexual affair. Edward soon suspects something when his wife increases the frequency of her visits to Manhattan. She uses her work on a charity event as an excuse, but Edward finds holes in her stories when he speaks with mutual friends. She shows less interest in him, *i.e.,* removing her wedding ring to wash the dishes. Eventually, one of Edward's business partners catches a glimpse of Connie and Paul fawning over each other in a cafe and tells Edward, who hires a detective (Chianese) to follow Connie. On a day when Edward was out of town, Connie and Paul enjoyed time in a movie theatre, leading her to forget to pick up her son from the school. The detective returns with pictures of Connie and Paul, which devastate Edward.

Connie sees Paul with another woman and attacks him, but he denies that the woman is special. She is enraged and they begin to fight in his building, but their anger turns into passion . Edward decides to visit Paul's apartment but leaves when unable to enter, and misses seeing Connie leave. He returns moments later, gets in and confronts Paul. Already upset, he is stunned to see a snow globe there, which he recognizes as his own gift to Connie. Paul says that Connie bought it for him as a gift, and Edward hits the other man with the globe and kills him. Edward cleans up the blood, wipes away his fingerprints and wraps Paul's body in a rug. As he works, the phone rings, and Edward hears Connie leaving a message that she must end the affair. Edward erases the message and leaves, putting the body in his car's trunk. Later that night, he drops it off at a dump.

Two police detectives arrive at the Sumner home. They explain that Paul's wife had reported him missing and they had found Connie's phone number in his apartment. She claims to have met him only once. A week later, the detectives return and tell Connie that they found Paul's body. She becomes upset while repeating her earlier story; Edward backs her up and adds that he never met Paul. Later that night, collecting Edward's clothes for the dry cleaner's, Connie finds the private detective's photos and realizes that Edward knows about the affair. She concludes that he murdered Paul after noticing the snow globe has been returned to their home. Underneath the globe, she discovers a hidden compartment containing a photograph of her, Edward and Charlie, with an anniversary message from Edward, which causes Connie to cry.

Edward and Connie confront each other. She burns the photographs; he offers to turn himself in. Connie rejects this and insists they will get through the crisis together. Later the couple are shown in their car stopped at an intersection, debating their next move; outside, the traffic lights change several times from red to green and back. The camera pulls back to reveal their car in front of a police station.

Cast

- Richard Gere as Ed Sumner
- Diane Lane as Connie Sumner
- Olivier Martinez as Paul Martel
- Erik Per Sullivan as Charlie Sumner
- Michelle Monaghan as Lindsey
- Chad Lowe as Bill Stone
- Erich Anderson as Bob Gaylord
- Kate Burton as Tracy
- Margaret Colin as Sally
- Željko Ivanek as Detective Dean
- Gary Basaraba as Detective Mirojnick
- Dominic Chianese as Frank Wilson
- Michael Emerson as Josh
- Joseph Badalucco Jr. as a Train Conductor

Production

According to actor Gere, an early draft of the screenplay, which he read several years ago, presented the Sumners as suffering from a dysfunctional sexual relationship. It gave Connie some justification for having an affair. According to the actor and to director Lyne, the studio wanted to change the storyline so that the Sumners had a bad marriage with no sex, to create greater sympathy for Connie. Both men opposed the change; Lyne in particular felt that the studio's suggestions would have robbed the film of any drama: "I wanted two people who were perfectly happy. I loved the idea of the totally arbitrary nature of infidelity." The Sumners' relationship was rewritten as a good marriage, with her affair the result of a chance meeting.[1]

Adrian Lyne while directing *Unfaithful*

Pre-production

During pre-production, the producers received a video-taped audition from Olivier Martinez, who was selected for Paul. His character was portrayed as French once Martinez was cast. Lyne said, "I think it helps one understand how Connie might have leapt into this affair--he's very beguiling, doing even ordinary things." Once cast in the role, Martinez, with Lyne's approval, changed some of his dialogue and the scene in which he first seduces Lane's character, while she is looking at a book in braille. According to Martinez, "The story that was invented before was much more sensual, erotic and clear."[2]

Lyne cast Lane in the role of Constance after seeing her in the film, *A Walk on the Moon*.[1] He felt that the actress "breathes a certain sexuality. But she's sympathetic, and I think so many sexy women tend to be tough and hard at the same time."[3] Lyne also wanted Gere and Lane to gain weight in order to portray the comfort of a middle-age couple. In particular, he wanted Gere to gain 30 pounds and left donuts in the actor's trailer every morning.[4]

Lyne asked director of photography Peter Biziou, with whom he made *9½ Weeks*, to shoot *Unfaithful*. After reading the script, Biziou felt that the story was appropriate for the classic 1.85:1 aspect ratio because, "so often has two characters working together in the frame." During pre-production, Biziou, Lyne and production designer Brian Morris used a collection of still photographs as style references. These included photos from fashion magazines and shots by prominent photographers.[5]

Principal photography

Initially, the story was set against snowy exteriors, but this idea was rejected early on. Principal photography started on March 22, 2001 and wrapped on June 1, 2001 with Lyne shooting in continuity whenever possible. The film was primarily shot in New York City. During the windstorm sequence where Connie first meets Paul, it rained and Lyne used the overcast weather conditions for the street scenes. The director also preferred shooting practical interiors on location so that the actors could "feel an intimate sense of belonging", Biziou recalls. The cinematographer also used natural light as much as possible.[5]

At times, Lyne's directing took its toll on the cast and crew. In a scene taking place in an office, the director pumped it full of smoke, an effect that "makes the colors less contrasty, more muted".[1] According to Biziou, "The texture it gives helps differentiate and separate various density levels of darkness farther back in frame".[5] The smoke was piped in for 18 to 20 hours a day and Gere remembers, "Our throats were being blown out. We had a special doctor who was there almost all the time who was shooting people up with antibiotics for bronchial infections". Lane acquired an oxygen bottle in order to survive the rigorous schedule.[1]

The film has many explicit sex scenes, including a tryst in a restaurant bathroom and a passionate exchange in an apartment building hallway. Lyne's repeated takes for these scenes were demanding for the actors, especially for Lane, who had to be emotionally and physically fit for the scenes.[1] To prepare for the initial love scene between Paul and Constance, Lyne had the actors watch clips from *Fatal Attraction*, *Five Easy Pieces*, and *Last Tango in Paris*.[4] Lane and Martinez would also talk over the scenes in his trailer beforehand. Once on the set, they felt uncomfortable until several takes in. She said, "My comfort level with it just had to catch up quickly if I wanted to be the actress to play it."[6] Martinez was not comfortable with nudity. Lane said that Lyne would often shoot a whole magazine of film, "so one take was as long as five takes. By the end, you're physically and emotionally shattered."[7]

Lane had not met Martinez before filming, and they did not get to know each other well during the shoot, mirroring the relationship between their characters.[8] A full four weeks of the schedule was dedicated to the scenes in Paul's loft, which was located on the third floor of a six-story building located on Greene Street. Biziou often used two cameras for the film's intimate scenes to reduce the number of takes that had to be shot.[5]

Post-production

Lyne shot five different endings to *Unfaithful* based on his experiences with *Fatal Attraction*, whose initial ending was rejected by the test audience.[4] According to Lyne, he had some debate with the 20th Century-Fox officials, who wanted to "make the marriage gray, the sex bad. I fought that. I tried to explore the guilt, the jealousy—that's what I'm interested in".[9] The studio did not like the film's "enigmatic" ending, which they felt failed to punish crimes committed by the characters. It imposed a "particularly jarring 'Hollywood' final line," which angered Gere.

Following negative reactions from test audiences, the studio reinstated the original ending;[7] a few weeks before the film was to open in theaters, Lyne asked Gere and Lane to return to Los Angeles for re-shoots of the ending.[1] Lyne claimed that the new ending was more ambiguous than the original and was the original one by screenwriter Alvin Sargent. Lyne also thought the new ending would "it would be more interesting and provoke more discussion".[10]

Reception

Unfaithful opened on May 10, 2002 in 2,617 theaters and grossed USD $14 million with an average of $5,374 per screen. It made $52 million in North America and a total of $119 million worldwide, well above its $50 million budget.[11]

Critical response

The film received largely mixed reviews, though Diane Lane earned widespread praise for her performance. It currently has a rating of 47% on Rotten Tomatoes (48% for their "Cream of the Crop" designation). CNN film critic Paul Tatara wrote, "The audience when I saw this one was chuckling at all the wrong times, and that's a bad sign when they're supposed to be having a collective heart attack."[12] *Entertainment Weekly* critic Owen Gleiberman awarded the film an "A-" grade and praised Lane for delivering "the most urgent performance of her career", writing that she "is a revelation. The play of lust, romance, degradation, and guilt on her face is the movie's real story."[13] Roger Ebert, of the *Chicago Sun-Times* wrote, "Instead of pumping up the plot with recycled manufactured thrills, it's content to contemplate two reasonably sane adults who get themselves into an almost insoluble dilemma."[14] In the *Los Angeles Times*, the critic Kenneth Turan wrote, "The only performer who manages to get inside her character is Lane. Whether it's her initial half-distrustful tentativeness, her later sensual abandon or her never-ending ambivalence, Lane's Constance seems to be actually living the role in a way no one else matches, a way we can all connect to."[15]

Stephen Holden in the *New York Times* praised the "taut, economical screenplay" that "digs into its characters' marrow (and into the perfectly selected details of domestic life) without wasting a word. That screenplay helps to ground a film whose visual imagination hovers somewhere between soap opera and a portentous pop surrealism."[16] *USA Today* gave the film three-and-a-half stars out of four and Mike Clark wrote, "Diane Lane also reaches a new career plateau with her best performance since 1979's *A Little Romance*."[17] In his review for the *Washington Post*, Stephen Hunter wrote, "In the end, *Unfaithful* leaves you dispirited and grumpy: All that money spent, all that talent wasted, all that time gone forever, and for what? It's an ill movie that bloweth no man to good."[18] David Ansen, in his review for *Newsweek*, wrote, "*Unfaithful* shows what a powerful, sexy, smart filmmaker Lyne can be. It's a shame he substitutes the mechanics of suspense for the real suspense of what goes on between a man and a woman, a husband and a wife."[19] Andrew Sarris, in his review for *The New York Observer*, wrote, "Ultimately *Unfaithful* is escapism in its purest form, and I am willing to experience it on that level, even though with all the unalloyed joy on display, there's almost no humor," and concluded that it was "one of the very few mainstream movies currently directed exclusively to grown-ups."[20]

Awards and nominations

The studio campaign's theme consisted of what the studio called the film's "iconic scene": Constance recalling her first tryst with Paul as she takes a train home. According to Tom Rothman, chairman of Fox Filmed Entertainment, "That scene captured the power of her performance. It's what everyone talked about after they saw her." Four days before the New York Film Critics Circle's vote, Lane was given a career tribute by the Film Society of Lincoln Center. A day before that, Lyne held a dinner for the actress at the Four Seasons Hotel. Critics and award voters were invited to both.[21] Lane won the National Society of Film Critics, the New York Film Critics Circle awards and was nominated for a Golden Globe and an Academy Award for Best Actress. *Entertainment Weekly* ranked *Unfaithful* the 27th on their "50 Sexiest Movies Ever" list.[22]

References

[1] Kobel, Peter (2002-05-05). "Smoke to Go With the Steam" (http://www.nytimes.com/2002/05/05/movies/film-smoke-to-go-with-the-steam.html). *The New York Times.* . Retrieved 2008-06-19.

[2] Topel, Fred (2002). "Olivier Martinez Interview – *Unfaithful*" (http://movies.about.com/library/weekly/aa050102c.htm). *About.com: Hollywood Movies.* . Retrieved 2007-08-24.

[3] Wolk, Josh (2002). "Meet Unfaithful's Diane Lane" (http://www.ew.com/ew/article/0,,238385~1~0~,00.html). *Entertainment Weekly.* . Retrieved 2007-08-24.

[4] Whipp, Glenn (2002-05-10). "Uncovered". *Los Angeles Times.*

[5] Martin, Kevin H (2002-06). "Broken Vows". *American Cinematographer.*

[6] Murray, Rebecca (2002). "Diane Lane Interview – *Unfaithful*" (http://movies.about.com/library/weekly/aa050102b.htm). *About.com: Hollywood Movies.* . Retrieved 2007-08-24.

[7] Bhattacharya, Sanjiv (2002-05-26). "Memory Lane" (http://film.guardian.co.uk/interview/interviewpages/0,6737,722253,00.html). *The Guardian.* . Retrieved 2007-08-24.

[8] Iley, Chrissy (2002-06-10). "Always In and Out of Passion". *The Times.*

[9] Wloszczyna, Susan (2002-05-09). "Director Adrian Lyne, faithful to sexual themes" (http://www.usatoday.com/life/movies/2002/2002-05-09-lyne.htm). *USA Today.* .

[10] "Director Tweaks *Unfaithful* Ending" (http://articles.latimes.com/2002/may/06/entertainment/et-1know6). *Los Angeles Times.* 2002-05-06. . Retrieved 2010-06-10.

[11] "*Unfaithful*" (http://www.boxofficemojo.com/movies/?id=unfaithful.htm). *Box Office Mojo.* . Retrieved 2007-08-24.

[12] Tatara, Paul (2002-05-09). "Sexually charged *Unfaithful* falls flat" (http://archives.cnn.com/2002/SHOWBIZ/Movies/05/09/review.unfaithful/index.html). *CNN.* . Retrieved 2007-08-24.

[13] Gleiberman, Owen (2002-05-17). "*Unfaithful*" (http://www.ew.com/ew/article/0,,237208,00.html). *Entertainment Weekly.* . Retrieved 2007-08-24.

[14] Ebert, Roger (2002-05-10). "*Unfaithful*" (http://rogerebert.suntimes.com/apps/pbcs.dll/article?AID=/20020510/REVIEWS/205100306/1023). *Chicago Sun-Times.* . Retrieved 2007-10-03.

[15] Turan, Kenneth (2002-05-08). "*Unfaithful*" (http://www.calendarlive.com/movies/reviews/cl-movie000032467may08,0,3886120.story). *Los Angeles Times.* . Retrieved 2009-01-22.

[16] Holden, Stephen (2002-05-08). "Day in Town Takes an Unexpected Tryst" (http://query.nytimes.com/gst/fullpage.html?res=9807E0D81430F93BA35756C0A9649C8B63). *The New York Times.* . Retrieved 2009-01-22.

[17] Clark, Mike (2002-05-11). "*Unfaithful* turns torrid affair scary" (http://www.usatoday.com/life/movies/2002/2002-05-08-unfaithful-review.htm). *USA Today.* . Retrieved 2009-01-22.

[18] Hunter, Stephen (2002-05-10). "*Unfaithful*: Unfathomable Attraction" (http://www.washingtonpost.com/ac2/wp-dyn/A63172-2002May9). *The Washington Post.* . Retrieved 2009-01-22.

[19] Ansen, David (2002-05-13). "Lust And Consequences" (http://www.newsweek.com/id/64509). *Newsweek.* . Retrieved 2009-01-22.

[20] Sarris, Andrew (2002-05-12). "Diane Lane Stumbles, Smolders-Richard Gere Plays the Square" (http://www.observer.com/node/45983). *The New York Observer.* . Retrieved 2009-03-20.

[21] Bowles, Scott (2003-01-15). "Studio keeps *Unfaithful* out in open" (http://www.usatoday.com/life/music/news/2003-01-15-unfaithful_x.htm?loc=interstitialskip). *USA Today.* . Retrieved 2007-08-24.

[22] "50 Sexiest Movies Ever" (http://www.ew.com/ew/gallery/0,,20241620_23,00.html). *Entertainment Weekly.* 2008-11-29. . Retrieved 2008-11-21.

External links

- *Unfaithful* (http://www.imdb.com/title/tt0250797/) at the Internet Movie Database
- *Unfaithful* (http://www.allrovi.com/movies/movie/v261807) at AllRovi
- *Unfaithful* (http://www.rottentomatoes.com/m/unfaithful/) at Rotten Tomatoes
- *Unfaithful* (http://www.boxofficemojo.com/movies/?id=unfaithful.htm) at Box Office Mojo

The Mothman Prophecies (film)

The Mothman Prophecies	
Theatrical release poster	
Directed by	Mark Pellington
Produced by	Tom Rosenberg Gary W. Goldstein Richard Hatem Gary Lucchesi Richard S. Wright Terry McKay Adrienne Gruben Rachel Hudgins
Screenplay by	Richard Hatem
Based on	Novel: John Keel
Starring	Richard Gere Laura Linney Debra Messing Will Patton Lucinda Jenney
Music by	tomandandy
Cinematography	Fred Murphy
Editing by	Brian Berdan
Distributed by	Screen Gems
Release date(s)	January 25, 2002
Running time	119 minutes
Country	United States
Language	English
Budget	$42 million
Box office	$54,639,865[1]

The Mothman Prophecies is a 2002 psychological horror film directed by Mark Pellington, based on the 1975 book of the same name by parapsychologist and Fortean author John Keel. The screenplay was written by Richard Hatem. The film stars Richard Gere as John Klein, a reporter who researches the legend of the Mothman.

The film claims to be based on actual events that occurred between November 1966 and December 1967 in Point Pleasant, West Virginia. Critical reviews were mixed, but the film was a modest financial success.

Plot

John Klein (Richard Gere) is a hotshot Washington, D.C. reporter whose life suddenly takes a turn after he and his wife Mary (Debra Messing) are involved in a car accident after she apparently tried to avoid something on the road. Although she suffers a non-fatal head injury, Mary's CAT scans show that she has an inoperable brain tumor diagnosed as glioblastoma. After she dies, John discovers an assortment of cryptic drawings she made of a strange black winged creature she saw on the night of the fateful accident.

Two years later, while driving to Richmond, Virginia, John gets lost and inexplicably finds himself almost five hours off-course, arriving in the small town of Point Pleasant, West Virginia. He soon becomes entangled in the personal stories of residents and in a chain of mysterious events, wherein townspeople report strange supernatural encounters, along with weird lights and phone calls. With the help of town sheriff Connie Mills (Laura Linney), John begins to investigate. He determines that the common link is an apparently supernatural creature known as the Mothman, whose appearances seem to foretell disasters. Things take a decidedly personal and frightening turn when he realizes the eerie connections between his wife's drawings, eyewitness accounts of the Mothman, and phone calls from an other-worldly, seemingly malevolent entity named Indrid Cold.

The Mothman becomes a personal obsession for Klein. He meets an expert on the subject, Alexander Leek (Alan Bates), who convinces him that there may be a tragedy in store for the small town.

Production

Kittanning Citizens Bridge

Filming

The budget was cut by $2,000,000 before filming began. [2] Aside from a few opening scenes filmed in Washington, D.C., the entire movie was filmed in the areas of Pittsburgh and Kittanning in Pennsylvania. The scenes of Gere sitting on a park bench are on the University of Pittsburgh campus. Road montages were filmed on Pennsylvania Route 28, and the Chicago scenes are completely shot in downtown Pittsburgh's Mellon Square and Trinity Churchyard environs as well as the entrance to the Duquesne Club. The "Chemical Plant" featured in the movie is actually a power station owned by Reliant Energy in Elrama, Pennsylvania. Point Pleasant scenes were shot in Kittanning, Pennsylvania. The collapse of the Silver Bridge was actually filmed at the Kittanning Citizens Bridge in downtown Kittanning. Scenes shot at Gordon Smallwood's house were filmed in Washington County on Pennsylvania Route 917. Pittsburgh's Allegheny County Airport serves as backdrop for the airfield scenes. Despite this relocation, several police officers from Point Pleasant appeared as extras.[3]

Direction

Director Mark Pellington had a cameo role as a bartender.

Music

Several artists contributed music to the venture. A remix single of "Halflight" by the band, Low, was featured in the movie.

Reception

The Mothman Prophecies received mixed reviews from critics. Review aggregate website Rotten Tomatoes reports 52% of critics gave the film positive write-ups based on 135 reviews, with a rating of 5.5/10.[4] Roger Ebert of the *Chicago Sun-Times* gave it two stars out of four, calling it "unfocused" and "meandering," but praised the direction by Mark Pellington "whose command of camera, pacing and the overall effect is so good, it deserves a better screenplay."[5]

Differences from the book

The film adaptation of *The Mothman Prophecies* concentrates more on the personal stories and personalities of the characters and less on the investigation of UFOs and other strange phenomena upon which much of the book is based. Also, it is set in the modern day rather than in the 1960s, when the alleged sightings of the Mothman entity occurred.

The majority of the characters are also re-imagined. All have been renamed and in some cases, several characters have been merged into one or altered in some other way. Several have been removed entirely, such as the newspaper editor Mary Hyre, although her death somewhat mirrors one of the characters in the movie. The Men in Black, or "MIBs," in the book are removed; Indrid Cold, a relatively benign being in the book, is something more sinister in the film; and the Mothman itself rarely appears in the film. Instead, it is used to evoke subtle notes of supernatural horror for the filmgoer, versus functioning as the central, mysterious and provocative character as in the book.

In reality, 46 people died in the collapse of the Silver Bridge, not 36. Also, the film's claim at the end credits of the collapse of the Silver Bridge never being explained is incorrect, the incident was found to be caused by the failure of an eye-bar in a suspension chain.[6]

Home media

Mothman Prophecies was released on DVD on June 2002, with a two-disc Special Edition DVD set released later, in May 2003.[7]

References

[1] "The Mothman Prophecies - Box Office Data, Movie News, Cast Information" (http://www.the-numbers.com/movies/2002/MOTHM.php). The Numbers. . Retrieved 2009-07-27.

[2] "The Mothman Prophecies - Special Edition Dvd" (http://www.filmfreakcentral.net/dvdreviews/mothmanprophecies.htm). Filmfreakcentral.net. . Retrieved 2009-07-27.

[3] Spiderweb 2000 Solutions. "Point Pleasant Register - Mothman" (http://www.mothmanmuseum.com/MothmanLives/mothmanmovie/register/pointpleasantregister1.html). Mothmanmuseum.com. . Retrieved 2009-07-27.

[4] *The Mothman Prophecies (film)* (http://www.rottentomatoes.com/m/mothman_prophecies/) at Rotten Tomatoes.

[5] "The Mothman Prophecies" (http://rogerebert.suntimes.com/apps/pbcs.dll/article?AID=/20020125/REVIEWS/201250305/1023). *Chicago Sun-Times*. .

[6] "The Collapse of the Silver Bridge-by Chris LeRose" (http://www.wvculture.org/history/wvhs1504.html). Wvculture.org. . Retrieved 2009-07-27.

[7] "The Mothman Prophecies" (http://www.slantmagazine.com/dvd/review/the-mothman-prophecies/136). DVD Review. .

External links

- *The Mothman Prophecies* (http://www.imdb.com/title/tt0265349/) at the Internet Movie Database
- *The Mothman Prophecies* - History vs. Hollywood at Chasing the Frog (http://www.chasingthefrog.com/reelfaces/mothmanprophecies.php)
- Science Fiction, Horror and Fantasy Film Review (http://www.moria.co.nz/horror/mothman.htm)
- A website discussing the film (http://www.mothmanlives.com/)
- Q&A with director Mark Pellington (http://hollywoodgothique.com/pellington.htm)

Shall We Dance? (2004 film)

Shall We Dance?	
Theatrical release poster	
Directed by	Peter Chelsom
Produced by	Simon Fields Bob Weinstein Harvey Weinstein James Tyler
Written by	Audrey Wells Masayuki Suo (original screenplay)
Narrated by	Richard Gere
Starring	Richard Gere Jennifer Lopez Susan Sarandon Stanley Tucci Lisa Ann Walter Richard Jenkins Bobby Cannavale Omar Benson Miller Mya Harrison Ja Rule Nick Cannon
Music by	John Altman Gabriel Yared
Cinematography	John de Borman
Editing by	Robert Leighton
Distributed by	Miramax Films
Release date(s)	October 15, 2004
Running time	106 minutes
Country	United States
Language	English
Budget	$50 million
Box office	$170,128,460

Shall We Dance? is a 2004 American film. It is a remake of the award-winning Masayuki Suo 1996 Japanese film, *Shall We Dance?*. The film made its US premier at the Hawaii International Film Festival.[1]

Plot

John Clark (Richard Gere) is a lawyer with a charming wife (Beverly, played by Susan Sarandon) and loving family, who nevertheless feels that something is missing as he makes his way every day through the city. Each evening on his commute home through Chicago, John sees a beautiful woman staring with a lost expression through the window of a dance studio. Haunted by her gaze, John impulsively jumps off the train one night, and signs up for ballroom dancing lessons, hoping to meet her.

At first, it seems like a mistake. His teacher turns out to be not Paulina (Jennifer Lopez), but the older Miss Mitzi (Anita Gillette), and John proves to be just as clumsy as his equally clueless classmates [Chic (Bobby Cannavale) and Vern (Omar Miller)] on the dance-floor. Even worse, when he does meet Paulina, she icily tells John she hopes he has come to the studio to seriously study dance and not to look for a date. But, as his lessons continue, John falls in love with dancing. Keeping his new obsession from his family and co-workers, John feverishly trains for Chicago's biggest dance competition. His friendship with Paulina blossoms, as his enthusiasm rekindles her own lost passion for dance. But the more time John spends away from home, the more his wife Beverly (Susan Sarandon) becomes suspicious. She hires a private investigator to find out what John is doing, but when she finds out the truth, she chooses to discontinue the investigation and not invade her husband's privacy.

John is partnered with Bobbie (Lisa Ann Walter) for the competition, although his friend Link (Stanley Tucci) steps in to do the Latin dances. Link and Bobbie do well in the Latin dances, and while John and Bobbie's waltz goes well, John hears his wife and daughter in the crowd during the quickstep, and is distracted by trying to find them. He and Bobbie fall and are disqualified, and John and Beverly argue in the parking structure. John quits dancing, to everyone's dismay.

Paulina, having been inspired by John to take up competing again, is leaving to go to Europe, and is having a going-away party at the dance studio. She sends John an invitation, but he's not convinced to go until his wife leaves out a pair of dancing shoes that she bought him. He goes and meets Beverly at work, convinces her that while he loves dancing, he still loves her just as much, and they dance. They go to the party and John and Paulina have one last dance before she leaves.

The end scene shows everyone afterwards: Link and Bobbie are now together; Chic, who was actually gay, dances at a club with his partner; Miss Mitzi finds a new partner, and they are happy together; John and Beverly are back to normal and dance in the kitchen; Vern, newly married to his fiancée, dances with her at their wedding; the private investigator that Beverly hired, Devine (Richard Jenkins), starts up dance lessons; and Paulina, with a new partner, competes at Blackpool, the competition that she had lost years before.

Cast

- Richard Gere as John Clark
- Jennifer Lopez as Paulina
- Susan Sarandon as Beverly Clark
- Lisa Ann Walter as Bobbie
- Stanley Tucci as Link Peterson
- Anita Gillette as Miss Mitzi
- Bobby Cannavale as Chic
- Omar Miller as Vern
- Tamara Hope as Jenna Clark
- Stark Sands as Evan Clark
- Richard Jenkins as Devine
- Nick Cannon as Scott
- Karina Smirnoff as Link's Pouty Dance Partner
- Mya Harrison as Vern's Fiancée
- Ja Rule as Hip-Hop Bar Performer
- Tony Dovolani as Slick Willy
- Cesar Corrales as Dancer
- Slavik Kryklyvyy as Paulina's Pro Ballroom (finale)

Soundtrack

1. "Sway" - The Pussycat Dolls
2. "Santa Maria" (Del Buen Ayre) - Gotan Project
3. "Happy Feet" - John Altman
4. "España Cañí" - John Altman
5. "I Wanna (Shall We Dance)" - Gizelle D'Cole
6. "Perfidia" - John Altman
7. "Under The Bridges Of Paris" - John Altman
8. "Moon River" - John Altman
9. "Andalucia" - John Altman
10. "The Book Of Love" - Peter Gabriel
11. "The L Train" - Gabriel Yared
12. "I Could Have Danced All Night" - Jamie Cullum
13. "Wonderland" - Rachel Fuller
14. "Shall We Dance?" - Gotan Project
15. "Let's Dance" - Mýa

Reception

Shall We Dance received a 48% rating from Rotten Tomatoes (*Fresh*: 70 *Rotten*: 75).[2] Roger Ebert gave the film 3 out of 4 stars, stating "I enjoyed the Japanese version so much I invited it to my Overlooked Film Festival a few years ago, but this remake offers pleasures of its own."[3]

Box office performance

The movie debuted on October 15, 2004, grossing $11,783,467 in the opening weekend, placing fourth at the North American box office. Despite its 27% decline in gross earnings, the film managed to climb to the third spot the following week. The movie ran for 133 days, grossing $57,890,460 domestically and $112,238,000 in the foreign market. Its international total stands at $170,128,460.

Filming

Parts of *Shall We Dance* were filmed in Winnipeg, Manitoba, in a dance studio located on campus at the University of Manitoba.

References

[1] http://www.hawaiireporter.com/story.aspx?f943c058-5936-47dc-ab5c-91df436a68fb
[2] Shall We Dance @ [[Rotten Tomatoes (http://www.rottentomatoes.com/m/shall_we_dance/)].]
[3] Roger Ebert review (http://rogerebert.suntimes.com/apps/pbcs.dll/article?AID=/20041014/REVIEWS/40921008/1023)

External links

- *Shall We Dance?* (http://www.imdb.com/title/tt0358135/) at the Internet Movie Database
- *Shall We Dance?* (http://www.allrovi.com/movies/movie/v288231) at AllRovi
- *Shall We Dance?* (http://www.boxofficemojo.com/movies/?id=shallwedance.htm) at Box Office Mojo

Bee Season (film)

Bee Season	
Theatrical release poster	
Directed by	Scott McGehee David Siegel
Produced by	Mark Romanek Arnon Milchan
Screenplay by	Naomi Foner Gyllenhaal
Based on	*Bee Season* by Myla Goldberg
Starring	Richard Gere Juliette Binoche
Music by	Peter Nashel
Cinematography	Giles Nuttgens
Editing by	Lauren Zuckerman
Studio	Regency Enterprises
Distributed by	Fox Searchlight Pictures
Release date(s)	November 11, 2005
Running time	104 minutes
Country	United States
Language	English Hebrew
Budget	$14 million[1]
Box office	$6,856,989[1]

Bee Season is a 2005 American drama film adaptation of the 2000 novel of the same name by Myla Goldberg. The film was directed by Scott McGehee and David Siegel and written by Naomi Foner Gyllenhaal. It stars Richard Gere and Juliette Binoche.

Plot

Saul Naumann (Gere) is a somewhat controlling Jewish husband and father. A Religious Studies professor at UC Berkeley, Saul wrote his graduate thesis on the Kabbalah. A devout Jew, his wife Miriam (Binoche) converted to Judaism when they married, and he nurtured his son Aaron (Max Minghella) into a traditional studious Jew like him. When Eliza (Flora Cross) wins her class spelling bee, they embark on a course of Kabbalah study to help her win. The film follows the family and the spiritual quests upon which they journey, in large part because of Saul: Miriam's attempt to make herself whole, Aaron's religious uncertainty, and Eliza's desire to be closer to her father.

Miriam lives a secret life throughout her entire marriage to Saul, trying to fulfill the religious idea she learned from him, *tikkun olam,* or "repairing the world" and "reuniting its shards." She takes this meaning literally and slowly collects trinkets she finds beautiful (sometimes breaking into people's houses and stealing them) and storing them in a warehouse, trying to hold the light of God in them. Saul's son, Aaron, grows unsure of the Judaism foisted on him by his father, and in trying to find a faith he personally believes in, he becomes a Hare Krishna after meeting a woman named Chali in the park. For Eliza, her experience begins with a desire to be as close to her father as he and Aaron are; the two would often have discussions about Judaism and play music together. Saul's graduate thesis on Kabbalah writer Abraham Abulafia (who believed that careful analysis of words could lead to contact with God) brings Saul and Eliza closer together when Saul learns Eliza has won the district spelling bee.

Upon learning of her success Saul takes control of Eliza's life, trying to coach her with the Kabbalah teachings he knows so well. Eliza enjoys the renewed attention of her father and pursues the competition with her father's involvement. This comes at the expense of Aaron, who receives less time with Saul, even as he falls deeper into his religious dubiosity. At the center of the film, Eliza becomes Saul's newest religious project. Eliza continues to do well at spelling bees seemingly because of a higher spiritual connection with God, as Abraham Abulafia wrote about; visions appear to her and help her spell the word, no matter how difficult.

Saul's obsession with his daughter's gift and the opportunities it presents to him consume him to the point that he is callously ignorant of the collapse of his family occurring around him. He is forced to face it when Miriam is caught entering a home and ultimately checks herself into a psychiatric ward. Aaron comes to reject his father's religion and eventually leave the household. Eliza is implicitly aware of how her gift has contributed to this deterioration and her attempts to achieve spiritual awareness become terrifying.

In the final scene, Eliza deliberately misspells the word origami (a word she had practiced with Saul the night before) to place second at the National Spelling Bee.

Cast

- Richard Gere as Saul
- Juliette Binoche as Miriam
- Flora Cross as Eliza
- Max Minghella as Aaron
- Kate Bosworth as Chali
- Anna Maria Perez de Taglé as Bee Season #1

Production

The regional bee was filmed at the Albany High School gym. Also seen filmed in the downtown section on Park st. in Alameda, California.

Writing

While the literal plot simply follows a girl from a somewhat dysfunctional family moving through the world of competitive spelling, the actual plot of *Bee Season* is a much more complex one on personal religious views. Saul can be seen a Kabbalistic figure himself, desperately trying to become closer to God while remaining, ironically, entirely oblivious to Eliza's natural gift for connecting to God, and to his family's deepening troubles. Instead of using knowledge (as one does in Kabbalah), Saul uses each of his family members in a (mostly vain) attempt to deepen his own religious sense (an act finally uncovered by Aaron near the film's end). Meanwhile, his wife, Miriam, is caught stealing and is sent to a mental institution. The relationships between all members of the family, which were shallow and disconnected to begin with, fall apart.

Differences between film and novel

The film generally follows the plot of Goldberg's novel, but with some notable changes. In the novel, Saul is a cantor, not a college professor. Miriam was born Jewish, rather than being a convert. Eliza did not get second place in the national spelling bee, though she did well. It was not until months later, when it came time at her school spelling bee to make her second attempt at the National Spelling Bee, that Eliza decided to get a word wrong on purpose. Chali, the person who introduces Aaron to the Hare Krishna religion, is a man in the novel. Also, in the novel, Aaron and Saul both play the guitar, whereas in the film, Aaron plays the cello, while Saul plays the violin.

Reception

Critical response

Rotten Tomatoes gives the film a score of 42% based on 104 reviews.[2] Metacritic gives the film as score of 54% based on reviews from 32 critics.[3]

Box office

As of January 29, 2006 *Bee Season* had taken a gross of $1,177,082 in the United States, with an opening American weekend of $120,544.[4]

Awards

Bee Season's single award nomination was a Broadcast Film Critics Association Awards Young Actress nomination for Flora Cross.[5]

Home media

The DVD was released in the US April 4, 2006.[6]

References

[1] http://www.boxofficemojo.com/movies/?id=beeseason.htm Box Office Mojo Amazon.com
[2] "Bee Season" (http://www.rottentomatoes.com/m/bee_season/). *Rotten Tomatoes*. Flixster. .
[3] "Bee Season" (http://www.metacritic.com/movie/bee-season). *Metacritic*. CBS. .
[4] Business details for *Bee Season* (http://imdb.com/title/tt0387059/business) for IMDb, retrieved March 24, 2006
[5] Awards details for *Bee Season* (http://imdb.com/title/tt0387059/awards) for IMDb, retrieved March 24, 2006
[6] Bee Season: DVD (http://www.amazon.com/gp/product/B000E6ES8U)

External links

- Official website (http://foxsearchlight.com/beeseason/)
- *Bee Season* (http://www.imdb.com/title/tt0387059/) at the Internet Movie Database
- *Bee Season* (http://www.boxofficemojo.com/movies/?id=beeseason.htm) at Box Office Mojo

The Hoax

The Hoax	
Theatrical poster	
Directed by	Lasse Hallström
Produced by	Mark Gordon Bob Yari Betsy Beers Leslie Holleran Joshua Maurer
Screenplay by	William Wheeler
Based on	*The Hoax* by Clifford Irving
Starring	Richard Gere Alfred Molina Marcia Gay Harden
Music by	Carter Burwell
Cinematography	Oliver Stapleton
Editing by	Andrew Mondshein
Distributed by	Miramax Films
Release date(s)	April 6, 2007
Running time	116 minutes
Country	United States
Language	English
Budget	$25 million
Box office	$11,772,183

The Hoax is a 2007 American drama film directed by Lasse Hallström. The screenplay by William Wheeler is based on the book of the same title by Clifford Irving and focuses on the autobiography Irving supposedly helped Howard Hughes write. Many of the events Irving described in his book were changed or completely eliminated from the film, and the author later said, "I was hired by the producers as technical adviser to the movie, but after reading the final script I asked that my name be removed from the movie credits."[1]

Plot

Although *Fake!*, his previous work about art forger Elmyr de Hory, sold poorly, executives at McGraw-Hill express interest in Clifford Irving's new effort, a novel called *Rudnick's Problem*, and he believes he has his breakout work at last, only to be told the publishing house has decided against releasing the book after a *Life* editor deems it unsatisfactory.

Vacationing with his friend and researcher Richard Suskind, Irving is ejected from his hotel at 1:00am when Howard Hughes arrives and demands the entire building be vacated. Returning to New York City to meet with his publishers, he is upset to find that he has been fobbed off onto one of the assistants. He storms into the board room and announces that his new project will be the "book of the century", and threatens to take it elsewhere if McGraw-Hill is not interested. He then struggles to come up with a suitable topic for his grandiose claim, rejecting numerous suggestions from Suskind. After catching sight of a magazine cover picturing Hughes, he decides to make him the subject of his book.

Irving approaches McGraw-Hill and claims he has been summoned by Hughes to help him write his autobiography and provides forged handwritten notes from Hughes as proof. When handwriting experts wrongly conclude the notes are genuine, the publishers strike a $500,000 deal for the book.

Because Hughes is so reclusive and notoriously wary of legal action, he is unlikely to sue Irving, and his eccentricities also mean any denials of the book's authenticity likely will be treated as misdirection. Irving is convinced his hoax is the perfect crime.

Irving is having marital problems with his artist wife Edith. His affair with actress/singer Nina Van Pallandt left Edith hurt and skeptical about her husband's ability to remain monogamous. Irving assures her he will remain faithful, and leaves to begin researching the book with Suskind. In order to create an authenticity that will fool even the experts, the two men devote days to studying documents pertaining to Hughes. They illicitly obtain a copy of a draft biography of Noah Dietrich, a retired Hughes aide, which provides details that add to the apparent authenticity of the work. Irving begins reciting passages for the book into a tape recorder in character as Hughes, going so far as to dress as Hughes and draw a Hughes-like mustache on himself during these sessions.

As work on the book progresses, a box containing explosive information about questionable dealings between Hughes and Richard Nixon is delivered to Irving. He assumes the package is from Hughes and convinces himself Hughes wants the damaging material included in the book, a sign he supports the autobiography.

As the publication date draws near, Irving steps up his pretense, including staging an aborted meeting between Hughes and the publishers. Denials that Hughes is involved in any way with the book are issued from his headquarters, but the McGraw-Hill executives are convinced it is a genuine work. Irving uses their increasing desire for the guaranteed bestseller to leverage larger payments for himself and (purportedly) Hughes, and he and Edith concoct a scheme for her to deposit Hughes' check, payable to H.R. Hughes, into a Swiss bank account using a forged passport with the name Helga R. Hughes.

Irving begins to become paranoid and experiences alcohol-fueled fantasies about being kidnapped by Hughes' people. His affair with Van Pallandt has continued, and the pressure of keeping up a pretense of fidelity with his wife adds to his stress.

In what is implied to be a favor to Nixon, Hughes goes public via a televised conference call and denies any knowledge of Irving or the book. Irving ultimately is arrested and agrees to cooperate if Edith is granted immunity. At a press conference, a government spokesman announces Irving, Edith, and Suskind have received short jail sentences. An overheard radio report details a sudden wave of legal decisions in favor of Hughes in a short period of time, ambiguously implying that Irving's book had indeed been used to create a situation placing Nixon in debt to Hughes. A fleeting scene from inside the Nixon White House shows that Nixon's preoccupation with Hughes led directly to the burglary and wiretapping of Democratic Headquarters at the Watergate Hotel, a historically disputed point and not a new one.

Cast

- Richard Gere as Clifford Irving
- Alfred Molina as Richard Suskind
- Marcia Gay Harden as Edith Irving
- Hope Davis as Andrea Tate
- Julie Delpy as Nina van Pallandt
- Stanley Tucci as Shelton Fisher
- Eli Wallach as Noah Dietrich

Critical reception

On Rotten Tomatoes, the film received an 86% positive rate, based on 139 reviews,[2] while on Metacritic, the film scored 70 out of 100, based on 37 reviews.[3]

A.O. Scott of the *New York Times* said the film was "for the most part a jumpy, suspenseful caper, full of narrow escapes, improbable reversals and complicated intrigue. But it has a sinister, shadowy undertow, an intimation of dread that lingers after Irving's game is up."[4]

Kenneth Turan of the *Los Angeles Times* called the film "an unexpectedly satisfying fantasia of reality and imagination, a meditation on the nature of lies and deception, on how we come to embrace not the truth but what it suits us to believe . . . sharply written . . . and gracefully directed."[5]

Peter Travers of *Rolling Stone* rated the film 3 1/2 out of four stars and called it a "devilish and devastating satire." He added, "Gere gives 'em the old razzle-dazzle with his roguish charm and sharp comic timing. The surprise is the unexpected feeling he brings to this challenging role."[6]

Deborah Young of *Variety* called the film a "breezy, fast-paced, somewhat loose-ended account [that] offers a surprisingly layered vehicle for a maniacally conniving Richard Gere, backed up by a superb Alfred Molina as his accomplice."[7]

Box office

The Hoax was given a limited opening in 235 theaters in the United States and Canada on April 6, 2007 and earning $1,449,320 on its opening weekend. It eventually grossed $7,164,995 in the US and Canada and $4,607,188 in foreign markets for a total worldwide box office of $11,772,183.[8]

Accolades

The London Film Critics Circle nominated Alfred Molina for British Supporting Actor of the Year, and Richard Gere was nominated for the Satellite Award for Best Actor - Motion Picture Musical or Comedy.

Accuracy

While the major events portrayed in the film actually occurred, the film takes several dramatic liberties and completely eliminates all scenes set in Ibiza, where Irving wrote much of his book in a farmhouse he owned there. The author described the film as "a historically cockeyed story" and decried the film's characterizations as inaccurate. He was unhappy with being portrayed as "desperate and humorless, a washed-up hack writer who lives in a conservative New York suburb." He observed, "The movie misses the point that the Howard Hughes hoax was a live-action adventure story concocted by two middle-aged hippie expat writers and a Swiss heiress. Edith, my then-wife, a woman of great zest, is portrayed as a dull hausfrau; and Nina van Pallandt, my Danish mistress, as barely one level above a New York hotel hooker. Dick Suskind, witty friend and co-conspirator, is offered to the public as a self-righteous, sweaty buffoon. The scenes that deal with Movie Clifford feuding with Movie Dick, getting him drunk and hiring a bargirl to seduce him, are totally fictional. The Hughes people mailing the package of files to me is also made up."[1]

References

[1] CliffordIrving.com (http://web.archive.org/web/20071224024956/www.cliffordirving.com/movie.php)
[2] "RottenTomatoes.com" (http://www.rottentomatoes.com/m/hoax/). RottenTomatoes.com. 2007-09-25. . Retrieved 2011-03-13.
[3] "Metacritic.com" (http://www.metacritic.com/film/titles/hoax). Metacritic.com. 2007-04-06. . Retrieved 2011-03-13.
[4] By A. O. Scott (2007-04-06). ""New York Times" review" (http://movies.nytimes.com/2007/04/06/movies/06hoax.html). Movies.nytimes.com. . Retrieved 2011-03-13.
[5] ""Los Angeles Times" review" (http://www.calendarlive.com/printedition/calendar/cl-et-hoax6apr06,0,1743288.story). Calendarlive.com. 2007-04-06. . Retrieved 2011-03-13.
[6] *Rolling Stone* review (http://www.rollingstone.com/reviews/movie/9474909/review/14030358/the_hoax)
[7] Young, Deborah (2006-10-15). ""Variety" review" (http://www.variety.com/review/VE1117931886.html?categoryid=31&cs=1&p=0). Variety.com. . Retrieved 2011-03-13.
[8] "BoxOfficeMojo.com" (http://www.boxofficemojo.com/movies/?id=hoax.htm). BoxOfficeMojo.com. . Retrieved 2011-03-13.

External links

- *The Hoax* (http://www.imdb.com/title/tt0462338/) at the Internet Movie Database
- *The Hoax* (http://www.allrovi.com/movies/movie/v331703) at AllRovi
- *The Hoax* (http://www.rottentomatoes.com/m/1159135-hoax/) at Rotten Tomatoes

The Hunting Party (2007 film)

The Hunting Party	
Promotional poster	
Directed by	Richard Shepard
Produced by	Mark Johnson Scott Kroopf Paul Hanson
Written by	Richard Shepard
Starring	Richard Gere Terrence Howard Jesse Eisenberg Diane Kruger James Brolin Dylan Baker
Music by	Rolfe Kent
Cinematography	David Tattersall
Editing by	Carole Kravetz
Distributed by	The Weinstein Company, Intermedia
Release date(s)	September 7, 2007
Running time	101 minutes
Country	United States
Language	English
Budget	US$40 million
Box office	$969,869 (USA only) $6,674,540 (foreign) $7,644,409 (total)

The Hunting Party is a 2007 American action-adventure-thriller film starring Richard Gere, Terrence Howard, Diane Kruger and Jesse Eisenberg. The working title for this film was *Spring Break in Bosnia* before being changed to *The Hunting Party* during post-production. *The Hunting Party* had its world premiere at the 64th Venice International Film Festival on September 3, 2007. The movie turned out to be a huge disappointment domestically, grossing only US$969,869 in US theatres.

Plot

After years of covering one war after another, journalist Simon Hunt (Richard Gere) loses his composure during a live broadcast covering the Bosnian War. While his career spirals downhill, that of his long-time camera man Duck (Terrence Howard) goes in the opposite direction. Duck gets a cushy job at the network, while Hunt is left following war after war, unemployed, in an attempt to get back on top. Years later, Duck returns to Bosnia to shoot a "puff piece" of the network anchor Franklin Harris (James Brolin) covering the fifth peace treaty anniversary celebrations, along with fresh young journalist (and son of the network vice-president) Benjamin (Jesse Eisenberg). Duck runs into Simon—by this point, a desperate, cynical freelancer who needs a story big enough to propel him back to the realm of credibility. He tells Duck that, through a source, he has located Radoslav Bogdanović—known as "The Fox"—who is a wanted war criminal with a US$5 million bounty on his head: he is assumed to be in the village of

Čelebići in Republika Srpska (Serbian entity in Bosnia and Herzegovina), near the border with Montenegro.

Convinced by Simon, Duck comes along to shoot the interview, with Benjamin in tow. On the way, Simon confesses his plan to capture the Fox—something Duck and Benjamin consider insane even to think about. Along the way, the group is mistaken for a CIA hit squad by several groups, including the United Nations police force and the Serbs themselves; at one point, at the initiative of Benjamin, they claim to be CIA agents themselves, using a threat to avoid paying a fee for a tip. Simon, Duck, and Benjamin are then captured by the Fox's guards and taken to a barn to be executed. At the last moment, a team of CIA assassins storms the barn and frees the journalists, but Fox escapes. It quickly becomes evident to the journalists that, even in the international community, there are people who do not wish the Fox to be captured. The CIA orders the journalists to board an airplane bound for the US, but they run away to carry out their plan to catch the Fox. They capture him while he is hunting in the woods without his guards. The journalists then release him, with his hands securely bound, in a village called Polje filled with the surviving family members of victims of his war crimes.

Cast and characters

- Richard Gere as Simon Hunt
- Terrence Howard as Duck
- James Brolin as Franklin Harris
- Jesse Eisenberg as Benjamin Strauss
- Ljubomir Kerekeš as The Fox
- Kristina Krepela as Marta
- Diane Kruger as Mirjana
- Mark Ivanir as Boris
- Zdravko Kocevar as Sascha
- Snežana Marković as Una
- Goran Kostic as Srdjan
- R. Mahalakshmi Devaraj as Miriam
- Joy Bryant as Duck's Girlfriend
- Damir Saban as Gert
- Nitin Ganatra as Indian Officer
- Dylan Baker as the CIA man
- Aleksandra Grdić as TriBeCa Loft Girl

The *Esquire* article

The trailer for the Bosnia-set movie *The Hunting Party* announces it as being "based on a true story", which is, in fact, very loosely based on the events depicted in an *Esquire* magazine article by American journalist Scott Anderson.[1][2] Published in October 2000 under the title "What I Did on My Summer Vacation",[2] the article talks about a group of five Western war-reporters (in addition to Anderson, the group consisted of two more Americans, Sebastian Junger and John Falk, as well as Dutchman Harald Doornbos and Philippe Deprez from Belgium) who reunited in Sarajevo during April 2000 and over some drinks at a local bar one night decided to make a halfhearted attempt at catching the accused war criminal and fugitive Radovan Karadžić. In addition to alcohol, the starting point for their "manhunt" was an article in local weekly newsmagazine *Slobodna Bosna* notorious for sensationalist reporting that claimed Karadžić, along with his heavily armed security detail, had been spotted in the village of Čelebići in Republika Srpska (Serbian entity within Bosnia and Herzegovina) near the border with Montenegro.

Before going into Čelebići, the party of five journalists first came to the nearby town of Foča where they inquired about the safety of their trip among the locally stationed UN personnel. They soon caught the eye of a well-connected local UN officer from Ukraine who became convinced they were a covert crew sent in to apprehend

Karadžić and decided to help them out by putting them in touch with a supposedly high-ranking Serbian secret police officer. The journalists decided to play along, and after returning from an uneventful visit to Čelebići, they arranged a meeting with the Serbian secret policeman who, too, was convinced they were a CIA Black Operations team. He also claimed to have an intimate knowledge of Karadžić's movements and whereabouts and in return for ratting him out he wanted American passports for himself, his wife, and their four kids, as well as a cut of the bounty prize.

Despite being not at all convinced of the honesty and sincerity of either the Ukrainian UN officer or the Serbian secret policeman, the journalists decided to play along even further, thus setting in motion an interesting chain of events that in the end led to local NATO officials, American embassy personnel, and apparently even top American security officials from overseas getting involved.

Scott Anderson's conclusion at the end of the article was that UN and NATO not only exhibited precious little interest in actually finding Karadžić, but they also actively sabotaged any such meaningful attempt from within their own ranks.

When he was discovered, however, Karadžić turned out to be hiding in disguise and alone.

Reception and reaction

United States

Critical reaction to *The Hunting Party* was mixed. The film critic site Rotten Tomatoes gave the film a 53% rating, or "Rotten", based on 90 reviews; the "Cream of the Crop" rating was 46% based on 24 reviews.[3] The site Metacritic showed a rating of 54 out of 100, qualifying as "Average or Mixed Reviews", based on 34 ratings.[4] *New York Times* reviewer Manohla Dargis called the film: "A misfired, misguided would-be satire."[5] Owen Gleiberman for *Entertainment Weekly* stated, on the other hand:

> "What makes The Hunting Party an original, gonzo treat is the way that Shepard plants the movie's tone somewhere between hair-trigger investigative danger and the from-the-frying-pan-into-the-fire glee of a Hope/Crosby picture."[6]

Elvis D'Silva of Rediff India, in his article "Fails to entertain", has questioned how much the movie reflects reality of the War in Bosnia and Herzegovina.[7]

Richard Gere promoted *The Hunting Party* with guest appearances on the *Late Show with David Letterman* and *Late Night with Conan O'Brien*. Still, the movie turned out to be a disappointment domestically, grossing only US$969,869 in US theatres.

It opened small, on September 7, 2007, initially being shown only on four screens in New York City and Los Angeles. It gradually expanded to other parts of USA over the following weeks - first to 40 screens, and then to 329. It ended its US theatrical life some six weeks after its release.

Europe

Almost simultaneously to the US, *The Hunting Party* was released in Turkey on September 14, 2007. Released as *Av Partisi*, in its two months at Turkish theaters, the movie managed to gross US$424,048.[8]

Next up was Germany on November 29, 2007, where it was released as *Hunting Party – Wenn der Jäger zum Gejagten wird* ("When the Hunter Becomes the Hunted") and grossed US$203,705 during just under a month at the theaters.[8]

On November 29, 2007, the movie was also released in Croatia. Its release in that country is particularly notable because most of the movie was shot there and the only two non-Hollywood actors with significant roles in it are Croats Kristina Krepela and Ljubomir Kerekeš. However, the movie received mostly lukewarm reviews in the Croatian media with mainstream print daily *Jutarnji list* reviewer Nenad Polimac criticizing the stock character portrayal of its villain - The Fox - as a stereotypical Hollywood baddie while suggesting the end product would've been a lot better had the movie been shot verbatim according to Anderson's original magazine article without the application of the Hollywood makeover. Additionally, Polimac's review longs for the days when "prestigious films like *Fiddler on the Roof* and *Sophie's Choice* were being shot here".[9] The movie didn't fare much better in Croatian cyberspace as Film.hr's Boško Picula complains that "despite its smooth plot, rounded-off characters, comendable attempts at reaching the virtue of genuineness, and welcome flirting with the absurd, *The Hunting Party* fails when all of that needs to be put together into a logical unit"[10] while Film-Mag.net's Robert Jukić refers to the overall product as "interestingly conceived, but poorly executed".[11] At present, there is no box-office data for Croatia.

The release in Bosnia-Herzegovina's Bosniak-Croat part where the movie was partly shot was originally scheduled for December 7, 2007, but one day before the premiere, it had to be postponed for a week due to technical difficulties.[12] The movie was finally released on December 14, 2007 with a premiere showing at Sarajevo's Meeting Point cinema attended by businessman Selen Balić, film directors Danis Tanović, and Elmir Jukić, as well as politician Bakir Izetbegović, among others. The premiere was also attended by local actors Miraj Grbić, Snežana Marković, and Semir Krivić, all of whom had minor roles in the movie as Thug #1, Una, and Roadhouse Waiter, respectively.[13] Translated as *Lov u Bosni* (Hunting in Bosnia), the movie garnered generally positive reviews in the country's Bosniak media with *Dnevni Avaz* reviewer Anila Gajević extoling its "important political message" and further seeing the movie as an example of "American fiction with emphasized altruism".[14]

In mid-January 2008, the movie was released in the country's Serbian part where audiences largely ignored it with a premiere in Banja Luka's Kozara theater attended by fewer than 15 people.[15] The reviews in the country's Serb media were generally negative: *Nezavisne novine*'s Davor Pavlović refers to the film as being "poorly directed" and concludes that its main flaws lay in "neither being able to treat the subject matter with sufficient seriousness nor to raise its dramaturgical level above that of a typical Hollywood action movie".[16]

Premieres

The Hunting Party has been released around the world, premiering in a number of countries in 2007 and 2008:

Premieres

Date	Country	Notes
September 7, 2007	United States	Initially shown on four screens in NYC and LA; first run ended after six weeks.
September 14, 2007	Turkey	Released as *Av Partisi*; grossed US$424,048 over two months.
October 4, 2007	Israel	The movie opened in Israel between its Turkish and German premieres. (No Israeli box office data is currently available.)
November 29, 2007	Germany	Released as *Hunting Party – Wenn der Jäger zum Gejagten wird* ("When the Hunter Becomes the Hunted"); grossed US$203,705 in one month.
November 29, 2007	Croatia	
December 14, 2007	Federation of Bosnia and Herzegovina	Released in mid-January 2008 in Republika Srpska.
December 27, 2007	Austria	The movie lasted in the theatres until roughly mid-January 2008, making only US$52,967.[8]
January 3, 2008	Slovenia	
January 4, 2008	Spain	
January 25, 2008	Romania	
January 31, 2008	Russia	
March 6, 2008	Portugal	
March 13, 2008	Argentina	
April 30, 2008	Italy	
May 10, 2008	Japan	
December 12, 2008	India	

References

[1] "Karadzic-hunting now going Hollywood: "Spring Break in Bosnia" due for 2006 release" (http://findingkaradzic.blogspot.com/2004_04_01_archive.html). Findingkaradzic.blogspot.com. 2004-04-22. . Retrieved 2010-05-21.

[2] Anderson, Scott (2000-10-01). "What I Did on My Summer Vacation" (http://www.esquire.com/features/summer-vaction-1000). Esquire. . Retrieved 2010-05-21.

[3] "The Hunting Party" (http://web.archive.org/web/20080129113111/http://www.rottentomatoes.com/m/10008441-hunting_party/). *RottenTomatoes.com*. Archived from the original (http://www.rottentomatoes.com/m/10008441-hunting_party/) on January 29, 2008. . Retrieved 2008-01-30.

[4] "The Hunting Party" (http://www.metacritic.com/film/titles/huntingparty?q=The Hunting Party). *Metacritic.com*. . Retrieved 2008-01-30.

[5] Dargis, Manohla (September 7, 2007). "The Hunting Party" (http://movies.nytimes.com/2007/09/07/movies/07hunt.html?ref=movies). *New York Times*. . Retrieved 2008-01-30.

[6] "The Hunting Party" (http://www.ew.com/ew/article/0,,20054830,00.html). *Entertainment Weekly*. . Retrieved 2008-01-30.

[7] D'Silva, Elvis (November 14, 2008). "The Hunting Party fails to entertain" (http://www.rediff.com/movies/2008/nov/14fails-to-entertain.htm). Rediff India Abroad. . Retrieved 2010-05-21.

[8] "The Hunting Party" (http://www.boxofficemojo.com/movies/?page=intl&id=huntingparty.htm). Box Office Mojo. 2009-04-12. . Retrieved 2010-05-21.

[9] "Promašena tema o lovu na Kardžića" (http://www.jutarnji.hr/clanak/art-2007,11,28,hunting_party,99885.jl) (in Croatian). Jutarnji. 2007-11-28. . Retrieved 2010-05-21.

[10] Picula, Boško. "Lov u Bosni" (http://www.film.hr/vijest.php?tekst_id=718&PHPSESSID=9b0e4957db8c3a9846db20f20) (in Croatian). Film.hr. . Retrieved 2010-05-21.
[11] Jukić, Robert (4 December 2007). "KINO: LOV U BOSNI, avantura" (http://www.film-mag.net/content.php?review.3295) (in Croatian). F.I.L.M.. . Retrieved 2010-05-21.
[12] "Pomjerena premijera filma "Lov u Bosni"" (http://www.sarajevo-x.com/clanak/071206075). Sarajevo-x.com. 2007-12-06. . Retrieved 2010-05-21.
[13] "Priča o hapšenju ratnog zločinca" (http://web.archive.org/web/20080319124100/http://www.dnevniavaz.ba/kultura/film/prica-o-hapsenju-ratnog-zlocinca). Dnevniavaz.ba. 2007-03-15. Archived from the original (http://www.dnevniavaz.ba/kultura/film/prica-o-hapsenju-ratnog-zlocinca) on 2008-03-19. . Retrieved 2010-05-21.
[14] "Ko (ne)će uhvatiti Karadžića?!" (http://web.archive.org/web/20080319110855/http://www.dnevniavaz.ba/kultura/film/ko-nece-uhvatiti-karadzica). Dnevniavaz.ba. 2007-03-15. Archived from the original (http://www.dnevniavaz.ba/kultura/film/ko-nece-uhvatiti-karadzica) on 2008-03-19. . Retrieved 2010-05-21.
[15] "Debakl filmskog "lova" na Karadžića" (http://web.archive.org/web/20080616092050/http://www.mtsmondo.com/news/vesti/text.php?vest=83054) (in Serbian). MTS Mondo. 2008-01-11. Archived from the original (http://www.mtsmondo.com/news/vesti/text.php?vest=83054) on 2008-06-16. . Retrieved 2010-05-21.
[16] Pavlovic, Davor (2008-01-16). "Lov u Bosni: Lov ćorcima na gledaoce" (http://www.nezavisne.com/vijesti.php?vijest=18889&meni=29) (in Serbian). Nezavisne Movine. . Retrieved 2010-05-21.

External links

- Official website (http://www.thehuntingpartymovie.com/)
- *The Hunting Party* (http://www.imdb.com/title/tt0455782/) at the Internet Movie Database
- *The Hunting Party* (http://www.rottentomatoes.com/m/1183674-hunting_party/) at Rotten Tomatoes
- *The Hunting Party* (http://www.metacritic.com/movie/huntingparty) at Metacritic
- *The Hunting Party* (http://www.boxofficemojo.com/movies/?id=huntingparty.htm) at Box Office Mojo
- *The Hunting Party* (http://www.allrovi.com/movies/movie/v374909) at AllRovi
- The Esquire article written by the journalist Scott Anderson October 1, 2000 (http://www.esquire.com/features/summer-vaction-1000)
- eFilmCritic.com Interview with writer-director Richard Shepard (http://efilmcritic.com/feature.php?feature=2256/)

I'm Not There

I'm Not There	
Theatrical release poster	
Directed by	Todd Haynes
Produced by	Christine Vachon John Goldwyn
Written by	Todd Haynes Oren Moverman
Narrated by	Kris Kristofferson
Starring	Christian Bale Cate Blanchett Marcus Carl Franklin Richard Gere Heath Ledger Ben Whishaw
Music by	Bob Dylan
Cinematography	Edward Lachman
Editing by	Jay Rabinowitz
Studio	Celluloid Dreams
Distributed by	The Weinstein Company (US) Paramount Pictures (UK)
Release date(s)	November 21, 2007
Running time	135 minutes
Country	Germany United States
Language	English
Budget	$20 million (est.)
Box office	$11,523,779

I'm Not There is a 2007 biographical musical film directed by Todd Haynes, inspired by iconic American singer-songwriter Bob Dylan. Six actors depict different facets of Dylan's life and public persona: Christian Bale, Cate Blanchett, Marcus Carl Franklin, Richard Gere, Heath Ledger, and Ben Whishaw.[1][2] At the start of the film, a caption reads: "Inspired by the music and the many lives of Bob Dylan".[1] Besides song credits, this is the only time Dylan's name appears in the film.

The film tells its story using non-traditional narrative techniques, intercutting the storylines of the six different Dylan-inspired characters. The title of the film is taken from the 1967 Dylan Basement Tape recording, "I'm Not There", a song that had not been officially released until it appeared on the film's soundtrack album. The film received a generally favorable response, and appeared on several top ten film lists for 2007, topping the lists for *The Village Voice*, *Entertainment Weekly*, *Salon* and *The Boston Globe*. Particular praise went to Cate Blanchett for her performance, culminating in a Volpi Cup from the Venice Film Festival, the Golden Globe Award for Best Supporting Actress, along with an Academy Award for Best Supporting Actress nomination.

The film was released two months prior to the death of the actor Heath Ledger, and was one of his last films.

Plot

The film opens with Jude Quinn (Cate Blanchett) (representing Dylan circa 1966)[3] walking on stage to perform at a concert, before cutting to him riding on a motorcycle and then crashing. The film then cuts to Quinn's body on a mortuary slab and an autopsy begins. (This opening sequence refers to Bob Dylan's motorcycle accident in July 1966).[4]

Woody Guthrie (Marcus Carl Franklin), an 11-year old African American boy, is seen carrying a guitar in a case labeled "This machine kills fascists" as he travels the country, pursuing his dream of becoming a singer. (Folk singer Woody Guthrie had an identical label on his guitar.)[5] Woody befriends the African-American Arvin family, who give him food and hospitality, and Woody in turn performs Bob Dylan's 1965 song "Tombstone Blues", accompanied by Richie Havens (as Old Man Arvin). At dinner, Mrs. Arvin advises Woody: "Live your own time, child, sing about your own time".

Later that night, Woody leaves the Arvins' home, leaving behind a note thanking them, and catches a ride on a train, where a group of thieves attempt to rob him. He jumps from the speeding train and dives into a river, where a white couple rescue him and take him to a hospital, before bringing him home. They receive a phone call from a juvenile correction center in Minnesota from which Woody had escaped. The phone call prompts Woody's swift departure, and he takes a Greyhound bus to Greystone Park Hospital in New Jersey, where he visits (the real) Woody Guthrie, leaving flowers at Guthrie's bedside and playing his guitar. (Over the hospital sequence, Bob Dylan performs his song "Blind Willie McTell".)

Ben Whishaw plays a young man who shares his name with the nineteenth century French poet Arthur Rimbaud. Arthur is solely seen in an interrogation room where he gives oblique answers to (unseen) questioners.

Christian Bale plays Jack Rollins, a young folk singer, whose story is framed as a documentary and told by interviewees such as fictional folk singer named Alice Fabian—described by some critics as a Joan Baez-like figure[6][7]—played by Julianne Moore. Rollins is praised by folk fans who refer to his songs as anthems and protest songs, whereas Jack himself calls them finger-pointing songs. When Rollins accepts the "Tom Paine Award" from a civil rights organization, a drunken Rollins insults the audience and claims that he saw something of himself in JFK's alleged assassin Lee Harvey Oswald. (Rollins's speech quotes from a speech Dylan made when receiving the Tom Paine Award from the National Emergency Civil Liberties Committee in December 1963.)[8]

Bale also plays Pastor John, a Born Again Christian preacher, who appears to be the Jack Rollins character several years later, having traveled to California and entered a church to engage in Bible studies. He becomes a preacher and is seen declaring his faith to his fellow church members, where he performs "Pressing On" – a song written and performed by Dylan on his 1980 gospel-influenced album *Saved*.

Heath Ledger plays Robbie Clark, an actor who is starring in a biopic about the life of Jack Rollins (the folk singer played by Christian Bale). This film-within-a-film is entitled *Grain of Sand*. (The film's title is a reference to the Dylan song "Every Grain of Sand".) We see how Robbie met his French artist wife Claire, played by Charlotte Gainsbourg, in a Greenwich Village diner and they fell in love. (The scene in which Robbie and Claire run romantically through the streets of New York re-enacts the cover of the 1963 album *The Freewheelin' Bob Dylan* which depicts Dylan arm in arm with his then-girlfriend Suze Rotolo walking down West 4th Street in Greenwich Village.)[9] Robbie and Claire attend the premiere of the movie, which turns out to be a disappointment for Claire and the audience. Robbie and Claire's relationship begins to unravel, as Claire glimpses Robbie touching another woman at a party and is disturbed by his misogynistic attitude in comments such as "chicks can never be poets". At the end of their marriage, Robbie and Claire argue over custody of their children and Robbie and Claire file for divorce. The result of the custody battle seems to be in Claire's favor, but Robbie leaves taking his daughters on a boat trip while archival clips show Henry Kissinger and Le Duc Tho signing the Paris Peace Accords. (Bob Dylan was divorced from his first wife, Sara Dylan, on June 29, 1977 and the divorce involved legal wrangling over the custody of their children.)[10] In the film, the relationship between Robbie and Claire lasts precisely as long as American involvement in the Vietnam War.

Cate Blanchett plays Jude Quinn, seen at a concert in a New England town, performing a rock version of "Maggie's Farm" to the outraged folk music fans. (Dylan performed this song at the Newport Folk Festival in 1965, which provoked booing and controversy.) Jude is seen arriving at a press conference in London and answering questions. (Some of these questions are quotes from Dylan's KQED press conference in San Francisco on December 3, 1965.)[11][12] Later, in his hotel suite, Jude is threatened by a hotel waiter brandishing a knife, who is knocked out by Jude's lover with a vase. Jude's operations in London are supervised by his manager, Norman (who bears a resemblance to Bob Dylan's 1960s manager Albert Grossman), played by Mark Camacho. In a surreal episode, Jude is seen gambolling at high speed in a park with the Beatles, following a cloud of smoke presumed to represent Dylan's introducing the band to cannabis. (The speeded-up film echoes the style of Dick Lester's direction in *A Hard Day's Night*). Jude is then confronted by BBC cultural reporter, Keenan Jones, played by Bruce Greenwood (The name of this character echoes Dylan's song "Ballad of a Thin Man" with its chorus: "Something is happening here/ And you don't know what it is, do you Mr. Jones?").

Jude and his entourage meet the poet Allen Ginsberg, played by David Cross, who suggests that Jude may be "selling out" to God. Keenan Jones later asks Jude whether he cares about what he sings about every night, to which Jude replies, "How can I answer that if you've got the nerve to ask me?" and walks out of the interview. (Dylan made a similar response to a reporter from *Time* magazine in D. A. Pennebaker's documentary covering Dylan's 1965 English tour, *Dont Look Back*). The Dylan song "Ballad of a Thin Man" plays as Keenan Jones moves through a surreal episode in which he appears to act out the song's lyrics.[13] Jones is seen obtaining a copy of Jude Quinn's high school year book. In concert, Jude performs "Ballad of a Thin Man", when one of his outraged fans shouts "Judas!" Jude replies "I don't believe you". (This scene re-enacts the "Judas!" shout at Dylan's Manchester concert on May 17, 1966.[4] The moment is captured on Dylan's album *Live 1966*.) As the fans rush the stage in an apparent attempt to attack Jude, he narrowly escapes with his band.

Back in his hotel suite, Jude watches Keenan Jones on television reveal that the true identity of Jude Quinn is "Aaron Jacob Edelstein" (In October 1963, *Newsweek* published a hostile profile of Dylan, revealing that he was originally named Robert Zimmerman, and implying that he had lied about his middle-class origins.[14]). Jude later throws a party where his guests include Brian Jones, The Rolling Stones guitarist, and wealthy socialite and "queen of the underground" Coco Rivington, whom Jude insults. (The description of Rivington as "Andy's new bird" suggests that this character is modeled on Edie Sedgwick, a socialite and actress within Andy Warhol's circle.) As Jude's condition from drug usage worsens, he vomits in his friend's lap. Jude and Allen Ginsberg are later seen at the foot of a huge crucifix, apparently talking to Jesus. Jude shouts at the figure on the cross: "Why don't you do your early stuff?" and "How does it feel?!". After being whisked off in a car, Jude passes out on the floor while his friends stare down at him. Jude's manager, Norman observes: "I don't think he *can* get back on stage. He's gotten inside so many psyches – and death is just such a part of the American scene right now." Jude is last seen in his car directly addressing the viewer, "Everyone knows I'm not a folk singer".

Richard Gere portrays the outlaw Billy the Kid. Billy searches unsuccessfully for his dog, Henry, and then meets his friend, Homer. Homer tells Billy about Pat Garrett's destruction of Riddle County and the high incidence of suicide and murder. As the townspeople celebrate Halloween, a funeral takes place and a band performs Dylan's Basement Tapes song "Goin' to Acapulco" (sung by Jim James and backed by the band Calexico). Following the service, Pat Garrett (Bruce Greenwood – who earlier in the film played Keenan Jones, a journalist who had tried to interrogate Jude Quinn) arrives and confronts the townspeople. Billy dons a mask to disguise himself and tells Garrett to stay clear of Riddle County. Garrett then orders the authorities to arrest Billy and he is taken to the county jail. Billy escapes from the jail (with the help of Homer) and hops a ride on a train. Billy then sees his dog, Henry, one last time. Billy finds a guitar on the train that reads "This Machine kills Fascists", the same guitar that Woody Guthrie played at the beginning of the film. Billy's final words are "People are always talking about freedom, the freedom to live a certain way without being kicked around. 'Course the more you live a certain way the less it feels like freedom. Me? I can change during the course of a day. When I wake I'm one person, when I go to sleep I know for certain I'm somebody else. I don't know who I am most of the time. It's like you got yesterday, today and tomorrow all in the same room. There's no telling what can happen."[15]

The film ends with a close-up of the real Bob Dylan playing an extended harmonica solo during a live performance of "Mr. Tambourine Man". The footage was shot by D. A. Pennebaker during Dylan's 1966 World Tour.

Cast

- Marcus Carl Franklin as "Woody Guthrie". This character refers to Dylan's youthful obsession with folk singer Woody Guthrie.[16] Woody also reflects the fictitious autobiographies that Dylan constructed during his early career as he established his artistic identity.
- Christian Bale as Jack Rollins / Pastor John. Rollins is a portrayal of Dylan during the acoustic *Freewheelin' Bob Dylan* and *The Times They Are a-Changin'* period. Pastor John refers to Dylan's "born-again" period when he recorded *Slow Train Coming* and *Saved*.

Richard Gere, Todd Haynes, Charlotte Gainsbourg and Heath Ledger at the Venice Film Festival, September 2007.

- Cate Blanchett as Jude Quinn. Quinn is a portrayal of Dylan in 1965–1966, when he controversially played electric guitar at the Newport Folk Festival, toured the UK with a band and was booed. This phase of Dylan's life was documented by D.A. Pennebaker in the films *Dont Look Back* and *Eat the Document*.
- Richard Gere as "Billy the Kid". Billy refers to Dylan's appearance in Sam Peckinpah's film *Pat Garrett and Billy the Kid* and to Dylan's descriptions of himself as an outsider, a trait he believed he shared with the outlaw Henry McCarty (better known as Billy the Kid). The Billy sequences also allude to ways in which Dylan tried to evade the spotlight of unwanted attention, and employ Americana-style images from songs on *The Basement Tapes*.
- Heath Ledger as Robbie Clark, an actor who portrays Jack Rollins in a biopic and becomes as famous as the person he portrays; he navigates the course of a dissolving marriage (as well as flashbacks to their courtship), reflecting Dylan's own personal life roughly around the time of 1975's *Blood on the Tracks*.
- Ben Whishaw as "Arthur Rimbaud". Rimbaud is depicted as a man being questioned and responding with quotes from Dylan's interviews and writings. Dylan has referred frequently to the influence of Rimbaud's poetry.[17]

The above six characters represent different aspects of Bob Dylan's life and music.[1][7]

- Charlotte Gainsbourg as Claire, wife of Robbie Clark (a representation of Sara Dylan and Suze Rotolo)
- David Cross as Allen Ginsberg
- Eugene Brotto as Peter Orlovsky
- Bruce Greenwood as Keenan Jones, a fictional reporter who interrogates Jude Quinn, and as Pat Garrett, nemesis of Billy the Kid
- Julianne Moore as Alice Fabian, friend of Jack Rollins in his protest days (a representation of Joan Baez)[6]
- Michelle Williams as Coco Rivington (a representation of Andy Warhol it-girl, Edie Sedgwick)
- Kim Gordon as Carla Hendricks
- Alison Folland as Grace
- Mark Camacho as Norman, the manager of Jude Quinn (a representation of Dylan's manager until 1970, Albert Grossman)
- Benz Antoine as Bobby Seale, the Black Panther leader, and as Rabbit Brown
- Craig Thomas as Huey Newton, the Black Panther leader
- Richie Havens as Old Man Arvin
- Kim Roberts as Mrs. Arvin
- Tyrone Bensin as Mr. Arvin

- Yolonda Ross as Angela
- Peter Friedman as Barker/Morris Bernstein
- Joe Cobden as Sonny
- Kristen Hager as Mona
- Fanny La Croix as Actress playing Alice Fabian
- Dennis St. John as Captain Henry/The Admiral
- Kris Kristofferson as The Narrator
- Don Francks as Hobo Joe
- Vito DeFilippo and Susan Glover as Mr. and Mrs. Peacock, a middle-class couple who temporarily take "Woody Guthrie" in after a near-drowning incident
- Paul Spence as Homer, Billy the Kid's friend.

Conception

Todd Haynes and his producer, Christine Vachon, approached Bob Dylan's manager, Jeff Rosen, to obtain permission to use Dylan's music and to fictionalize elements of Dylan's life. Rosen suggested that Haynes should send a one page synopsis of his film for submission to Dylan. Rosen advised Haynes not to use the word 'genius'.[7] The page Haynes submitted began with a quote from Arthur Rimbaud: "I is someone else", and then continued:

> If a film were to exist in which the breadth and flux of a creative life could be experienced, a film that could open up as oppose to consolidating what we think we already know walking in, it could never be within the tidy arc of a master narrative. The structure of such a film would have to be a fractured one, with numerous openings and a multitude of voices, with its prime strategy being one of refraction, not condensation. Imagine a film splintered between seven separate faces — old men, young men, women, children — each standing in for spaces in a single life.[7]

Dylan gave Haynes permission to proceed with his project. Haynes developed his screenplay with writer Oren Moverman. In the course of writing, Haynes has acknowledged that he became uncertain whether he could successfully carry off a film which deliberately confused biography with fantasy in such an extreme way. According to the account of the film that Robert Sullivan published in the *New York Times*: "Haynes called Jeff Rosen, Dylan's right hand, who was watching the deal-making but staying out of the scriptwriting. Rosen, he said, told him not to worry, that it was just his own crazy version of what Dylan is."[7]

In a comment on why six actors were employed to portray different facets of Dylan's personality, Haynes wrote:

> The minute you try to grab hold of Dylan, he's no longer where he was. He's like a flame: If you try to hold him in your hand you'll surely get burned. Dylan's life of change and constant disappearances and constant transformations makes you yearn to hold him, and to nail him down. And that's why his fan base is so obsessive, so desirous of finding the truth and the absolutes and the answers to him – things that Dylan will never provide and will only frustrate.... Dylan is difficult and mysterious and evasive and frustrating, and it only makes you identify with him all the more as he skirts identity.[18]

A seventh character, a Charlie Chaplin-like incarnation of Dylan, was present in the script but was dropped before filming began.[19]

Production and premiere

The production began filming in late July 2006 in Montreal, Quebec, Canada.

The film premiered at the 34th Telluride Film Festival on August 31, 2007. It opened in theaters in Italy and played the Toronto International Film Festival in September 2007. It opened in limited release in the United States and Canada in November, and was released in Australia on Boxing Day 2007. It was rated R by the Motion Picture Association of America for language, some sexuality, nudity and drug use.

Critical reception

I'm Not There received generally positive reviews from critics. The review aggregator Rotten Tomatoes reported that 78% of critics gave the film positive reviews, based on 141 reviews.[20] Metacritic reported the film had an average score of 73 out of 100, based on 35 reviews.[21]

Writing in *The Chronicle of Higher Education*, critic Anthony DeCurtis said that casting six different actors, including a woman and an African-American child, to play Dylan was "a preposterous idea, the sort of self-consciously 'audacious'—or reassuringly multi-culti—gambit that, for instance, doomed the Broadway musical based on the life and music of John Lennon. Yet in *I'm Not There,* the strategy works brilliantly." He especially praised Blanchett:

> [H]er performance is a wonder, and not simply because, as Jude Quinn, she inhabits the twitchy, amphetamine-fired Dylan of 1965–66 with unnerving accuracy. Casting a woman in this role reveals a dimension to the acerbic Dylan of this era that has rarely been noted. Even as she perfectly mimics every jitter, sneer, and caustic put-down, Blanchett's translucent skin, delicate fingers, slight build, and pleading eyes all suggest the previously invisible vulnerability and fear that fueled Dylan's lacerating anger. It's hard to imagine that any male actor, or any less-gifted female actor for that matter, could have lent such rich texture to the role.[3]

Several reviewers praised Blanchett's performance as the mid-60s Dylan. *Newsweek* magazine described Blanchett as "so convincing and intense that you shrink back in your seat when she fixes you with her gaze."[22] The *Charlotte Observer* called Blanchett "miraculously close to the 1966 Dylan."[23] The film won the Grand Jury Prize and Best Actress honors for Blanchett at the 64th Venice Film Festival.[24] Blanchett also won the Golden Globe Award for her performance, in addition to several critics awards. She was nominated for a Screen Actors Guild Award and an Academy Award.

Ed Siegel's piece in the *Boston Globe* called the film "A noble failure in grasping Dylan," but finds Haynes' film worthy to be considered part of "the wealth of high-quality material that Dylan has allowed to emerge in recent years." His article is equally focused on Dylan, whose ambiguity has inspired a variety of interpretations, compelling Siegel to suggest his own interpretation: "I'm All Here."[25]

Luke Davies, film critic for The Monthly, declared it "a beautiful failure of a film" with "so much to love in it" but "unintentionally comical and inadvertently pretentious." Davies labelled the film a "biopic as kaleidoscopic poem rather than historical interpretation." Davies acclaims Blanchett's performance as the greatest success within the film, but claims that Blanchett's performance "actually draws energy inwards, creating a split between the failed Haynes film, and the successful Blanchett mini-film." However, Davies says such joy is inaccessible for non-fans of Dylan, because "*I'm Not There* would be utterly incomprehensible if you knew nothing of the Dylan story" as it is "an encyclopaedic poem of all that Bob Dylan passed through, in grand sweeps, over two decades."[26]

Todd McCarthy, writing in the film trade magazine *Variety*, concluded that the film was well-made, but was ultimately a speciality event for Dylan fans, with little mainstream appeal. He wrote: "Dylan freaks and scholars will have the most fun with *I'm Not There*, and there will inevitably be innumerable dissertations on the ways Haynes has both reflected and distorted reality, mined and manipulated the biographical record and otherwise had a field day with the essentials, as well as the esoterica, of Dylan's life. All of this will serve to inflate the film's significance by ignoring its lack of more general accessibility. In the end, it's a specialists' event."[1]

For Roger Ebert, the film was enjoyable cinematically, yet never sought to resolve the enigmas of Dylan's life and work: "Coming away from *I'm Not There*, we have, first of all, heard some great music (Dylan surprisingly authorized use of his songs both on his own recordings and performed by others). We've seen six gifted actors challenged by playing facets of a complete man. We've seen a daring attempt at biography as collage. We've remained baffled by the Richard Gere cowboy sequence, which doesn't seem to know its purpose. And we have been left not one step closer to comprehending Bob Dylan, which is as it should be."[6]

Top ten lists

The film appeared on several critics' lists of the top ten films of 2007.[27]

- 1st – J. Hoberman, *The Village Voice*[27]
- 1st – Owen Gleiberman, *Entertainment Weekly*[27]
- 1st – Stephanie Zacharek, *Salon*[27]
- 1st – Ty Burr, *The Boston Globe*[27]
- 1st – Philip Martin, *Arkansas Democrat-Gazette*
- 3rd – Lisa Schwarzbaum, *Entertainment Weekly*[27]
- 3rd – Marc Mohan, *The Oregonian*[27]
- 4th – A.O. Scott, *The New York Times*[27]
- 4th – Nathan Lee, *The Village Voice*[27]
- 4th – Shawn Levy, *The Oregonian*[27]
- 5th – Steven Rea, *The Philadelphia Inquirer*[27]
- 5th – Best Musical, *Rotten Tomatoes*[28]
- 6th – Kevin Crust, *Los Angeles Times*[27]
- 7th – Marjorie Baumgarten, *The Austin Chronicle*[27]
- 9th – Glenn Kenny, *Premiere*[27]
- 9th – Peter Travers, *Rolling Stone*[29]
- 10th – Ann Hornaday, *The Washington Post*[27]
- 10th – Desson Thomson, *The Washington Post*[27]
- 10th – Keith Phipps, *The A.V. Club*[27]
- 10th – Tasha Robinson, *The A.V. Club*[27]

Awards and nominations

- **Academy Awards**:
  - Best Supporting Actress (Cate Blanchett, nominee)
- Broadcast Film Critics:
  - Best Supporting Actress (Cate Blanchett, nominee)
- Central Ohio Film Critics:
  - Best Supporting Actress (Cate Blanchett, **winner**)
- Chicago Film Critics:
  - Best Supporting Actress (Cate Blanchett, **winner**)
- Chlotrudis Awards:
  - Best Supporting Actress (Cate Blanchett, **winner**)
- **Golden Globe Awards:**
  - Best Supporting Actress (Cate Blanchett, **winner**)
- Independent Spirit Awards
  - Robert Altman Award (cast and crew, **winner**)
  - Best Director (Todd Haynes, nominee)
  - Best Film (nominee)
  - Best Supporting Actor (Marcus Carl Franklin, nominee)
  - Best Supporting Actress (Cate Blanchett, **winner**)
- Las Vegas Film Critics:
  - Best Supporting Actress (Cate Blanchett, **winner**)
- Los Angeles Film Critics:

- Best Supporting Actress (Cate Blanchett, runner-up)
- New York Film Critics Online:
  - Best Supporting Actress (Cate Blanchett, **winner**)
- National Society of Film Critics:
  - Best Supporting Actress (Cate Blanchett, **winner**)
- Nilsson Awards for Film
  - Best Supporting Actress (Cate Blanchett, **winner**)
  - Best Cinematography
  - Best Compiled Soundtrack
- Satellite Awards:
  - Best Actress – Comedy or Musical (Cate Blanchett, nominee)
- Screen Actors Guild (SAG):
  - Best Supporting Actress (Cate Blanchett, nominee)
- Southeastern Film Critics:
  - Best Supporting Actress (Cate Blanchett, runner-up)
- Venice Film Festival:
  - CinemAvvenire Award – Best Film (**winner**)
  - Golden Lion (Todd Haynes, nominee)
  - Special Jury Prize (Todd Haynes, **winner**)
  - Volpi Cup Best Actress (Cate Blanchett, **winner**)

DVD release

I'm Not There was released on DVD as a 2-disc special edition on May 6, 2008. The DVD special features include audio commentary from Haynes, deleted scenes, featurettes, a music video, audition tapes for Marcus Carl Franklin and Ben Whishaw, a gag reel, a tribute to Heath Ledger, a series of unreleased trailers featuring the six actors re-enacting the "Subterranean Homesick Blues" promo film and a Bob Dylan filmography and discography.

Soundtrack

The film features numerous songs by Dylan, performed by Dylan and also recordings by other artists. The songs feature as both foreground—performed by artists on camera (e.g. "Goin' to Acapulco", "Pressing On")—and background accompaniment to the action. A notable non-Dylan song in the movie is "(I'm Not Your) Steppin' Stone" by The Monkees, which plays in the background of a party scene set in London.

Notes

[1] Todd McCarthy (2009-09-04). "*I'm Not There*" (http://www.variety.com/review/VE1117934602.html?categoryid=31&cs=1&p=0). *Variety.*. Retrieved 2009-02-05.
[2] A. O. Scott (2007-11-07). "*I'm Not There*" (http://movies.nytimes.com/2007/11/21/movies/21ther.html?ref=movies). *The New York Times.*. Retrieved 2009-02-10.
[3] DeCurtis, Anthony (2007-11-23). "6 Characters in Search of an Artist" (http://chronicle.com/free/v54/i13/13b01401.htm). *The Chronicle of Higher Education.*.
[4] "Bob Dylan Timeline" (http://www.bbc.co.uk/bbcfour/music/bobdylan/timeline/timeline_html.shtml). BBC.. Retrieved 2009-02-05.
[5] Gray, 2006, *The Bob Dylan Encyclopedia*, pp. 287–289.
[6] Ebert, Roger (21 November 2007). "I'm Not There" (http://rogerebert.suntimes.com/apps/pbcs.dll/article?AID=/20071120/REVIEWS/711200304). rogerebert.com.. Retrieved 5 July 2010.
[7] Sullian, Robert (2007-10-07). "This Is Not A Bob Dylan Movie" (http://www.nytimes.com/2007/10/07/magazine/07Haynes.html?pagewanted=all). New York Times.. Retrieved 2009-02-06.

[8] Part of Dylan's speech went: "There's no black and white, left and right to me any more; there's only up and down and down is very close to the ground. And I'm trying to go up without thinking of anything trivial such as politics."; see, Shelton, *No Direction Home*, pp. 200–205.
[9] "NYC Album Art: The Freewheelin' Bob Dylan" (http://gothamist.com/2006/04/18/nyc_album_art_t.php). Gothamist. 2006-04-18. . Retrieved 2009-03-01.
[10] Gray, *The Bob Dylan Encyclopedia*, pp. 198–200.
[11] Heylin, 1996, *Bob Dylan: A Life In Stolen Moments*, p. 87.
[12] Dylan's 1965 press conference reproduced in: Hedin (ed.), 2004, *Studio A: The Bob Dylan Reader*, pp. 51–58.
[13] "You walk into the room/ With your pencil in your hand/ You see somebody naked / And you say: 'Who is that man?'"
[14] Heylin, 2000, *Bob Dylan: Behind the Shades Revisited*, pp. 128–133.
[15] In his 1997 interview with David Gates of *Newsweek*, Dylan said: "I don't think I'm tangible to myself. I mean, I think one thing today and I think another thing tomorrow. I change during the course of a day. I wake and I'm one person, and when I go to sleep I know for certain I'm somebody else. I don't know who I am most of the time. It doesn't even matter to me."Gates, David (1997-10-06). "Dylan Revisited" (http://www.newsweek.com/id/97107/output/print). *Newsweek*. . Retrieved 2008-10-13.
[16] Dylan, *Chronicles, Volume One*, pp. 243–246.
[17] Dylan, *Chronicles, Volume One*, p. 146
[18] "Haynes in Weinstein Company press notes for "I'm Not There", quoted in *Footnote fetishism & "I'm Not There"* by Jim Emerson" (http://blogs.suntimes.com/scanners/2007/10/how_does_it_feel_footnote_feti.html). Jim Emerson's scanners::blog. 2007-10-10. .
[19] "Dylan Director Comes Clean" (http://www.mojo4music.com/blog/2007/12/dylan_director_comes_clean.html). *Mojo*. . Retrieved 2008-09-07.
[20] "I'm Not There Movie Reviews, Pictures – Rotten Tomatoes" (http://www.rottentomatoes.com/m/im_not_there_suppositions_on_a_film_concerning_dylan/). Rotten Tomatoes. . Retrieved 2008-05-19.
[21] "I'm Not There (2007): Reviews" (http://www.metacritic.com/film/titles/imnotthere). Metacritic. . Retrieved 2008-05-19.
[22] David Gates, "The Roles They Are A-Changin': In Todd Haynes's film, one Dylan's not enough" (http://www.newsweek.com/id/70994) from *Newsweek*, November 26, 2007.
[23] Lawrence Toppman, "Everybody's 'There' except Bob D." (http://ae.charlotte.com/entertainment/ui/charlotte/movie.html?id=987014) from *The Charlotte Observer*, November 23, 2007.
[24] "Blanchett wins top Venice award" (http://news.bbc.co.uk/2/hi/entertainment/6985422.stm). BBC News Online. 8 September 2007. . Retrieved 2007-09-08.
[25] Siegel, Ed (2007-12-04). "A noble failure in grasping Dylan" (http://www.boston.com/bostonglobe/editorial_opinion/oped/articles/2007/12/04/a_noble_failure_in_grasping_dylan/). Boston Globe. . Retrieved 2007-12-04.
[26] Luke Davies. "Let the Bird Sing, Let the Bird Fly: Todd Haynes's 'I'm Not There'" (http://www.themonthly.com.au/film-luke-davies-let-bird-sing-let-bird-fly-todd-haynes-s-i-m-not-there-746). *The Monthly*. .
[27] "Metacritic: 2007 Film Critic Top Ten Lists" (http://web.archive.org/web/20080102102034/http://www.metacritic.com/film/awards/2007/toptens.shtml). Metacritic. Archived from the original (http://www.metacritic.com/film/awards/2007/toptens.shtml) on 2008-01-02. . Retrieved 2008-01-05.
[28] Best musical Im not there (http://www.rottentomatoes.com/features/rtawards/?category=musical&rank=5)
[29] Travers, Peter, (December 19, 2007) "Peter Travers' Best and Worst Movies of 2007" (http://www.rollingstone.com/news/story/17686508/peter_travers_best_and_worst_movies_of_2007/9) *Rolling Stone*. Retrieved 2007-12-20

References

- Dylan, Bob (2004). *Chronicles: Volume One*. Simon and Schuster. ISBN 0-7432-2815-4.
- Gray, Michael (2006). *The Bob Dylan Encyclopedia*. Continuum International. ISBN 0-8264-6933-7.
- Hedin, Benjamin (ed.) (2004). *Studio A: The Bob Dylan Reader*. W.W.Norton & Co.. ISBN 0-393-32742-6.
- Heylin, Clinton (1996). *Bob Dylan: A Life In Stolen Moments*. Book Sales. ISBN 0711956693.
- Heylin, Clinton (2003). *Bob Dylan: Behind the Shades Revisited*. Perennial Currents. ISBN 0-06-052569-X.
- Shelton, Robert, *No Direction Home*, Da Capo Press, 2003 reprint of 1986 original, 576 pages. ISBN 0-306-81287-8

External links

- Official website (http://www.imnotthere-movie.com)
- *I'm Not There* (http://www.imdb.com/title/tt0368794/) at the Internet Movie Database
- *I'm Not There* (http://www.allrovi.com/movies/movie/v1:335936) at AllRovi
- *I'm Not There* (http://www.boxofficemojo.com/movies/?id=imnotthere.htm) at Box Office Mojo
- *I'm Not There* (http://www.rottentomatoes.com/m/im_not_there_suppositions_on_a_film_concerning_dylan/) at Rotten Tomatoes
- *I'm Not There* (http://www.metacritic.com/movie/imnotthere) at Metacritic
- Director Todd Haynes talks about *I'm Not There* at the 2007 New York Film Festival (http://blog.spout.com/2007/10/04/nyff-todd-haynes-meets-the-press/)

The Flock (film)

The Flock	
Promotional movie poster	
Directed by	Andrew Lau
Produced by	Philippe Martinez Elie Samaha Jenette Kahn Adam Richman Andrew Lau
Written by	Hans Bauer Craig Mitchell
Starring	Richard Gere Claire Danes KaDee Strickland
Music by	Cutting Edge
Cinematography	Enrique Chediak
Editing by	Martin Hunter
Distributed by	Bauer Martinez Entertainment
Release date(s)	22 November 2007
Country	USA
Language	English
Budget	US$35,000,000[1]

The Flock is a 2007 American thriller film directed by Andrew Lau, the co-director of the *Infernal Affairs* trilogy. The film, which marks his first English-language film, stars Richard Gere and Claire Danes.

Plot

A hyper-vigilant agent of the Department of Public Safety Erroll Babbage (Richard Gere) checks on registered sex offenders. Burnt out after a long career, he has become frustrated with the system of sex offender monitoring. With little faith in humanity left he takes on one last job to find a missing girl (Kristina Sisco).

He is three weeks away from taking early retirement and his final job is to train his young female replacement Allison Lowry (Claire Danes). After being left a newspaper with his characteristic headline circling, he is convinced the case of kidnapping is connected to a paroled sex offender he's monitoring and he takes it upon himself to find the victim at all costs.

Errol is eventually forced to leave the department early due to his relentless interrogation of sexual offenders and occasional vigilante actions against them. His efforts center on Viola (KaDee Strickland), a woman who has a history of being abused but is known to have a connection to another culprit that Errol suspects to have taken the girl. Together with his partner they figure out that Viola has become an abuser herself and is the ringleader in a kidnapping and torture syndicate. They track her down to a deserted scrap heap where they find the latest kidnapped girl as well as corpses of previous victims. The movie ends with Viola being brought to book after Errol considers killing her. Errol and Allison realize that in fighting the monsters involved in sexual offenses, they must not become monsters themselves.

Cast
- Richard Gere – Agent Errol Babbage
- Claire Danes – Allison Lowry
- Avril Lavigne – Beatrice Bell (Suspect's Girlfriend)
- KaDee Strickland – Viola
- Paul McGowen – Det. Grant P. Stockdale
- Matt Sanford – James Ray Ward
- Carmen Serano – Colette
- Kristina Sisco – Harriet Wells
- Ray Wise – Robert Still
- French Stewart – Haynes Ownsby

Release
The film was released theatrically in several countries throughout the world in late 2007, early 2008, yet in the United States it premiered April 11, 2008 at the Palm Beach International Film Festival, before being released on DVD on May 20, 2008 by Genius Products.[2][3]

References
[1] The Flock – Box office / business (http://www.imdb.com/title/tt0473356/business). Internet Movie Database. Retrieved August 21, 2008.
[2] The Flock – Release dates (http://www.imdb.com/title/tt0473356/releaseinfo). Internet Movie Database. Retrieved August 21, 2008.
[3] The Flock – Company credits (http://www.imdb.com/title/tt0473356/companycredits). Internet Movie Database. Retrieved August 21, 2008.

External links
- *The Flock* (http://www.allrovi.com/movies/movie/v336642) at AllRovi
- *The Flock* (http://www.boxofficemojo.com/movies/?id=flock.htm) at Box Office Mojo
- *The Flock* (http://www.imdb.com/title/tt0473356/) at the Internet Movie Database
- *The Flock* (http://www.rottentomatoes.com/m/flock/) at Rotten Tomatoes
- *The Flock* (http://www.the-numbers.com/movies/2008/FLOCK.php) at The Numbers

Nights in Rodanthe

Nights in Rodanthe	
Theatrical release poster	
Directed by	George C. Wolfe
Produced by	Denise Di Novi
Written by	**Novel** Nicholas Sparks **Screenplay** Ann Peacock John Romano
Starring	Richard Gere Diane Lane
Music by	Jeanine Tesori
Cinematography	Alfonso Beato
Editing by	Brian A. Kates
Studio	Village Roadshow Pictures
Distributed by	Warner Bros.
Release date(s)	September 26, 2008
Running time	97 minutes
Country	United States Australia
Language	English Spanish
Box office	$84,375,061 [1]

Nights in Rodanthe (pronounced Roe-DANTH-ee[2]) is a 2008 American/Australian film adaptation of the novel with the same name by Nicholas Sparks. The film stars Richard Gere and Diane Lane in their third screen collaboration after *Unfaithful* (2002) and *The Cotton Club* (1984). The film is rated PG-13 by the MPAA for "some sensuality" and was released on September 26, 2008. It was filmed in the small seaside village of Rodanthe, the northernmost village of the inhabited areas of Hatteras Island as well as North Topsail Beach, North Carolina. The film's soundtrack features "Love Remains the Same", a song written by Gavin Rossdale for his 2008 debut solo album, despite the fact that it does not appear in the film.

Plot

While picking up his son and daughter for a weekend visit, Jack (Christopher Meloni) tells his estranged wife Adrienne (Diane Lane) that he wants to move back home. Adrienne says she needs time and space to think. It is made clear that Jack left his family for another woman.

Adrienne drives to Rodanthe, North Carolina to a friend's bed-and-breakfast for the weekend. The house is rustic, romantic and right on the beach and partially in the surf at high tide.

There is only one guest for the weekend, Paul (Richard Gere), a surgeon who arrives at the inn with his own emotional baggage. He has flashbacks of a surgery which ended tragically. The family of the patient, who live in Rodanthe, is suing him.

A storm moves in and the two team up to protect the inn. They dine together, share stories and eventually turn to each other for emotional comfort. A genuine romance is born. With Adrienne's advice and moral support, Paul opens up to the patient's widower and in doing so faces his own pain.

Paul very reluctantly leaves Adrienne and Rodanthe to fly to South America, where his estranged son Mark (James Franco) lives, to reconcile with him. Paul carries guilt for passing up a relationship with his son in favor of his career. He helps him practice medicine and take care of the natives there.

During their separation Adrienne and Paul exchange numerous handwritten letters expressing their longing to be with each other once again. Unfortunately, Paul is killed in a flash mudslide before he is able to be with her again. Mark arrives at Adrienne's door with the tragic news, a box of Paul's personal belongings and gratitude to Adrienne for giving him back his father.

Adrienne ultimately is left all alone with her nearly unbearable grief. There is nobody else available to offer her solace and comfort.

She finally is granted a respite from her heart-rending sadness when, during a solitary sojourn along the beach on a strikingly beautiful day, she looks up to see a small herd of magnificent wild horses go thundering on by her.

Cast

- Diane Lane as Adrienne Willis
- Richard Gere as Dr. Paul Flanner
- James Franco as Dr. Mark Flanner (uncredited)
- Scott Glenn as Robert Torrelson
- Christopher Meloni as Jack Willis
- Viola Davis as Jean
- Pablo Schreiber as Charlie Torrelson
- Mae Whitman as Amanda Willis
- Charlie Tahan as Danny Willis

The house in Rodanthe, North Carolina used in the movie.

Critical reception and box office

The film opened at #2 at the North American Box office making $13,418,454 in its opening weekend behind *Eagle Eye*. According to review aggregator Rotten Tomatoes, the critical consensus holds that the film is "derivative and schmaltzy" and "strongly mottled by contrivances that even the charisma of stars Diane Lane and Richard Gere can't repair". The site rates the movie as "rotten", with a score of 29% based on 106 reviews.[3] Metacritic scored the film as 39/100, with "generally negative reviews", based on 26 reviews.[4] Although the movie was critically panned, it grossed $84,375,061 worldwide.[5]

The *Times of London* included *Nights in Rodanthe* on its 100 Worst Films of 2008 list.[6]

References

[1] http://www.boxofficemojo.com/movies/?id=nightsinrodanthe.htm
[2] http://www.starnewsonline.com/apps/pbcs.dll/article?AID=/20070521/NEWS/705210319/1051/NEWS
[3] http://www.rottentomatoes.com/m/nights_in_rodanthe
[4] http://www.metacritic.com/film/titles/nightsinrodanthe
[5] http://www.boxofficemojo.com/movies/?id=nightsinrodanthe.htm
[6] http://entertainment.timesonline.co.uk/tol/arts_and_entertainment/film/article5245052.ece?token=null&offset=24&page=3

External links

- Official site (http://nightsinrodanthe.warnerbros.com/)
- *Nights in Rodanthe* (http://www.imdb.com/title/tt0956038/) at the Internet Movie Database
- *Nights in Rodanthe* (http://www.allrovi.com/movies/movie/v387784) at AllRovi
- *Nights in Rodanthe* (http://www.boxofficemojo.com/movies/?id=nightsinrodanthe.htm) at Box Office Mojo
- *Nights in Rodanthe* (http://www.rottentomatoes.com/m/nights_in_rodanthe/) at Rotten Tomatoes

Amelia (film)

Amelia	
Theatrical release poster	
Directed by	Mira Nair
Produced by	Ted Waitt Kevin Hyman Lydia Dean Pilcher **Executive Producers:** Ronald Bass Hilary Swank
Written by	Ronald Bass Anna Hamilton Phelan
Based on	*East to the Dawn* by Susan Butler and *The Sound of Wings* by Mary S. Lovell
Starring	Hilary Swank Richard Gere Ewan McGregor Christopher Eccleston
Music by	Gabriel Yared
Cinematography	Stuart Dryburgh
Editing by	Allyson C. Johnson Lee Percy
Studio	Fox Searchlight Pictures Avalon Pictures AE Electra Productions
Distributed by	Fox Searchlight Pictures
Release date(s)	October 23, 2009
Running time	111 minutes
Country	United States Canada
Language	English
Budget	$40 million
Box office	$19,233,908

Amelia is a 2009 biographical film of the life of Amelia Earhart, directed by Mira Nair and starring Hilary Swank[1] as Earhart along with Richard Gere, Christopher Eccleston[2] and Ewan McGregor.[3] It was written by Ronald Bass and Anna Hamilton Phelan, using research from sources such as *East to the Dawn* by Susan Butler and *The Sound of Wings* by Mary S. Lovell.[1] To date, the film has garnered predominantly negative reviews.

Plot

On July 2, 1937, Amelia Earhart (Swank) and her navigator, Fred Noonan (Eccleston), are on the last leg of an around-the-world flight. Moving in vignettes from her early years when Earhart was captivated by the sight of an aircraft flying overhead on the Kansas prairie where she grew up, her life over the preceding decade gradually unfolds. As a young woman, she is recruited by publishing tycoon and eventual husband George Putnam (Gere) to become the first woman to cross the Atlantic Ocean, albeit as a passenger. Taking command of the flight results in a success and she is thrust into the limelight as the most famous woman pilot of her time. Putnam helps Earhart write a book chronicling the flight, much like his earlier triumph with Charles Lindbergh's *We*, gradually falling in love with his charge, and they eventually marry, although she enacts a "cruel" pledge as her wedding contract.

Embarrassed that her fame was not earned, Earhart commences to set myriad aviation records, and in 1932, recreates her earlier transatlantic flight, becoming the first female pilot to fly solo across the Atlantic. Throughout a decade of notoriety, Earhart falls into an awkward love affair with pilot and future Federal Aviation administrator Gene Vidal (McGregor). In a display of romantic jealousy, Putnam quietly tells Amelia that he does not want Vidal in his house. Earhart is annoyed by the seemingly endless agenda of celebrity appearances and endorsements but Putnam reminds his wife that it funds her flying. They each acquiesce to the other's wishes and Earhart is drawn back to her husband on the eve of her last momentous flight, a round the world flight fraught with perils. Earhart's first attempt ends in a runway crash in Hawaii, due to collapsed landing gear. Earhart shuts off the fuel supply but her aircraft requires repairs before the flight can be attempted again. Eventually, she takes the repaired Lockheed Model 10 Electra "Flying Laboratory" in a reverse direction, leaving the lengthy transpacific crossing at the end of her flight.

Setting out to refuel at tiny Howland Island, radio transmissions between USCGC *Itasca*, a Coast Guard picket ship, and Earhart's aircraft reveal a rising crisis, as her fuel begins to run out. Her last message is a cryptic position report that the Coast Guard radio operators realize is not of sufficient length to provide a "fix". *Itasca* has a directional finder with a dead battery, and weak radio communications prevent Earhart and USCG *Itasca* from making contact. Earhart and Noonan continue to fly on, as the story ends.

Cast

- Hilary Swank as Amelia Earhart
- Richard Gere as George P. Putnam
- Ewan McGregor as Gene Vidal
- Christopher Eccleston as Fred Noonan
- Joe Anderson as Bill Stutz
- William Cuddy as Gore Vidal
- Mia Wasikowska as Elinor Smith
- Cherry Jones as Eleanor Roosevelt
- Virginia Madsen was cast as Dorothy Binney, Putnam's first wife, but her scenes were cut.[4]
- Divine Brown, Canadian Juno award-winning rhythm and blues and soul singer briefly appeared as the "Torch singer".[5]

Production

Hilary Swank took on the role of Executive Producer, working closely with Nair.[6] Filming took place in New York, Toronto, Parkwood Estate in Oshawa, Nova Scotia, Dunnville, Ontario and Niagara-on-the-Lake, Ontario as well as various locations in South Africa. Over the weekend of June 22, 2008, Swank was in Wolfville, Nova Scotia for filming at Acadia University. Although Swank is a pilot-in-training[7] and three other women pilots were contracted for the flying scenes,[8] Nair was concerned about insurance and liability issues, and opted for professional pilots, Jimmy Leeward and Bryan Regan to fly in the film.[9] Contemporary newsreel footage of Earhart was interspersed throughout the film while a combination of static, real aircraft and CGI effects was utilized for the flying sequences.[10] Numerous period aircraft, automobiles and equipment were obtained to provide authenticity, including the use of two replica aircraft, a Lockheed Vega and Fokker F.VIIb/3m Tri-motor *Friendship* (with limited ability to run up engines and taxi).[11] The Lockheed 12A Electra Junior "Hazy Lily" (F-AZLL) used alongside another Electra Junior, filled in for the much more rare Lockheed Electra 10E that Earhart used.[12] Despite the efforts to faithfully replicate the period, numerous historical inaccuracies were evident, as chronicled in some reviews.[13]

At the completion of filming, the two replica aircraft featured in the Earhart transatlantic flights were donated to museums. The Lockheed Vega is now in the collection of the San Diego Air & Space Museum[14] while the Fokker F. VIIB/3M tri-motor is now housed at the Canadian Bushplane Heritage Centre in Sault Ste. Marie, Ontario where it was unveiled in 2009 with a local Amelia Earhart reenactor Kathie Brosemer recounting the story of Earhart's flight in 1928.[15]

Writing

Oscar-winning screenwriter Ronald Bass wrote seven drafts of the script for aviation buff and Gateway founder Ted Waitt, who has funded expeditions to search for Earhart's plane, and was prepared to finance the film himself.[16] Bass used research from books on Earhart such as biographies by Susan Butler, *East to the Dawn* and Mary S. Lovell's *The Sound of the Wings* as well as Elgen and Mary Long's *Amelia Earhart: The Mystery Solved*.[1] Although not intended to be a documentary, Bass incorporated many of Earhart's actual words into key scenes.[17] Oscar-nominated screenwriter Anna Hamilton Phelan did a re-write, taking a different approach from the original screenplay..[16]

Reception

Critical response

Amelia received mixed to negative reviews from film critics, with a 20% "rotten" rating on the Rotten Tomatoes website based on 102 reviews with an average score of 4.4/10.[18] Among Rotten Tomatoes' "Cream of the Crop", which consists of popular and notable critics from the top newspapers, websites, television, and radio programs, the film holds an overall approval rating of 11% based on 28 reviews.[19] Another review aggretator, Metacritic, which assigns a normalized rating of 100 reviews from mainstream critics, gave the film a score of 37% based on 34 reviews (a weighted average of the score of 46.1%).[20]

Echoing the majority view, Martin Morrow's review on the *Canadian Broadcasting Corporation* website was very critical of the film, labeling it "a dud," declaring: "Hilary Swank may look the spitting image of Earhart in those vintage newsreels, but her performance is more insipid than inspiring. Mira Nair directs as if she were piloting an overloaded plane on an endless runway – the film lumbers along interminably, never achieving takeoff... As the film limps to a close, *Amelia* has accomplished a feat we didn't think possible: it has made us indifferent to this real-life heroine's tragic fate."[21] Most critics decried the inconsistencies and lack of focus in the film; Manohla Dargis of the *The New York Times* wrote, "The actors don't make a persuasive fit, despite all their long stares and infernal smiling. ...the movie is a more effective testament to the triumphs of American dentistry than to Earhart or aviation."[22] Ric Gillespie, author of *Finding Amelia*, wrote that "...Swank, under Nair's direction, accomplishes the amazing feat of making one of the most complex, passionate, ferociously ambitious, and successful women of the 20th century seem shallow, weepy, and rather dull."[13]

A small number of positive reviews included Ray Bennett of the *Hollywood Reporter* who characterized the film as an "instant bio classic," stressing the production values in which "director Nair and star Swank make her quest not only understandable but truly impressive."[23] Matthew Sorrento of *Film Threat*, gave the film 4 stars, and wrote: "Director Mira Nair trusts her oldschool filmmaking style enough to inspire a fresh take on a legend."[24] Roger

Ebert of the *Chicago Sun-Times*, however, gave the film a positive review and gave it 3 stars out of 4, and called it "a perfectly sound biopic, well directed and acted".[25] In pre-release publicity, Hilary Swank had been touted as a candidate for a third Oscar, but later that prospect was viewed as distant.[7] Carrie Rickey of the *Philadelphia Inquirer*, however, awarded the film 3 stars, praising Swank's performance in her review stating that "like Maggie in *Million Dollar Baby*, [Swank] is unwavering in her gaze, ambition, and drive," and "in Nair's evocatively art-directed (and sensationally costumed) film, Earhart comes alive."[26]

Home media release

On February 2, 2010, Fox Home Entertainment released *Amelia* in DVD and Blu-ray versions. Extras on the DVD include deleted scenes and "The Power of Amelia Earhart", "Making Amelia" and "Movietone News" featurettes. The Blu-ray release also has two additional featurettes: "The Plane Behind the Legend" and "Re-constructing the Planes of Amelia" along with a digital copy of the film.[27]

References

Notes

[1] Fleming, Michael. "Hilary Swank to play Amelia Earhart". (http://www.variety.com/article/VR1117980470.html?categoryid=13&cs=1) *Variety*, February 7, 2008. Retrieved: October 8, 2008.
[2] Fleming, Michael. "Christopher Eccleston joins 'Amelia'". (http://www.variety.com/article/VR1117987374.html?categoryid=1236&cs=1) *Variety*, June 12, 2008. Retrieved: October 8, 2008.
[3] Siegel, Tatiana. "Ewan McGregor flies with 'Amelia'". (http://www.variety.com/article/VR1117986462.html?categoryid=13&cs=1) *Variety*, May 26, 2008. Retrieved: October 8, 2008.
[4] Siegel, Tatiana. "Virginia Madsen added to 'Amelia'." (http://www.variety.com/article/VR1117984375.html?categoryid=13&cs=1) *Variety*, April 21, 2008. Retrieved: October 8, 2008.
[5] "Divine Brown." (http://www.divinebrown.ca) *divinebrown.ca*. Retrieved: October 27, 2010.
[6] Zohn 2009, p. 118.
[7] Coles 2009, p. 172.
[8] "Lucknow Native involved in production of 'Amelia' film." (http://ameliaearhart.com/news/2009/10/lucknow-native-involved-in-production-of-amelia-film/) *Lucknow Sentinel* via *ameliaearhart.com*, October 21, 2009. Retrieved: October 25, 2009.
[9] Rozemeyer, Karl. "Interview: Hilary Swank Discusses Playing Amelia Earhart." (http://www.cinemaspy.com/article.php?id=3423) *cinemaspy.com*, October 22, 2009. Retrieved: October 25, 2009.
[10] Braser, Bryant. "Amelia Flies With Subtle VFX: Nothing Flashy as Mr. X Recreates Period Planes and Settings for Earhart." (http://www.studiodaily.com/filmandvideo/projects/11436.html) *studiodaily.com*, October 22, 2009. Retrieved: October 25, 2009.
[11] O'Leary 2009, pp. 12–13.
[12] "Star of the silver screen visits Duxford." (http://www.aeroplanemonthly.co.uk/news/Star_of_the_silver_screen_visits_Duxford_news_285219.html) *aeroplanemonthly.co.uk*, June 29, 2009. Retrieved: October 24, 2009.
[13] Gillespie, Ric. " 'Amelia' – a film by Mira Nair starring Hilary Swank as Amelia Earhart and Richard Gere as George Palmer Putnam." (http://tighar.org/news/) *tighar.org*, October 23, 2009. Retrieved: October 24, 2009.
[14] "Lockheed Vega 5B ." (http://www.aerospacemuseum.org/collections/collection_item.php?id=30) *aerospacemuseum.org*. Retrieved: November 14, 2010.
[15] Stares, Bob. "Amelia flies again." (http://www.soonews.ca/viewarticle.php?id=22948) *SooNews.ca*, October 29, 2009. Retrieved: November 14, 2010.
[16] Thompson, Anne. "'Amelia': When biopics go bad." (http://blogs.indiewire.com/thompsononhollywood/2009/10/23/amelia_when_biopics_go_bad/) *Thompson on Hollywood*, October 23, 2009. Retrieved: December 13, 2011.
[17] O'Leary 2009, p. 12.
[18] " 'Amelia' Reviews, Pictures." (http://www.rottentomatoes.com/m/amelia_2009/) *Rotten Tomatoes, IGN Entertainment*.
[19] " 'Amelia' Reviews, Pictures – Cream of the Crop." (http://www.rottentomatoes.com/m/amelia_2009/?critic=creamcrop) *Rotten Tomatoes, IGN Entertainment*. Retrieved: October 15, 2010.
[20] " 'Amelia' (2009): Reviews." (http://www.metacritic.com/film/titles/amelia) *Metacritic*. Retrieved: October 15, 2010.
[21] Morrow, Martin. "Review: 'Amelia' – Hilary Swank's evocation of legendary pilot Amelia Earhart just doesn't fly." (http://www.cbc.ca/arts/film/story/2009/10/22/f-amelia-review.html) *cbc.ca*, October 22, 2009. Retrieved: October 24, 2009.
[22] Dargis, Manohla. "An Adventurer Takes Flight, Blinding Smile and All." (http://movies.nytimes.com/2009/10/23/movies/23amelia.html) *The New York Times*, October 23, 2009. Retrieved: October 24, 2009.

[23] Bennett, Ray. " 'Amelia': Film Review." (http://www.hollywoodreporter.com/hr/film-reviews/amelia-film-review-1004023274.story?imw=Y) *Hollywood Reporter*, October 18, 2009. Retrieved: October 24, 2009.

[24] Sorrento, Matthew. " 'Amelia' Current Movie Reviews, Independent Movies." (http://www.filmthreat.com/index.php?section=reviews&Id=11955) *Film Threat*, October 23, 2009. Retrieved: October 25, 2009.

[25] Ebert, Roger. "'Amelia' (PG)." (http://rogerebert.suntimes.com/apps/pbcs.dll/article?AID=/20091021/REVIEWS/910219989) *Chicago Sun-Times*, October 21, 2009. Retrieved: October 25, 2009.

[26] Rickey, Carrie. "Swank soars as flier Amelia Earhart." (http://www.philly.com/inquirer/columnists/carrie_rickey/20091023_Swank_soars_as_flier_Amelia_Earhart.html) *Philadelphia Inquirer*, October 22, 2009. Retrieved: October 25, 2009.

[27] Woodward, Tom. "Fox Home Entertainment announces DVD and Blu-ray releases of the movie." (http://www.dvdactive.com/news/releases/amelia.html) *dvdactive.com*, December 15, 2009. Retrieved: March 2, 2010.

Bibliography

- Butler, Susan. *East to the Dawn: The Life of Amelia Earhart*. Reading, MA: Addison-Wesley, 1997. ISBN 0-306-80887-0.
- Coles, Joanna. " Hilary Swank is Ready for Takeoff." *Marie Claire*, November 2009.
- Goldstein, Donald M. and Katherine V. Dillon. *Amelia: The Centennial Biography of an Aviation Pioneer*. Washington, DC: Brassey's, 1997. ISBN 1-57488-134-5.
- Long, Elgen M. and Marie K. *Amelia Earhart: The Mystery Solved*. New York: Simon & Schuster, 1999. ISBN 0-684-86005-8.
- Lovell, Mary S. *The Sound of Wings*. New York: St. Martin's Press, 1989. ISBN 0-312-03431-8.
- O'Leary, Michael, ed. "Amelia on the Silver Screen." *Air Classics*, Volume 45, No. 11, November 2009.
- Rich, Doris L. *Amelia Earhart: A Biography*. Washington, DC: Smithsonian Institution Press, 1989. ISBN 1-56098-725-1.
- Zohn, Patricia. "Oh So Swank." *Town and Country*, October 2009.

External links

- Official website (http://www.foxsearchlight.com/amelia)
- *Amelia* (http://www.allrovi.com/movies/movie/v431074) at AllRovi
- *Amelia* (http://www.imdb.com/title/tt1129445/) at the Internet Movie Database
- BBC interview with Mary S Lovell and history report on Amelia Earhart landing in Southampton, UK (http://news.bbc.co.uk/local/hampshire/hi/people_and_places/history/newsid_8346000/8346866.stm)

Hachi: A Dog's Tale

Hachi: A Dog's Tale	
Japanese Theatrical Poster	
Directed by	Lasse Hallström
Produced by	Richard Gere Bill Johnson Vicki Shigekuni Wong
Written by	Stephen P. Lindsey
Starring	Chico Layla Forrest Richard Gere Joan Allen Cary-Hiroyuki Tagawa Sarah Roemer Jason Alexander Erick Avari
Music by	Jan A. P. Kaczmarek
Editing by	Kristina Boden
Studio	Hachiko,LLC Grand Army Entertainment,LLC Opperman Viner Chrystyn Entertainment Scion FilmsInferno Production
Distributed by	Stage 6 Films
Release date(s)	June 13, 2009 (Seattle)
Running time	104 minutes
Country	United States
Language	English
Budget	$16 million[1]
Box office	$46,671,235

Hachi: A Dog's Tale (or ***Hachiko: A Dog's Story*** outside the United States) is a 2009 American drama film based on the true story of the faithful Akita Hachikō. It is a remake of the 1987 movie *Hachi-kō (Hachikō Monogatari)* ハチ公物語 (literally "The Tale of Hachiko"). It was directed by Lasse Hallström, written by Stephen P. Lindsey and stars Richard Gere, Joan Allen and Sarah Roemer.

The first foreign premiere was on August 8, 2009, in Japan. To date the film has opened in over 25 countries and continued to open in foreign territories throughout 2010.[2] In the United States the movie was first shown at the Seattle International Film Festival on June 13, 2009. Sony Pictures Entertainment decided to forgo a U.S. theatrical release. According to the Odeon Cinema website the film was given a UK theatrical release on March 12, 2010, courtesy of Entertainment Film Distributors.[3] Box Office Mojo reports that total foreign box office had reached $46.7million as of June 2010.[4]

Short Summary

A drama based on the true story of a college professor's bond with the abandoned dog he takes into his home.

Plot

Based on a true story from Japan, *Hachiko Monogatari* ハチ公物語 *(literally "The Tale of Hachiko")* is a moving film about loyalty and the rare, invincible bonds that occasionally form almost instantaneously in the most unlikely places.

In the modern day, a class full of young students are giving oral presentations about personal heroes. A boy named Ronnie (Kevin DeCoste) stands up and begins to tell of 'Hachiko', his grandfather's dog. Years before, an Akita puppy is sent from Japan to the United States, but his cage falls off the baggage cart at an American train station, where he is found by college professor Parker Wilson (Richard Gere). Parker is instantly captivated by the dog. When Carl (Jason Alexander), the station controller, refuses to take him, Parker takes the puppy home overnight. His wife Cate (Joan Allen) is insistent about not keeping the puppy.

The next day Parker expects that someone will have contacted the train station, but no one has. He sneaks the pup onto the train and takes him to work, where a Japanese college professor, Ken (Cary-Hiroyuki Tagawa), translates the symbol on the pup's collar as 'Hachi', Japanese for 'good fortune', and the number 8. Parker decides to call the dog 'Hachi'. Ken points out that perhaps the two are meant to be together. Parker attempts to play fetch with Hachi, but he refuses to join in. Meanwhile Cate receives a call about someone wanting to adopt Hachi. After seeing how close her husband has come to Hachi, however, Cate tells the caller that Hachi has already been adopted.

A few years later, Hachi and Parker are as close as ever. Parker, however, is still mystified by Hachi's refusal to do normal, dog-like things like chase and retrieve a ball. Ken advises him that Hachi will only bring him the ball for a special reason. One morning, Parker leaves for work and Hachi sneaks out and follows him to the train station, where he refuses to leave until Parker walks him home. That afternoon, Hachi sneaks out again and walks to the train station, waiting patiently for Parker's train to come in. Eventually Parker relents and walks Hachi to the station every morning, where he leaves on the train. Hachi leaves after Parker's safe departure, but comes back in the afternoon to see his master's train arrive and walk with him home again. This continues for some time, until one afternoon Parker attempts to leave, but Hachi barks and refuses to go with him. Parker eventually leaves without him, but Hachi chases him, holding his ball. Parker is surprised but pleased that Hachi is finally willing to play fetch the ball with him. Worried that he will be late for the college, Professor Parker leaves on the train despite Hachi barking at him. At work that day Parker, still holding Hachi's ball, is teaching his music class when he suddenly suffers a fatal heart attack.

At the train station, Hachi waits patiently as the train arrives, but there is no sign of Parker. He remains, lying in the snow, for several hours, until Parker's son-in-law Michael (Ronnie Sublett) comes to collect him. The next day, Hachi returns to the station and waits, remaining all day and all night. As time passes, Cate sells the house and Hachi is sent to live with her daughter Andy (Sarah Roemer), Michael, and their new baby Ronnie. However, at the first opportunity, he escapes and eventually finds his way back to his old house and then to the train station, where he sits at his usual spot, eating hot dogs given to him by Jasjeet (Erick Avari), a local vendor. Andy arrives soon after and takes him home, but lets him out the next day to return to the station.

For the next nine years, Hachi waits for his owner. His loyalty is profiled in the local newspaper. Years after Parker's death, Cate comes back to visit Parker's grave when she catches sight of Hachi, now old and achy, waiting at the station. She gets emotional and sits next to Hachi until the next train comes. Hachi returns to the train station late at night and closes his eyes for the last time. Then, Parker walks out of the station and greets him as if nothing has changed at all, and the two reunite as their spirits rise up to Heaven to be together forever.

The film then shows Ronnie, back in his classroom, making his conclusion of why Hachi will forever be his hero. Ronnie's story has clearly moved the class, with some holding back tears. The boy after school sees his own Akita puppy, also named Hachi, to walk down the same tracks where Parker and Hachi spent so many years together.

The closing cards reveal information about the real Hachikō, who was born in Ōdate in 1923. After the death of his owner, Hidesaburo Ueno, in 1925, Hachikō returned to the Shibuya train station the next day and every day after that for the next nine years. The final card reveals that the real Hachikō died in 1934 (in fact, he died in 1935). A photo of his statue in the Shibuya train station is the last image shown before the credits roll.

Cast

- Richard Gere as Parker Wilson, the professor[5]
- Joan Allen as Cate Wilson, the professor's wife[5]
- Cary-Hiroyuki Tagawa as Ken Fujiyoshi
- Sarah Roemer as Andy Wilson, the professor's daughter
- Jason Alexander as Carl Boilins
- Erick Avari as Jasjeet, the Indian vendor
- Davenia McFadden as Mary Anne
- Kevin DeCoste as Ronnie
- Tora Hallstrom as Heather
- Robbie Sublett as Michael
- Robert Capron as Student
- Abhisek Bhaumik as Himself
- Frank Aronson as The Butcher
- Hachiko is played by three Akitas named Chico', Layla and Forrest — each playing a different period in Hachiko's life and his home

Differences

The film is set in present-day United States rather than Shōwa Era Japan, as the true story. The Hachi puppy is played by a Shiba Inu puppy, while the new Hachi in the end is an Akita Inu puppy.

Hachi: A Dog's Story bears similarity in theme to the 1961 Walt Disney feature film *Greyfriars Bobby*, also based on a true story, in which a Skye Terrier guards the grave of his departed master who is interred at Greyfriers Cemetery. There is a statue in Edinburgh, Scotland, to honor Bobby's loyalty.

Production

The film was shot primarily in Woonsocket, Rhode Island and Bristol, Rhode Island. The newspaper reporter, Teddy, states he is from the Woonsocket Call, the daily newspaper published in Woonsocket. This is the only spoken reference to the actual location where filming took place. The majority of filming took place in Bristol, and Woonsocket, both in the State of Rhode Island. Additional locations included the University of Rhode Island in Kingston, RI, along the Providence and Worcester Railroad Mechanical, and the Columbus Theater located in Providence, RI.[6] A second production unit filmed some scenes on-location in Japan.

Reception

As of May 31, 2011, the film has a 58% score at Rotten Tomatoes.[7]

References

[1] Film folks eat well on state's tab | Rhode Island news | projo.com | The Providence Journal (http://www.projo.com/news/content/film_office_spending_04-20-08_H99M8R3_v142.3663a87.html). projo.com (April 20, 2008). Retrieved on August 7, 2010.
[2] Release info on IMDb (http://www.imdb.com/title/tt1028532/releaseinfo)
[3] Hachi: A Dog's Tale (http://www.odeon.co.uk/fanatic/film_info/m12647/Hachi:_A_Dog's_Tale). ODEON. Retrieved on August 7, 2010.
[4] Hachiko: A Dog's Story (2009) (http://boxofficemojo.com/movies/intl/?page=&wk=2010W8&id=_fMADEINDANMARK01). Boxofficemojo.com. Retrieved on August 7, 2010.
[5] Michael Fleming (December 10, 2007). "Joan Allen fetches a 'Dog's' tale" (http://www.variety.com/article/VR1117977455.html?categoryid=1236&cs=1). Variety. . Retrieved July 24, 2008.
[6] IMDb, Filming locations (http://www.imdb.com/title/tt1028532/locations), IMDb
[7] *Hachiko: A Dog's Tale* at Rotten Tomatoes.com (http://www.rottentomatoes.com/m/hachiko_a_dogs_story/)

External links

- *Hachi: A Dog's Tale* (http://www.imdb.com/title/tt1028532/) at the Internet Movie Database
- *Hachi: A Dog's Tale* (http://www.rottentomatoes.com/m/hachiko_a_dogs_story/) at Rotten Tomatoes

Brooklyn's Finest

Brooklyn's Finest	
Theatrical release poster	
Directed by	Antoine Fuqua
Produced by	Basil Iwanyk John Langley John Thompson Elie Cohn
Written by	Michael C. Martin
Starring	Richard Gere Don Cheadle Ethan Hawke Wesley Snipes Will Patton Vincent D'Onofrio Shannon Kane Lili Taylor
Music by	Marcelo Zarvos
Cinematography	Patrick Murguia
Editing by	Barbara Tulliver
Studio	Millenium Films Thunder Road Film Productions Nu Image
Distributed by	Overture Films
Release date(s)	January 16, 2009 (SFF) March 5, 2010 (United States)
Running time	132 minutes
Country	United States
Language	English
Budget	$17 million[1]
Box office	$36,027,986

Brooklyn's Finest is a 2009 American crime film starring Richard Gere, Don Cheadle, Ethan Hawke, and Wesley Snipes in his first theatrical film since 2004's *Blade: Trinity*. The film also stars Will Patton, Ellen Barkin and Vincent D'Onofrio. It is directed by Antoine Fuqua, and written by Michael C. Martin, a one-time subway flagman from East New York.[2] The film was released in North America on March 5, 2010.

Plot

The film takes place within the notoriously rough Brownsville section of Brooklyn and especially within the Van Dyke housing projects in the NYPD's (fictional) 65th precinct. The action revolves around three policemen whose relationships to their jobs are drastically different.

The opening scene shows two men sitting in a parked car having a conversation, the man in the driver's seat, Carlo (Vincent D'Onofrio) is then shot unexpectedly in the face by the passenger, Detective Salvatore "Sal" Procida (Ethan Hawke). Sal grabs a bag of money out of Carlo's lap and runs away. Sal immediately confesses to a priest, not seeking God's forgiveness but his help with his situation, which he sees as dire. His wife (Lili Taylor) is pregnant with twins. His house is too small for the four children he already has, and it also has wood mold, which is jeopardizing his wife's health and the twins'. Desperate to move, Sal has arranged to purchase a larger home through a woman who owes him a favor. The down payment is due the following Tuesday, and Sal is still short. Sal appears to be a highly skilled and accomplished narcotics detective, but he has begun to try to pocket money from police raids.

Officer Eddie Dugan (Richard Gere) is a week from retirement after twenty-two years of less than exemplary service to the force when he is assigned to oversee rookies in the tough neighborhoods. His life in shambles, Eddie is barely hanging on, swilling whiskey in the morning to get out of bed. His only friend is a prostitute he frequents.

Detective Clarence "Tango" Butler (Don Cheadle) is an undercover cop working the drug beat. Losing himself in his role as a drug dealer, he is tired of the kind of attention that a black man in a black car attracts. Having been promised a promotion and a desk job for years, he is finally offered a way out but it means betraying a close friend Caz, a known criminal (Wesley Snipes) recently released from federal prison. Federal Agent Smith (Ellen Barkin) instructs Tango to set up the drug deal that will assure Caz's arrest and return to federal prison.

Eddie's first rookie assignment (Logan Marshall-Green) is a former Marine, who becomes disgusted with Eddie's lack of professionalism and cynical outlook, and asks to be reassigned – only to be killed on his next assignment. Eddie's second rookie assignment (Jesse Williams) accidentally fires his gun near a teenager during a petty theft investigation causing him to go deaf, leaving the NYPD facing a public relations nightmare. During the investigation, Eddie is remorseful for what happened, but refuses to play along with his superiors' attempts to imply that the teenager was a drug dealer.

When Tango goes to warn Caz to abort their upcoming drug deal, they are ambushed and Caz is shot dead on the street, under orders from Red (Michael K. Williams), a gangster Tango had humiliated earlier in a rooftop incident. After Agent Smith makes a racist remark and refuses to pursue Red, Tango lunges at her, but is restrained by fellow officers.

Eddie turns in his badge and visits his regular hooker, Chantal (Shannon Kane), who does not want to change her life by moving with him to Connecticut. On his way home, Eddie sees a woman, (Sarah Thompson), who was reported missing being shoved into a van. He follows the van to the Van Dyke housing projects. Meanwhile, Sal's latest raid on the complex is cancelled, but he decides to go to the location and rob the money he needs for his house. One of his team members, Detective Ronny Rosario (Brían F. O'Byrne), tries to stop him but fails. As he approaches the building, Sal passes Tango, who has come there to kill Red.

Sal raids the apartment. After killing three people and finding their stockpile of cash, Sal is shot in the back and killed by a young man who became suspicious when he saw Sal enter the building. Meanwhile, Eddie locates the sex-slave dungeon in the basement. Eddie apprehends one of the men and is confronted by a second. Eddie tells the second man to get down, but the man threatens him. Eddie shoots the man in the chest, and a big fight ensues in which Eddie eventually chokes him with a zip tie. Tango gets his vengeance on Red, but he is mistaken for a gangster and is shot by Rosario. Only after shooting Tango does Rosario realize he has shot another law officer. Rosario, still determined to stop Sal, is forced to continue his search for him. He witnesses the young man who shot Sal running away from the crime scene and is devastated when he finds Sal's body in the drug dealers' apartment.

The closing scene shows Eddie, having found redemption by rescuing the three missing girls.

Cast

- Richard Gere as Officer Edward "Eddie" Dugan, a veteran cop, 7 days from retirement.
- Don Cheadle as Detective Clarence "Tango" Butler, a cop struggling to keep his cover.
- Ethan Hawke as Detective Salvatore "Sal" Procida, a cop desperate to support his large family.
- Wesley Snipes as Casanova "Caz" Phillips, Tango's prison buddy and one of Brooklyn's most infamous drug lords.
- Brían F. O'Byrne as Officer Ronny Rosario
- Jesse Williams as rookie Officer Eddie Quinlan
- Will Patton as Bill Hobarts, the lieutenant watching over Tango's undercover work.
- Lili Taylor as Angela Procida, Sal's wife.
- Shannon Kane as Chantel, a prostitute that Eddie visits regularly.
- Ellen Barkin as Federal Agent Smith
- Michael K. Williams as Red
- Vincent D'Onofrio as Bobby "Carlo" Powers, an informant.
- Tobias Truvillion as Gutta
- Logan Marshall-Green as Melvin Panton, a former Marine.
- Raquel Castro as Katherine

Production

The film was filmed in three boroughs in New York City: Manhattan, Queens, and Brooklyn. In Brooklyn, locations included Brownsville and there, among others, the Van Dyke Houses. In Queens, locations included Rego Park.[2] Michael Martin's script originally took place primarily in the Louis H. Pink Houses in East New York, which were near where the writer and a couple of his friends grew up.[3]

The total budget for the film was in the $17 million range, and many of the actors took large pay cuts to make the movie.[2] The part of Man Man was given to Zaire Paige, a gang member from the neighborhood; three months after filming, he was involved in a murder, for which he was sentenced to 107 years in prison.[4]

Writer

Michael C. Martin, the writer of the screenplay, went to South Shore High School, where a film appreciation course sparked his interest and an ACL injury derailed a possible future basketball career. He went on to study film at Brooklyn College. He originally wrote the *Finest* script for a screenwriter's contest after having been injured in a car accident in 2005. He did not win the contest but his second prize included a subscription to the IFP newsletter. The script also continued to gain attention. Martin found an agent interested in him writing a *New Jack City* sequel, and finally, interested in producing the original script. Martin was paid $200,000 for the script.[2]

In an interview at the time of the movie's release, Martin detailed the development of the film: "Jeanne O'Brien-Ebiri and Mary Viola are responsible for getting this movie made. Jeanne was the first person in the industry to read the script and she was responsible for getting me an agent and the staff job (as a staff writer on the Showtime series *Sleeper Cell*). And once the script was out there, it came across Mary Viola's desk at Thunder Road as a writing sample for *New Jack City 2*. Mary, a native New Yorker, worked like hell to sell it to the head of Thunder Road, Basil Iwanyk. Basil was an executive on *Training Day*, he had a great relationship with Antoine. And once Antoine attached himself to the script ... Richard Gere, Don Cheadle, Wesley Snipes, and Ethan Hawke followed. Within weeks it received a greenlight."

By way of inspirations for the *Finest* script, Martin named three Italian neorealist films – *Nights of Cabiria*, *Umberto D.*, and *The Bicycle Thief* – and two directors, Vittorio De Sica who directed *Umberto* and *Thief* among others, and Jim Jarmusch.

In the interview, Martin identified his South Shore film teacher as Mr. Braun.[3][5]

Release

Brooklyn's Finest premiered at the Sundance Film Festival in January 2009, and was picked up by Senator Distribution with a price "in the low seven figures".[6] Due to some financial distress, Senator Distribution wasn't able to fund its release in 2009.[7] The film was sold again to Overture Films at the Venice Film Festival in September,[7] and was released in North America on March 5, 2010.

Critical reception

The film was met with mixed reviews. It currently holds a 43% approval rating based on 131 reviews collected by Rotten Tomatoes, with an average rating of 5.4/10.[8] The film also received a weighted average score of 43% at Metacritic, based on 33 reviews from mainstream critics.[9]

In his review for the *Chicago Sun-Times*, Roger Ebert gave the film three stars out of four, concluding that "The film has a basic strength in its performances and craft, but falls short of the high mark Fuqua obviously set for himself."[10] Mick LaSalle of the *San Francisco Chronicle* praised the actors for "bringing dimension to these stock characters", but criticized the film for being "a melodrama about three cliches in search of a bloodbath."[11]

A. O. Scott of the *New York Times* also gave the film a mixed review, stating that "the sheer charismatic force of much of the acting keeps you in the movie", but "Mr. Fuqua and Mr. Martin dig themselves into a pulpy predicament, and then find themselves unable to do anything but shoot their way out."[12] The *Los Angeles Times* reviewer commented that "*Brooklyn's Finest* is an old-style potboiler about desperate cops in dire straits that overcooks both its story and its stars."[13]

Box office

In its debut weekend in the United States, *Brooklyn's Finest* opened at #2 behind *Alice in Wonderland* with $13,350,299 in 1,936 theaters, averaging $6,896 per theater.[1][14] As of September 3, 2010, the film has grossed $27,163,593 in the United States theatrically,[1] – a good result for its United States distributor Overture Films which paid less than $3 million to acquire this film's United States rights.[15] The film also grossed $36,027,986 in theaters worldwide,[1] and achieved an eleventh-place on a "Cop – Dirty" genre ranking, 1973 – present.[16]

Home media

Brooklyn's Finest was released on DVD and Blu-ray in July 2010,[17] and topped the United States home video charts for its first week of release ended July 11.[18]

Awards/Nominations

- BET Awards
  - Nominee, Don Cheadle *Best Actor*
- Black Reel Awards
  - Nominee, *Best Picture*
  - Nominee, *Best Ensemble*
  - Nominee, Antoine Fuqua *Best Director*
  - Nominee, Michael C. Martin *Best Screenplay: Original or Adapted*

- Nominee, Don Cheadle *Best Actor*
- Nominee, Wesley Snipes *Best Supporting Actor*

References

[1] "Brooklyn's Finest (2010) – Box Office Mojo" (http://boxofficemojo.com/movies/?id=brooklynsfinest.htm). *Box Office Mojo*. . Retrieved March 8, 2010.

[2] Lee, Trymaine (August 10, 2008). "Brooklyn to Hollywood: That's Some Subway Ride" (http://www.nytimes.com/2008/08/10/movies/10Lee.html?scp=5&sq=Brooklyn's Finest&st=cse). *The New York Times*. . Retrieved February 8, 2010.

[3] "Q&A with *Brooklyn's Fines* screenwriter Michael C. Martin" (http://www.gointothestory.com/2010/03/q-with-brooklyns-finest-screenwriter.html) Interview by Scott Myers, March 5, 2010. Retrieved May 31, 2010.

[4] Elizabeth Dwoskin, Jason Parham (2011-1-26). "Zaire Paige Not Only Played a Movie Killer, He Became One in Real Life" (http://www.villagevoice.com/2011-01-26/news/zaire-paige-brooklyns-finest-actor-killed-ethan-hawke/). Village Voice. . Retrieved 2011-12-20.

[5] Aaron Braun page (http://www.ratemyteachers.com/aaron-braun/789431-t) at *RateMyTeacher.com*. Retrieved May 31, 2010.

[6] Cieply, Michael (January 26, 2009). "Movies Sell Slowly at Sundance" (http://www.nytimes.com/2009/01/26/business/media/26sundance.html?8dpc). *The New York Times*. . Retrieved February 4, 2010.

[7] Swart, Sharon (September 13, 2009). "Fuqua's 'Finest' to Overture" (http://www.variety.com/article/VR1118008535.html). *Variety*. . Retrieved February 4, 2010.

[8] "Brooklyn's Finest Movie Reviews – Rotten Tomatoes" (http://www.rottentomatoes.com/m/brooklyns_finest/). *Rotten Tomatoes*. Flixster. . Retrieved July 11, 2010.

[9] "Brooklyn's Finest reviews at Metacritic.com" (http://www.metacritic.com/film/titles/brooklynsfinest). *Metacritic*. Amazon.com. . Retrieved March 6, 2010.

[10] Roger Ebert (March 3, 2010). "Brooklyn's Finest :: rogerebert.com :: Reviews" (http://rogerebert.suntimes.com/apps/pbcs.dll/article?AID=/20100303/REVIEWS/100309991/1023). *Chicago Sun-Times*. . Retrieved March 5, 2010.

[11] Mick LaSalle (March 4, 2010). "Review: Cliches handcuff 'Brooklyn's Finest'" (http://www.sfgate.com/cgi-bin/article.cgi?f=/c/a/2010/03/04/MV851C9OM1.DTL). *San Francisco Chronicle*. . Retrieved March 5, 2010.

[12] A. O. Scott (March 5, 2010). "Movie Review - Brooklyn's Finest - NYTimes.com" (http://movies.nytimes.com/2010/03/05/movies/05brooklyn.html?ref=movies). *The New York Times*. . Retrieved March 5, 2010.

[13] Betsy Sharkey (March 5, 2010). "Review: 'Brooklyn's Finest' - latimes.com" (http://www.latimes.com/entertainment/news/la-et-brooklyn5-2010mar05,0,2865434.story). *Los Angeles Times*. . Retrieved March 5, 2010.

[14] "Weekend Report: Moviegoers Mad About 'Alice' – Box Office Mojo" (http://boxofficemojo.com/news/?id=2684&p=.htm). *Box Office Mojo*. . Retrieved June 20, 2010.

[15] "Overture Box-Office Profits: $50M-$60M" (http://www.thewrap.com/ind-column/overture-box-office-profits-50-60-million-15072). *TheWrap.com*. . Retrieved June 20, 2010.

[16] "Cop – Dirty Movies at the Box Office" (http://boxofficemojo.com/genres/chart/?id=dirtycop.htm). *Box Office Mojo*. Amazon.com. . Retrieved April 16, 2010.

[17] Kehr, Dave (July 4, 2010). "DVDS; A Lone Figure, Standing Upright Amid the Cyclone" (http://www.nytimes.com/2010/07/04/movies/homevideo/04kehr.html). *The New York Times*: p. 8. . Retrieved July 15, 2010.

[18] Arnold, Thomas K. (July 14, 2010). "'Brooklyn's Finest' dominates video charts" (http://www.hollywoodreporter.com/hr/content_display/news/e3i190b1d465625a16d1178f4cc9a736a83). *The Hollywood Reporter*. . Retrieved July 15, 2010.

External links

- Official website (http://www.brooklynsfinestthemovie.com/)
- *Brooklyn's Finest* (http://www.imdb.com/title/tt1210042/) at the Internet Movie Database
- *Brooklyn's Finest* (http://www.allrovi.com/movies/movie/v449183) at AllRovi
- *Brooklyn's Finest* (http://www.boxofficemojo.com/movies/?id=brooklynsfinest.htm) at Box Office Mojo
- *Brooklyn's Finest* (http://www.metacritic.com/movie/brooklyns-finest) at Metacritic
- *Brooklyn's Finest* (http://www.rottentomatoes.com/m/brooklyns_finest/) at Rotten Tomatoes
- *On Directing (Brooklyn's Finest) with Antoine Fuqua* (http://www.nthword.com/issue6/Interview_Antoine_Fuqua_Directing.php) nthWORD Magazine Interview by Gina Ponce, April 2010

The Double (film)

The Double	
Theatrical release poster	
Directed by	Michael Brandt
Produced by	Ashok Amritraj
Written by	Derek Haas Michael Brandt
Starring	Richard Gere Topher Grace Martin Sheen
Music by	John Debney
Cinematography	Jeffrey L. Kimball
Editing by	Steve Mirkovich
Studio	Hyde Park Entertainment Imagenation Abu Dhabi
Distributed by	Image Entertainment
Release date(s)	October 28, 2011
Running time	98 minutes
Country	United States
Language	English

The Double is a 2011 spy film, starring Richard Gere and Topher Grace, released on October 28, 2011.

Plot

A retired CIA operative is paired with a young FBI agent to unravel the mystery of a senator's murder, with all signs pointing to a Soviet assassin.

Cast

- Richard Gere as Paul Shepherdson
- Topher Grace as Ben Geary
- Martin Sheen as Tom Highland
- Odette Yustman as Joanie Geary
- Stephen Moyer as Brad
- Stana Katic as Amber
- Chris Marquette as Harrison
- Jeffrey Pierce as Agent Pierce
- Tamer Hassan as Boz
- Nicole Forester as Molly

Reception

The film received mostly negative reviews from critics, earning it a 14% on Rotten Tomatoes based on 37 reviews.

References

External links

- *The Double* (http://www.imdb.com/title/tt1646980/) at the Internet Movie Database
- *The Double* (http://www.rottentomatoes.com/m/the_double_2011/) at Rotten Tomatoes

Arbitrage (film)

Arbitrage	
Directed by	Nicholas Jarecki
Produced by	Laura Bickford Kevin Turen Justin Nappi Robert Salerno
Written by	Nicholas Jarecki
Starring	Richard Gere Brit Marling
Music by	Cliff Martinez
Cinematography	Yorick Le Saux
Studio	Green Room Films Treehouse Pictures Artina Films
Country	United States

Arbitrage is an upcoming financial drama film. Filming began in April 2011 in New York City.

Plot

A troubled hedge fund magnate is forced to turn to an unlikely person for help after a crucial mistake involving a sale in his trading empire.

Cast

- Tim Roth as Det. Michael Bryer
- Susan Sarandon as Ellen Miller
- Richard Gere as Robert Miller
- Brit Marling as Brooke Miller
- Monica Raymund as Reina
- Josh Pais as Aimes
- Nate Parker as Jimmy Grant
- Larry Pine as Jeffrey Greenburg

External links

- *Arbitrage (film)* [1] at the Internet Movie Database

References

[1] http://www.imdb.com/title/tt1764183/

Article Sources and Contributors

Richard Gere *Source*: http://en.wikipedia.org/w/index.php?oldid=468508979 *Contributors*: -Midorihana-, -^Glorfindel^-1, 42ndwalrus, Aaron Bowen, AaronY, Aaronp808, Abeg92, Abrech, Addicted, Adnghiem501, Adraeus, Agnosticraccoon, Ahoerstemeier, Ajraddatz, Akamad, Aksi great, Alakazam, Alan smithee, Alansohn, Alexf, AlexiusHoratius, Algabal, Alksub, All Hallow's Wraith, Allstarecho, Altenmann, Ameliorate!, Amitch, Ananaso, Anchoress, And we drown, Andrei G Kustov, Andrewlp1991, Andrewrp, Andycjp, AngelLatinoFL, Angr, AnonEMouse, Antandrus, Appraiser, Aranae, Arashk rp2, Arthur Rubin, Artrush, Asher196, Asience, Astorknlam, Astrosnlc, AuburnPilot, AustralianMelodrama, Avaarga, AzaToth, BCST2001, BD2412, Badgernet, Bagande, BarretB, Barticus88, BassBone, Bcorr, Becksguy, Belovedfreak, Bencey, Bencherlite, Big iron, Bill Bei, Bladestorm, BlastOButter42, BloodDoll, Bobo192, Bond007rh, Bookgrrl, Boothy443, BorgQueen, Bossk-Office, Bovineboy2008, Bradv, Brandon, Brian Brockmeyer, BrokenSegue, BuckwikiPDa535, CWii, Cablekids2010, CambridgeBayWeather, Can't sleep, clown will eat me, CapitalR, Capolinho, Catapult, Catsue, Cfailde, Cgingold, Ch'rihaan, Chasingsol, Chicheley, Chocolateboy, Christopher Parham, CioDu, Cla68, Closedmouth, Clpo13, Cobalty, Cometstyles, Comicist, Commander Keane, CommonsDelinker, Connormah, Cortonin, CovenantD, Crotchety Old Man, Ctbolt, Ctrl-Alt-Dimension, Cupivistine Noscere?, D6, DNewhall, Dane3, Daniel J. Leivick, Danielfolsom, Daren1132, DarkFalls, Darthmix, Darthveda, Darwinek, Daverodgers, Davewild, DavidOaks, Davidkuffer, Dawnseeker2000, Ddlfan, Debresser, Deflective, Delpino, Demonburrito, Demong, DeppFan03, DerHexer, Diannaa, Discospinster, Dismas, Divinstephen1, Django94, Djbj16, Djedwardsmith, Dobtoronto, DonalisaMcnichols, DowneyOcean, Downtown dan seattle, Dr. Blofeld, DuaneThomas, Duckie7, Dureo, Dycedarg, Dysepsion, Earl CG, Ecollins, Electron9, Elendil's Heir, ElinorD, Ellbeecee, Encyclopediaman1, Enpitsu, EntChickie, Erck, Espoo, Esurnir, Eug.galeotti, Evil Monkey, FCYTravis, FJPB, FNMF, Fallout boy, Farside6, Ferrie, Fifty pence, FisherQueen, FlyingPenguins, Flyingidiot, Fodient, Frecklefoot, Frigginawesomeimontv, Funnyfarmofdoom, Fwend, Gaius Cornelius, Garion96, Generalpoteito, George415, Gfoley4, GhostFace1234, GiantSnowman, Gogo Dodo, GoldCoaster, Good Olfactory, Gothmog.es, GraemeL, Grafen, Gran2, Grayfox1988, Greg Pandatshang, Ground, Gsarwa, Guat6, GusF, Gwernol, Gwguffey, Hariharan91, Heimstern, Helplessstar88207, Helpsome, Hemanshu, Herostratus, HexaChord, Hmwith, Hornplease, Hottentot, Hégésippe Cormier, Ian Pitchford, Ianboggs, Ibeowulf, IceCreamAntisocial, Ike-bana, Invertzoo, Irishguy, IronGargoyle, Ixfd64, J.J. Dilbert, J.delanoy, JFlin5, JGKlein, JJstroker, JRSP, JaGa, Jack Bhan, Jack O'Lantern, JackO'Lantern, JackofOz, Jagarin, JakeVortex, Jauhienij, Java7837, Javert, Jayjg, Jdavidb, Jeandré du Toit, Jedoand5, Jeff3000, Jeffrey O. Gustafson, Jeschutte, Jfitts, Jim Michael, Jim16, Jmh123, Jmlk17, John, Jojhutton, Jopgaard, Josiah Rowe, Jpers36, Jrdioko, Jredmond, Jtarr, Julia W, Jusjih, Justme89, Jwsleasman, Jzummak, KC0ZHQ, Kaiba, Kalmia, Kanonkas, Katalaveno, Kbdank71, Kbrest, Keilana, Kelly, Kevin, KevinTR, Kinu, Ko ko kovach, Koavf, Kralahome, Kurt Shaped Box, Kuru, Kwamikagami, LOL, LaBohemienne, Lamrock, Layla12275, Legalbeaver, Leifern, Levineps, Liamdaly620, Lilyha, LittleDan, Littleendian, Lixy, Llamabr, Lode Runner, Lol0075, Lord Cornwallis, Loren.wilton, Lovely Chris, LtMuldoon, Lugnuts, Lulugo, Luna Santin, Luv Dors, MJSS, MPerel, MZMcBride, Ma3nocum, Madchester, Madman Marz, Magnet For Knowledge, Mandarax, Mannafredo, MantaRay, Manticore126, Manway, MarcK, MarkSutton, Markcookney, Martarius, MastCell, Master Deusoma, MathewBrooks, MattLee90, Mawkish1983, Mayumashu, Maziotis, Mbc362, Mdob, Mephistophelian, Michael614, Mike 7, Mike Spiker, Mild Bill Hiccup, MithrandirAgain, Mm44, Modster, Momo san, Moncrief, MonoAV, MovieMadness, Mr oompapa on mars!, Mr oompapa on the edge of the Adromeda galaxy, Mrbluesky, Muntuwandi, Murph24, Musicpvm, Mwalimu59, NSH001, Nancy, Nano Dan, NeelAbodh, NeoChaosX, NiamhColl, Nibuod, Nichalp, Nick tempsperdu, Nishidani, NithinBekal, Nivix, Njchurchill, Noclador, Noodlez311, Noroton, Novalis, Nromo22, Nunh-huh, Oda Mari, Oden, OliverTwisted, Olivier, Ondenc, Onorem, Oommpapa, Opelio, Openmy, OwenX, Oxymoron83, PDH, Pacian, Paradiso, Paul A, Paul August, Paultantk, Pax:Vobiscum, Pearle, Pegship, PepperEarth, PhGustaf, Pharaoh of the Wizards, Philip Trueman, Philipculp, Phobetor, Phrankle, Pilif12p, Piperdown, Pitchka, Polutlas, Ponyo, Postcard Cathy, Ppareit, Ppt1973, Prodego, Pu mbit, Quentin X, RG2, RMHED, Ralphael, RattleandHum, Rawling, Realm of Shadows, Redzone175, Reedy, Regibox, Restecp, Rich Farmbrough, Risker, Rito Revolto, Rjasper499, Rjwilmsi, Rnb, RobertG, Roberta F., Rodhullandemu, Ronhjones, Roscoegino, Rossrs, Rulernumba1, Rustoleum2k, Ryeinn, Rédacteur Tibet, SCEhardt, SalilSBudhe, Sam, Sanchom, Scimitar, Scooteristi, Scott MacDonald, Scream clarity, SeanO, Seewolf, Sfan00 IMG, Sfmammamia, Shalom Yechiel, ShelfSkewed, Sholom, Shrigley, Silence, Sjc07, Skysmith, SlimVirgin, Slovenia10, Snow Goblin, Sophie albinson, Spamajama, Sparkzilla, SpuriousQ, Sry85, Steel, Stephenb, Steven Zhang, Stevenmitchell, Stwalkerster, Sunray, Sunseed, Sywsyw, T-borg, TEHodson, Tanglewood4, Tangurena, Tapir2001, Tbhotch, Tdmg, Tdxiang, Tejas81, Teleomatic, Tergum violinae, Tevus, Texasshiva, The Red Mask, The invisible force of darkness, The undertow, The wub, Theda, Thefourdotelipsis, Thehelpfulone, Thincat, Thiseye, Tide rolls, TigerShark, Tinton5, Tkondaks, Toddst1, Tomenes, Tommy2010, Tony1, Tonytam, Tool2Die4, Tregoweth, Trew231, Treybien, Turzh, Twir, Udzu, Ugur Basak, Ukexpat, Ulric1313, Universal Hero, Username7888, Utcursch, Varlaam, Vary, Vbdrummer0, Veinor, VeryVerily, Videmus Omnia, Violetriga, Voyagerfan5761, Vranak, Vulturell, WacoJacko, Wakuran, Warreed, Wasted Time R, WatchingYouLikeAHawk, Wdrev, WebHamster, West2East, Widmerpool, Wiki alf, Wildhartlivie, WilyD, Winhunter, Wiooiw, Wknight94, Wmahan, Wnick99, Wolverineblue, Woohookitty, Xenophrenic, Xiaoyu of Yuxi, Ymmv99, Yoko santoso, Z3u2, Zackg323, Zippoist, Zutopiaa, 777 anonymous edits

Report to the Commissioner *Source*: http://en.wikipedia.org/w/index.php?oldid=422873342 *Contributors*: Blair1000, JamesBWatson, Neutrality, Paisiello2, Teófilo Moraes Guimarães, WOSlinker, 4 anonymous edits

Baby Blue Marine *Source*: http://en.wikipedia.org/w/index.php?oldid=451846677 *Contributors*: Clarityfiend, Foofbun, NostalgiaBuff97501, Philipculp, Polisher of Cobwebs, TheMovieBuff, 1 anonymous edits

Looking for Mr. Goodbar (film) *Source*: http://en.wikipedia.org/w/index.php?oldid=462630779 *Contributors*: Arrowlikemouth, Bisbis, Bobak, Bovineboy2008, Donfbreed, Easchiff, Filmfluff, Heironymous Rowe, JerryFriedman, John, Kbdank71, LtMuldoon, Mathmo, Muzilon, Nbarth, R'n'B, Roxanne Smith, Sean D Martin, Sfan00 IMG, Tassedethe, Think outside the box, Treybien, TubularWorld, UnitedStatesian, Whoville, 34 anonymous edits

Bloodbrothers (1978 film) *Source*: http://en.wikipedia.org/w/index.php?oldid=470626430 *Contributors*: A. Carty, Bovineboy2008, ShelfSkewed, Tassedethe, TheMovieBuff, Treybien, 7 anonymous edits

Days of Heaven *Source*: http://en.wikipedia.org/w/index.php?oldid=471632192 *Contributors*: Abidjan227, Alcmaeonid, Ale And Quail, Andrzejbanas, Aquillion, Arkind, Artoasis, Atamata, Aurelien3381, Brasqueychutter, Ceoil, Chick Bowen, Cocopie, Colonies Chris, Contributor777, Cop 663, Count Ringworm, Croftscv, D6, Darrenhusted, Dbenbenn, Digitalme, Doctor Sunshine, Dominus, EFieg, Easchiff, Ef200, Ellsworth, Farsidehobbes, Harac, Hektor, Henchren, Hmains, Idaltu, Irishguy, J 1982, J.D., Jalepino Donkey-Boy, Jaydec, Jonathan F, Jordancelticsfan, Kernitou, Kinkyturnip, Kollision, Lugnuts, Malickfan86, McMuff, Noirish, Nv8200p, Oneiros, Otterfan, Parkwells, Paul Barlow, Phbasketball6, Polisher of Cobwebs, Promking, R'n'B, Richiekim, Rjwilmsi, Sevenarts, Shining.Star, Slowbeard, Snickers01, Supernumerary, TRBP, TallulahBelle, Template namespace initialisation script, TheLeopard, Tkreuz, Treybien, Ukas, Usernodunno, Wasted Sapience, Winkyburger, Yohowithrum, Zoicon5, 71 anonymous edits

Yanks *Source*: http://en.wikipedia.org/w/index.php?oldid=470344388 *Contributors*: 16@r, A. Carty, AN(Ger), After Midnight, Albireo223, Ball luss, Billy Hathorn, Binary TSO, Bob Castle, Bovineboy2008, Brian Crawford, Carl Logan, Carlossuarez46, Crzrussian, Cuchullain, DShamen, Davecrosby uk, Easchiff, EnBob08, FMAFan1990, Finavon, Hmains, Jay-W, Jhamez84, Jza84, King konger, MRSC, Mabzilla, Magioladitis, Mallanox, Markagoulden, Memberonetoone, MinghamSmith, Moh.trance, Mr Stephen, Orbicle, Oscarthecat, Ospalh, Pegship, Pollinosisss, THEN WHO WAS PHONE?, The Thing That Should Not Be, Thefourdotelipsis, Tony Sidaway, Txomin, Ume, Varlaam, WOSlinker, Wildroot, YUL89YYZ, Yamamoto Ichiro, 40 anonymous edits

American Gigolo *Source*: http://en.wikipedia.org/w/index.php?oldid=469588624 *Contributors*: AN(Ger), Amorfati00, Andrew69., Andromeda, Andrzejbanas, Betty Logan, Big Bird, BrotherFlounder, CaptainAmerica, Carax, Catamorphism, Catgut, Ccacsmss, D6, Dale Arnett, Djln, Docu, Dolphonia, Donmike10, Donreed, Donteatyellowsnow, Dreamer.se, DuaneThomas, Dutzi, Ezzex, Fizzerbear, Fuzheado, Gcstackmoney, Ghosts&empties, GoldCoaster, Grandpafootsoldier, Harley Hudson, Hektor, Hraefen, Hullaballoo Wolfowitz, Irishguy, JasonAQuest, Jedgeco, Kangaruu, KimChee, Kittybrewster, Kubigula, Lg16spears, M baptiste, Maciste, MartinVillafuerte85, Melaen, MichaelAWilson, Misza13, Myscrnnm, NYArtsnWords, Nightscream, Not a dog, Paul J, Pedro Cunha, PhilipC, Picapica, Polisher of Cobwebs, Prayerfortheworld, Radon210, Reedy, Rjwilmsi, Roaring Siren, Rodrigogomespaixao, Ron whisky, Scaranol, Shining.Star, SidP, SilkTork, Sky Captain, Stubblyhead, The JPS, The sock that should not be, TheCustomOfLife, TheMovieBuff, Thingg, Tieftaucher07, TonyTheTiger, Treknorth, Valenciano, Walloon, Wasted Sapience, Wmk0, YUL89YYZ, Yoursvivek, 96 anonymous edits

An Officer and a Gentleman *Source*: http://en.wikipedia.org/w/index.php?oldid=471857413 *Contributors*: Adambomb1701, Amylovesian99, Andromeda, Angr, Ataruzzolo, Bahamut0013, Before My Ken, Ben-Bopper, Bigchinalism, Biocyte, Birdmantd, Bobet, Bootkinero, Bovineboy2008, Brad, Btyner, Butchw1971, Cameronandre, Captain Kirk, Cburnett, Chemguy2, Clarityfiend, CobraWiki, ContiAWB, DJ Clayworth, Darkness2005, Deathphoenix, Dennette, Dickclarkfan1, DimitriL, Dismas, Donmike10, Dowew, Download, Downtown dan seattle, DuaneThomas, Eaglestorm, EamonnPKeane, Edlitz36, Edward, Ehayes, Eric444, Erik, Fgf2007, Fredrick day, FreewayDan, Freshh, Gamaliel, Glacier109, GoodDay, GusF, Hansh, Hiphats, Hongooi, Husnock, Imladros, IndulgentReader, Irishguy, ItsBatman, J.delanoy, JaGa, Jackfork, Jbl1975, Jblcn1042, Jeff Muscato, Jeffman52001, Jeffq, Jeffsmo, John of Reading, Jtpaladin, Judgesurreal777, Juliosham, Karaoke Prince, Karlchwe, Kbdank71, Kckoch, Kcwbar, Keeves, Keno, Khaosjr, KnightRider, Koman99, Kransky, Kumioko, Kusma, LGagnon, LegalEagleUSA, LorenzoB, Lots42, Lvr, Mallanox, MarnetteD, Mike hayes, MikeJ9919, Milepost53, Mynameisphil, Myscrnnm, NWill, Neutrality, NewWalmartLogoFanatic, Nikkimaria, Nutshack1, Platypus222, Plutonium27, RHodnett, Radosław10, Reservoirhill, Resqspc, Ricky81682, Ron whisky, Rossflock, SQL, Savolya, Sayerslle, Scorch.Dylan, ScottyBoy900Q, Sean0254, ShelfSkewed, Smetanahue, Smooth Nick, Somedaypilot, Sonlui, TV4Fun, Target for Today, Thrashmeister, Treybien, Uucp, Warreed, Wasted Sapience, Wikid77, WillC, Woohookitty, WurmWoode, Xnatedawgx, YUL89YYZ, Zoe, Zyrix, 215 anonymous edits

The Honorary Consul (film) *Source*: http://en.wikipedia.org/w/index.php?oldid=469652791 *Contributors*: ADwarf, Alexey2244, Andrzejbanas, B3t, Cybercobra, DagosNavy, JuliaVictoria, Lord Cornwallis, Lugnuts, Miguelemejia, PhilipC, Studerby, TheMovieBuff, 2 anonymous edits

Breathless (1983 film) *Source*: http://en.wikipedia.org/w/index.php?oldid=456344450 *Contributors*: Adam Berlin, AdamDeanHall, Andrei G Kustov, Andrzejbanas, Ask123, BullRangifer, Bvarady, Colonies Chris, Cop 663, David Gerard, Dnuniez, Echuck215, Erik9, FMAFan1990, Freshacconci, Gonioul, Hagerman, Hektor, ItsTheClimb17, J.D., Jeffman52001, Lacrymocéphale, Lugnuts, Marktreut, Olivier, Orbicle, PEJL, Plasticspork, Rlendog, Shining.Star, Sugar Bear, TheMovieBuff, Wikery, Wikid77, Шизомби, 33 anonymous edits

The Cotton Club (film) *Source*: http://en.wikipedia.org/w/index.php?oldid=469268141 *Contributors*: Adamreid86, Ahoerstemeier, Alan16, AndrewHowse, Aradek, Arcadian, Auntof6, BD2412, BGC, Brianyoumans, Captain Crawdad, ChristinaDunigan, Cliff1911, Comet Tuttle, Count Ringworm, Darwinek, David Rush, DeeP., Elipongo, Emperor, FMAFan1990, Fakechampion, Ffirehorse, FollowGuard, Freshh, Frut, Garion96, GregorB, Hedyfrancis, Inoculatedcities, J.D., Jeph paul, John K, John Prattley, Kuzosake, Laurinavicius, Lugnuts, MachoCarioca, Mahatma Randy, MarnetteD, Mrblondnyc, Pejorative.majeure, Philip Cross, Polisher of Cobwebs, Postcard Cathy, Radon210, RedWolf, RepublicanJacobite, Ronhjones, SFTVLGUY2, Schmiteye, Shir-El too, Shoessss, Silly Dan, Stefanomione, Swimdb, Tapir2001, Tassedethe, TenPoundHammer, The wub, Thefourdotelipsis, Thegerm, Theseniorеditor, Tim!, Tjmayerinsf, Tm3108, TracyLinkEdnaVelmaPenny, Treybien, Ulric1313, Vegaswikian, Veritasmaximal, WallyCuddeford, Ward3001, Wasted Sapience, Woohookitty, Wool Mintons, Yashveer r, Zoicon5, ²¹², 66 anonymous edits

King David (film) *Source*: http://en.wikipedia.org/w/index.php?oldid=470158066 *Contributors*: Adam Bishop, Ajshm, Andycjp, Bovineboy2008, Centrx, Cooksey, D6, Das Baz, Draikens, Easchiff, Eliyak, Fayenatic london, FollowGuard, Gdmercury, Good Olfactory, Iantresman, Jimmyzimms, Laurenticwave, Longhair, MarcK, Markoff Chaney, Matthew Dillenburg, Necrothesp, Nikkimaria, Orbicle, Paradiso, PigFlu Oink, Portillo, Robertjm, TheLastAmigo, TheMovieBuff, Tonyrex, Varlaam, Wilburanded, Yworo, 26 anonymous edits

No Mercy (film) *Source*: http://en.wikipedia.org/w/index.php?oldid=444750793 *Contributors*: After Midnight, Cliff1911, D.c.camero, FilmFemme, Grandpafootsoldier, IronGargoyle, Lugnuts, Martarius, Pegship, SGCommand, Schmiteye, Skb8721, The JPS, TheMovieBuff, Wnick99, 19 anonymous edits

Power (1986 film) *Source*: http://en.wikipedia.org/w/index.php?oldid=466476783 *Contributors*: ABCxyz, Bovineboy2008, Cliff1911, Easchiff, Erik9, FlagrantUsername, FollowGuard, HarringtonSmith, MovieMadness, Murph24, Nicholas0, Quentin X, Radosław10, Uhai, UnneededAplomb, 11 anonymous edits

Miles from Home *Source*: http://en.wikipedia.org/w/index.php?oldid=434475345 *Contributors*: AN(Ger), Andrzejbanas, Bockelj, BrainyIowan, Charles Matthews, Dr. Blofeld, Erik9, Grandpafootsoldier, JamesBurns, Lugnuts, Pixelface, QuasyBoy, Robofish, 11 anonymous edits

Internal Affairs (film) *Source*: http://en.wikipedia.org/w/index.php?oldid=470117249 *Contributors*: AN(Ger), AdamSmithee, Andrzejbanas, AngelLatinoFL, Arapaima, BRUTE, Belovedfreak, Beyond My Ken, Colin473, Dantesque1, David Gerard, Davidbspalding, DeWaine, Djln, Djrobgordon, Donmike10, DrFrench, Father Goose, FrankRizzo2006, Grey Shadow, Hamletarman2, IllaZilla, Kondziu15, Ladybirdintheuk, Larryblau, Madman Marz, Magnet For Knowledge, Marcus Brute, Martarius, Moffattsamantha, Mr Fist, Mr. Lefty, Mrschimpf, Murgh, Nehrams2020, Pagrashtak, Pearle, Piperdown, Pjoef, Poco a poco, Quentin X, Rito Revolto, Rjwilmsi, SidP, Sngnisfuk, Somerwind, Sophus Bie, TakuyaMurata, Treybien, Wasted Sapience, Woohookitty, Yashveer r, 58 anonymous edits

Pretty Woman *Source*: http://en.wikipedia.org/w/index.php?oldid=471638559 *Contributors*: 97198, AbsoluteGleek92, Academic Challenger, Access Denied, Adiagr, Aharmon1973, AlexWaelde, Alfie66, Alfio, Analoguedragon, Andreas Kaganov, Andromeda, Andycjp, Angel caboodle, Angel2001, Appraiser, Ar tamm, Archanamiya, Archola, Argonith, Arnon Chaffin, Art LaPella, Ashton 29, Aspects, Astorknlam, Auzzz24, Banej, Baroing, Belovedfreak, Bender235, Bensin, BigBin, BigBrightStars, BigT2006, Bloodlikefire, BlueAzure, Bob98133, Bobo192, Bonalaw, Bonehed, Bovineboy2008, Brown Shoes22, Callidior, Can't sleep, clown will eat me, Cburnett, Ccacsmss, CherryFlavoredAntacid, Chinthejackrabbit, Chris the speller, ChrisCork, Ckatz, Classicrockfan42, Cleduc, CloudSurfer, Coder Dan, Colfer2, Colonies Chris, Companionship, ContiAWB, Coopdawg0919, Cr8tiv, Cresix, Crywalt, DANE YOUSSEF, DONUTMONSTER, Darkness2005, Darwin16, David Gerard, David from Downunder, Deor, Derbent 5000, Dgmoran, Dick Shane, Discospinster, Donreed, Dr. Blofeld, Dramakid5485, Drpryr, Dycedarg, Eaglesk, EdRicardo, Edcolins, ElrRigby, EoGuy, Epbr123, Erik, Erik9, Esteffect, FMAFan1990, Faradayplank, FashVic, Fdewaele, Filpaul, Flamma, Fluffernutter, Fluffybun, FrankRizzo2006, Fredrick day, Freikorp, Frem3831, Freshh, Fwend, Fæ, Gaius Cornelius, Garywgoldstein, Geniac, GhostFace1234, Gogo Dodo, GoingBatty, GoldDragon, Grafen, Graham87, Gridge, Gringotsgoblin, GusF, Harley Hudson, Harsimrankaur, Herunar, Hessamnia, Hohockjim, Horkana, Humbert von Gikkingen, Ianbong, Icantbeliveijoindwiki, IllaZilla, Irishguy, JForget, JP Godfrey, Jaardon, Jaknouse, James Morton (User), JamesAM, Jbruin152, Jezhotwells, Jienum, JillandJack, Jimarey, Jimmy Bing, Joelehane, John Anderson, John Jacob Wilson Alueminous, John K, Joho777, JonMoore, Jonathan.s.kt, Jusdafax, Justme89, Jwy, Kakofonous, Karaoke Prince, Katetallyho, Kbdank71, Keeper76, Keith D, Khan3817, Khatru2, Koavf, Kongr43gpen, Krawunsel, Kusma, Kwamikagami, L'Aquatique, Lafuzion, Lemon-s, Lethe, Levineps, Lixxylu, Magioladitis, Malber, Mamawrites, Manway, MartinVillafuerte85, Massimo Macconi, Mattg82, McTools, MegX, Melaen, MikeyChalupa, Mlaffs, Mofs, NawlinWiki, Neilymon, Ner102, Nil Einne, Nino.shoshia, Niteowlneils, Nmadera, Noclevername, Noirish, Nono64, Northfox, Nsaa, Otto4711, Ozzieboy, Pacian, Pacomartin, Paige Barbeau, Panagea, Parsecboy, Patyo1994, Paul Barlow, Peanut4, Pere Serafi, Pnkrockr, Polarbear97, Polyhymnia, Power level (Dragon Ball), PrinceMyshkin, Psy guy, Quentin X, Quuxplusone, R Lowry, Radiohawk, Rakaha, RattyPussFACE, Rawling, Reginmund, RepublicanJacobite, RicJac, Rick7425, Rjanag, Rodrigogomespaixao, Ronz, Rudi argento, Runnermonkey, RuudZw, Rvn1966, Ryantb93, SJP, Saigalonly, Salathi, Salliesatt, SaltyBoatr, Sasquatch, Scientizzle, Sepguilherme, Serpent's Choice, Shakesphere17, Shannernanner, Shshshsh, SidP, Sjc07, Sje549977, Skarebo, Smalljim, SmartGuy, Smurdah, Soojmagooj, Sottolacqua, Speedoflight, Starionwolf, Stefanomione, Strongsauce, Suto, Sypherin, TAnthony, TMC1982, TPIRFanSteve, Taejo, Taochen, Ted Wilkes, The Giant Puffin, The Singing Badger, The Wild West guy, TheMadBaron, Thebluetowel, Themepark, Tigerghost, Timeineurope, Tokek, TracyLinkEdnaVelmaPenny, Trident13, Trusilver, Uruguayeze, Valgerdur, Vega84, Vonlyman, Wafulz, Wars, Wasted Sapience, Wasted Time R, Wildhartlivie, Willirennen, Winterheart, Wizardman, Woohookitty, Wsiegmund, Wxlfsr, Xiahou, Y2J 2212, Yamla, Yashveer r, Zeromaru, Zoltarpanaflex, Zotdragon, 580 anonymous edits

Rhapsody in August *Source*: http://en.wikipedia.org/w/index.php?oldid=468895014 *Contributors*: AGGoH, Andrei G Kustov, Ary29, Azucar, Bobet, Bobo12345, Cbrown1023, Cherryblossom1982, Chris the speller, David Gerard, Dekkappai, Doctor Sunshine, Drunken Pirate, Everyguy, Feitclub, Ffbear, Hmains, Jithin.jerald, Kihachi, Kummi, Levent, Lugnuts, MarnetteD, Marty Rockatansky, Morio, Mrblondnyc, Nehrams2020, Open2universe, Palm dogg, Paris By Night, Redfruits, Rockermatc, Sailor Titan, Seann, Staecker, 21 anonymous edits

Final Analysis *Source*: http://en.wikipedia.org/w/index.php?oldid=471824036 *Contributors*: AN(Ger), Andrzejbanas, Can't sleep, clown will eat me, Cliff1911, David Gerard, DepressedPer, Erik9, Feydey, FollowGuard, Haasofpain, Ifny, Intgr, JackofOz, Jwy, Ketiltrout, Lambiam, Lamro, Luigibob, Lunch, Mallanox, Merqurial, Okki, Peter.shaman, Polisher of Cobwebs, RepublicanJacobite, RoadTrain, Scanlan, Schwenkstar, Signalhead, Sonett72, Spike Wilbury, Tassedethe, The wub, TheMovieBuff, Treybien, Wnyxmcneal, 20 anonymous edits

Mr. Jones (film) *Source*: http://en.wikipedia.org/w/index.php?oldid=462150698 *Contributors*: Caponer, Closedmouth, DeWaine, DuckyBaby2, EnBob08, FollowGuard, FrankRizzo2006, Heffalump1974, Hermes the Merchant, IW.HG, JimVC3, Khaosjr, Mkill, Mr Fist, Paradoxsociety, Pegship, Prayudhi, RattleandHum, Responsible?, Rickyharder, Sreejithk2000, Static Universe, Steam5, Tassedethe, Treybien, Uucp, Xme, 21 anonymous edits

Sommersby *Source*: http://en.wikipedia.org/w/index.php?oldid=469014166 *Contributors*: 99shakes, AN(Ger), BD2412, Cabiria, Caiaffa, D6, Danleary25, Darrenhusted, Davecampbell, Dcfleck, Deadlock, Donmike10, DoubleCross, Dpv, Dwanyewest, ESkog, Escampadour, Evans1982, Everyking, FollowGuard, FrankRizzo2006, Freshh, GenderLine, Gongshow, Gonioul, Hajor, Hippo43, Jeandré du Toit, John of Reading, Johnakabean, Jordancelticsfan, Kerowyn, Kingstowngalway, Kuralyov, Kusma, Kyriosity, Llywrch, Lugnuts, Magnius, MarnetteD, MaxSem, Nietzsche 2, PC78, Quentin X, Rjwilmsi, Robertvan1, SKC, Skopelos-slim, Slark, Sreejithk2000, SteinbDJ, Tavilis, Tesi1700, TheMovieBuff, Thomasbp30, Tina85, Twas Now, Wasted Sapience, Yworo, Саша Стефановић, 61 anonymous edits

And the Band Played On (film) *Source*: http://en.wikipedia.org/w/index.php?oldid=465586833 *Contributors*: ABVR, Arrangement Guy, Bearcat, Belovedfreak, Bovineboy2008, Bristle-krs, Chinstrap1, Ckatz, DePiep, Donfbreed, Dreiss2, Eatcacti, Edonald, Emerson7, Goustien, Grandpafootsoldier, Guy M, Hedmark, Idinic, LOL, Loquax1975, MKSB, MovieMadness, Optigan13, RepublicanJacobite, SaRa, Sfan00 IMG, SilkTork, Softlavender, Somercet, Sottolacqua, TAnthony, TEHodson, Thefourdotelipsis, Tim!, TonyTheTiger, Treybien, UDScott, Werldwayd, William Allen Simpson, 26 anonymous edits

Intersection (film) *Source*: http://en.wikipedia.org/w/index.php?oldid=461810268 *Contributors*: AN(Ger), B3t, Cooksey, EnBob08, Everyking, FollowGuard, Gonioul, K1Bond007, Kingturtle, MarcK, Marcfl, McTools, NWill, OlEnglish, Oytun 73, Phil Boswell, Prayudhi, Pubdog, SISLEY, Sreejithk2000, Tassedethe, TheMovieBuff, Witchkraut, Xezbeth, Yunusware, 8 anonymous edits

First Knight *Source*: http://en.wikipedia.org/w/index.php?oldid=471213163 *Contributors*: 21stCenturyGreenstuff, A.T. Horsfield, ACKarzun, AN(Ger), ARUNKUMAR P.R, AbsoluteGleek92, Acjelen, Andrzejbanas, Angus Wright, Antaeus Feldspar, Areaseven, Attilios, Betacommand, Bluemoose, Bonehed, BoosterBronze, Bormoglot, Bovineboy2008, BrownHairedGirl, C mon, CWii, Cikmin, Contributor777, Cooksey, Cromwellt, Cst17, Cubs197, Cuchullain, Davesawyer, David Edgar, David Gerard, Doctorfluffy, Dolovis, Dupz, DutchDevil, Easchiff, Erik, FlamingSilmaril, Foofbun, Frecklefoot, FromtheWordsofBR, General Epitaph, GeoWPC, Gonnym, Hapleworth, Hoary, Hogyn Lleol, Iantresman, Icseaturtles, Irishguy, JCCamp, JamieJones, Jay-W, Jg2904, Juliancolton, Kartano, Katharineamy, Kghusker, Klapi, Knowledgeum, Krazykoolkat, Kuralyov, Limabeans, Marco Thomas, Marshall, Materialscientist, Moscow1971, Mysdaao, Pictureuploader, Polylerus, Puffin, Rmp1978, Rtkat3, Ryryrules100, SoSaysChappy, Solitude, Supernumerary, Tanner65, Tassedethe, Tim!, Triage, Typhin, Týr, Ultraexactzz, Uthanc, Voceditenore, Vranak, Wasted Sapience, Yashmanthegreat, 111 anonymous edits

Primal Fear (film) *Source*: http://en.wikipedia.org/w/index.php?oldid=471291348 *Contributors*: *drew, ADNghiem501, AP Shinobi, Afa86, Alansohn, Alpha Quadrant, Andrzejbanas, Angel caboodle, Ary29, Awaterl, BD2412, Beefcake32, Benzh, Bluerules, Bovineboy2008, CBM, Cburnett, Cliff1911, D0wN b0i, DJBullfish, DRosenbach, David Gerard, Davidsietsma, Deavenger, DepressedPer, Domingo Portales, Donmike10, DoubleCross, Dr. Blofeld, Edward321, Erik, FMAFan1990, Gaius Cornelius, Gmosaki, GregorB, HelloAnnyong, HitroMilanese, Inderonline1988, InfamousPrince, Jahangir23, Jaxl, Joelmills, Joseph A. Spadaro, Kbdank71, Kevinalewis, Kirbyrocks, Knoche, La Pianista, Latics, Lynch1000s, Lynch8000s, Marktreut, Master shepherd, MattyLite, Maxim, Mrwojo, NellieBly, Ondenc, Ostinato, P0p0, Pcap, Pegship, Phaldo, Pinethicket, QuasyBoy, Quentin X, Quixoto, RJaguar3, Radosław10, Ratchetcomand, RattleandHum, Rnb, Room429, Rossrs, Santryl, Schwenkstar, Shshshsh, Singingdaisies, SluggoOne, Sturmfuhrer, TakuyaMurata, Theprowier, Tony Sidaway, TracyLinkEdnaVelmaPenny, Treybien, Ultimahero, Uucp, Venicemenace, VirtualSteve, Ward3001, WatchAndObserve, Writesiriusly, Y2J 2212, Yankees10, Zerosis, أحمد.غامدي.24, 131 anonymous edits

The Jackal (1997 film) *Source*: http://en.wikipedia.org/w/index.php?oldid=471458104 *Contributors*: A Toyota's A Toyota, AdamSmithee, Andrzejbanas, AnmaFinotera, Azucar, Bearcat, Beck162, Beetstra, Bender235, Bluerules, Bovineboy2008, BrainyBroad, Brewcrewer, Bwiki, CheshireKatz, Commander Keane, Crotchety Old Man, Cubs Fan, Cyberpower678, DagosNavy,

Darkness2005, David Gerard, DeWaine, DennisA, Dep. Garcia, Descendall, Dismas, Djolds1, Doctor Sunshine, Donmike10, DoubleCross, Dtcdthingy, Dudesleeper, Easchiff, Egon Eagle, Elp gr, Epbr123, FergusM1970, FollowGuard, Foot Dragoon, GeorgeC, Gonzalo Diethelm, Gothicfilm, HighKing, Humus sapiens, Iantresman, Imacphee, Imladros, Jeff Muscato, Jfdwolff, Jibbideejibbish, Jonashart, JukoFF, Kafziel, Laketahoeblue, Lowellian, Mannerheim, Markshel, Martarius, Marychan41, Max rspct, Mike R, Millahnna, Misterkillboy, Moisanite, Morana, Mormegil, Morpose, Mr pand, Nicknackrussian, Nihil novi, Normalityrelief, Ntsimp, Number87, Physicistjedi, Pp0912, Premkudva, Quebec99, Quentin X, Radosław10, Rafaelrosa, RattleandHum, Remyvhw, RenniePet, Rich Farmbrough, Roaring Siren, Robertvan1, Robinson weijman, RutgerH, Saebhiar, Seidenstud, Sesshomaru, Shawn in Montreal, Sjyglm, SmartGuy, Smurfy, Space Mountain Mike, Sreejithk2000, Stefanomione, Sturmwehr, Swfong, Szumyk, Tantalizing Posey, Tassedethe, The Giant Puffin, TheMovieBuff, Thomas Blomberg, Thomasionus, Tills, Tomgibbons, Trans4mers, Treybien, TriiipleThreat, Tyræs, Ukexpat, Upsmiler, Vinnivince, Wasted Sapience, Waters13, Woohookitty, Woowah, Wyss, Xezbeth, Yvh11a, Zombie433, A. Погодин, 154 anonymous edits

Red Corner *Source*: http://en.wikipedia.org/w/index.php?oldid=469968183 *Contributors*: AN(Ger), AlexJW, Allan palmos, AmericanGringo, Andrzejbanas, Andrés D., ArcWriter, Commander Shepard, D6, Daniel J. Leivick, DeWaine, Donmike10, FCYTravis, Furrykef, GoonerDP, Itsmejudith, Ixfd64, Jusjih, Litalex, Lummie, MadDreamChant, Philip Cross, Prayudhi, Producercunningham, Qqr, Radosław10, RossF18, Shattered Gnome, Sinfanti, Sk5893, Sreejithk2000, Tapir2001, The wub, TheMovieBuff, ThylekShran, Tientao, Treybien, Ward3001, Wikiklrsc, Xerxes2k, Yug, Zephirum, Валерий Пасько, Ὁ οἶστρος, 44 anonymous edits

Runaway Bride (1999 film) *Source*: http://en.wikipedia.org/w/index.php?oldid=472048772 *Contributors*: AN(Ger), AbsoluteGleek92, After Midnight, Alakazam, Alexc922, AntonioMartin, Arvindn, Astorknlam, Babedacus, Ben-Bopper, Bencherlite, Bomkia, Candy156sweet, Coltsfan, CoolKatt number 99999, Darkness2005, David Gerard, Descriptive notes, Fluffybun, FrankRizzo2006, Freshh, Gaia Octavia Agrippa, Glenellyn, Hondasaregood, I c u trippin, Ianblair23, Idm04, John K, Keenan Pepper, Levineps, MarnetteD, Mike Payne, MilfordBoy991, Nmadera, Notmicro, Piano non troppo, Quentin X, Savolya, Semblance, Stibu, Strongbad1982, Swimdb, TAnthony, TKD, The JPS, TiffanyRohe, Timclare, Ulric1313, Wafulz, Warreed, Wasted Sapience, WillC, Woohookitty, Yopohari, Zenosparadox, 89 anonymous edits

Dr. T & the Women *Source*: http://en.wikipedia.org/w/index.php?oldid=462618808 *Contributors*: AN(Ger), Andycjp, Belovedfreak, Bovineboy2008, CanisRufus, Catamorphism, Damaavand, Doc Strange, Doctor Sunshine, GUllman, Gabbe, Gimmetrow, Hrvoje Simic, ItsTheClimb17, Jkelly, Leithp, Mrshayes, Mwalimu1, Nehrams2020, Nutmegger, Nv8200p, Ohinternet, PigFlu Oink, Popageorgio, Reaper Eternal, Redux, Shining.Star, Suckstobeabum, Th1rt3en, Volatile, Wasted Sapience, WhisperToMe, Wool Mintons, Xezbeth, ZayZayEM, 35 anonymous edits

Autumn in New York (film) *Source*: http://en.wikipedia.org/w/index.php?oldid=470882942 *Contributors*: Andycjp, ArcWriter, AtticusX, Bdulhanr, Bovineboy2008, Count Ringworm, Davemcarlson, Donmike10, FollowGuard, FrankRizzo2006, Hagerman, KLuebbers, Koppapa, Lighterside, LilHelpa, Monkeymanman, Nino.shoshia, Olivier, Qylecoop, Rich Farmbrough, Rosalbissima, SISLEY, Seansoo3, ShelfSkewed, SilkTork, Slipperyweasel, Sportsnut, Steave77, Suckstobeabum, Supernumerary, TheGerm, Tjmayerinsf, Tryptofeng, Uncle Milty, 35 anonymous edits

Chicago (2002 film) *Source*: http://en.wikipedia.org/w/index.php?oldid=471434976 *Contributors*: 17Drew, 23skidoo, 82766.music, A2Kafir, ARGOU, AbsoluteGleek92, Acroterion, Actryan, Ajd, Alan smithee, AlbertSM, Alex S, Alex43223, AlexDotta, All Hallow's Wraith, Amcguire12, Ameliorate!, Andrew0921, Andromeda, Andrzejbanas, Andy Marchbanks, Andycjp, Angel caboodle, Anime No Kyouran, Ankama, Applejaxs, Aramgutang, Arataman 79, ArkansasTraveler, Asciident, AshTFrankFurter2, Aspirex, B0OP, BSMellen, Bahar101, Beetstra, Before My Ken, Bevo, Bigs slb, Bill shannon, Billdanbury, Blake Burba, Blanchardb, Bob bobato, Bovineboy2008, Bzuk, Caknuck, Carl.bunderson, CarolGray, Cburnett, CharlotteWebb, Chill Pill Bill, Cholmes75, ChrisGriswold, ChristinaDunigan, Ciderbarrel, Circeus, ClockworkLunch, ClonedPickle, Coder Dan, Cop 663, Coverage1600, Cruz-iglesia, Ctrl190, Cxz111, Cypherpunk, D4, DaveFoster110@hotmail.com, Davemcarlson, DeWaine, DearPrudence, DearSeba, Delldot, Dopefish, Downtownstar, Dr. Blofeld, Dr. Conehead, Drbogdan, Dugwiki, Dynesclan, E. Ripley, EJBanks, Easchiff, Ebyabe, Enigmaman, EoGuy, Erebus555, Erik, Eruditionfish, Ewin, ExpressingYourself, Films addicted, Flockmeal, FriscoKnight, FuriousFreddy, Gadfium, Garden59, Gbelk08, Gevorg89, Ghost Akira, Grafen, Granburguesa, Grstain, Hal Raglan, Harikari, Harry811, Hawaiian717, Hearfourmewesique, HilaryB, Hullaballoo Wolfowitz, IAmTheCoinMan, Irk, ItsTheClimb17, JDDJS, JGKlein, JackFloridian, Jahangir23, JamesMLane, Jasonbres, Jazzymartini, Jc37, Jedd the Jedi, Jhsounds, Jiffy Clay, Joey80, Johnandmitchy, Jordan Brown, Joseph A. Spadaro, Jzummak, Kaisersanders, Katelin Helinsky, Kbdank71, Kgman, Kollision, Konlyg, L Kensington, LAX, Leszek Jańczuk, Levineps, Lewiscb, Liftarn, Lifung, LinkTiger, LinkToddMcLovinMontana, Logan, Lorenglassman, LostLeviathan, Lugnuts, Major 1986, Majorly, Mani1, Manop, Marblespire, MarnetteD, Martin451, MartinVillafuerte85, Martinsizon, Matlefebvre20, MattHucke, MearsMan, MegX, Meredyth, Metropolitan90, Mfmoviefan, Midhav Ravindran, Mightyfastpig, Millahnna, Mirmo!, Moni3, Morada1356, Moviefan, Mr. Comodor, Mtjaws, NWill, Nasnema, NeonDaylight, NiGHTS into Dreams..., Nunh-huh, Nymf, Ohconfucius, Opusaug, Ossmkitty, Ozzie425er, PC78, Paul A, Pb30, Pepso, Phbasketball6, Phe, Philip Trueman, Pinkninjarox, Pinktulip, Pjoef, Polylerus, Pwnage8, QuadrivialMind, QuasyBoy, Que-Can, RBBrittain, RPlunk2853, RRHadley, RattleandHum, RealityTelevisionFan, RedWolf, Reflex Reaction, RicJac, Richard D. LeCour, Rick Block, Ricky81682, Robert Merkel, Roberto Frana, Rodrigogomespaixao, Rogerd, Ronkonkaman, Ronniecat, Rossrs, Royboycrashfan, Ru-G Corp., RuED, SFTVLGUY2, Savidan, SchfiftyThree, ScudLee, Scuse me, what r u doin?, SeanO, Seeinggreen, Seeleschneider, Seresin, Sergeiarias, ShelfSkewed, Shsilver, Silverhorse, SiobhanHansa, Skiasaurus, Skydog892, Somblsaldoms69, Someone else, Sottolacqua, Soundofmusicals, Staticat369, Stefanomione, Stormie, Str1977, Sugar Bear, Supadog, Tassedethe, Tellyaddict, Template namespace initialisation script, The Duke of Waltham, The Man in Question, The Transhumanist, TheMovieBuff, TheRealFennShysa, Themepark, Theoldanarchist, Thismightbezach, Timeineurope, Tommy2010, TracyLinkEdnaVelmaPenny, Tregoweth, TuneyLoon, Tvfreak1, Twix1875, Txomin, UZiBLASTER7, Ummit, Unaiaia, Urbane Legend, Vicious 1990, VirtualSteve, Vivify, WAS, WIS, Wanengineer, Wapcaplet, Wasted Sapience, WayTooSerious, Wayne Slam, Weebiloobil, WhisperToMe, Wiki109, WikiMiss, Wikipeterproject, Wildhartlivie, Wknight94, Woohookitty, Wwestarwars, Xevior, Xezbeth, Yeyosmoka21, Ysangkok, Yvesnimmo, ZeroJanvier, ZeroOne, Zik2, Zzyzx11, Александър, 448 anonymous edits

Unfaithful (2002 film) *Source*: http://en.wikipedia.org/w/index.php?oldid=470868594 *Contributors*: *drew, Achin4aiken15, Ahoerstemeier, Alexandria, Alhutch, Americanhero, Andrzejbanas, Arbero, Ariya shookh, Ashravin, AtheWeatherman, Beast from da East, Bisbis, Bodnotbod, Bovineboy2008, Bubbachuck, Bunchofgrapes, CLW, Cburnett, CerealBabyMilk, Chris the speller, ClonedPickle, Composer321, Count Ringworm, Courtkittie, CrimeSetKenDoll, CuteLittleDoggie, Dansham, David Gerard, DeWaine, Djflem, Donmike10, Donteatyellowsnow, DuaneThomas, Dysepsion, EricRoubinek, Erik, FSG, FrankRizzo2006, Gabbe, Glane23, Gonioul, Gracefool, Granpuff, Hooriaj, Hullaballoo Wolfowitz, J. Van Meter, J.D., Jbmurray, Jjberzelius, Jmlk17, Jpu1000, Kariteh, Kfrogers, Ling.Nut, LolliapaulinaS1, LtMuldoon, M4bwav, Mickea, Momoricks, Nmital191, Noirish, Nt6614a, Olivier, Oshowski, OwenBlacker, Parkwells, Peteresch, PlatformerMastah, Polylerus, Qatter, Radosław10, Redrocket, RichF, Roberthope33, Simplemime, SunCreator, TashTish, The Parsnip!, The Thing That Should Not Be, TheMovieBuff, TheoloJ, Thomas Larsen, Tovojolo, Tregoweth, Treybien, Ward3001, Wasted Sapience, WhisperToMe, WwViNwW, Xineann, Zahir13, ماني, 115 anonymous edits

The Mothman Prophecies (film) *Source*: http://en.wikipedia.org/w/index.php?oldid=466253702 *Contributors*: + + Mythman or Mothman? + +, 6afraidof7, AdamSmithee, Alaniaris, All Hallow's Wraith, ArcWriter, Berniethomas68, Bk50in09, Bovineboy2008, BreakerLOLZ, Breakfastchief, Bronks, Chatfecter, Chris the speller, ChrisGriswold, Cliff1911, Czolgolz, DCincarnate, DM Jolly, DOHC Holiday, Dammit, David Gerard, DepressedPer, Dfsghjkgfhdg, DionysiusThrax, Discospinster, Donmike10, Doodleface, Downwards, Dream out loud, Empty2005, FMAFan1990, Felicity4711, FrankRizzo2006, Frecklefoot, Frightner, Frosted14, Garywgoldstein, Gaunt, GenQuest, GorgeCustersSabre, HandThatFeeds, Imbrown, Iridescent, Jcsmith65, Jtalledo, KConWiki, Kablekarrz, Kesh, Keyesc, Laser brain, Lontano, LuckyLouie, Mallanox, Master Deusoma, Mathroman, McGeddon, Mischa83, Moguaurobanazg, Moth1965, MurderWatcher1, Mvincec, NE2, Nuberger13, Ohnoitsjamie, Peepnklown, Pegship, Perfectblue97, Petereiley, Pharos, Philip Trueman, Pmberry, Pro Game Master87, Quentin X, RattleandHum, Rejectwater, Rich Farmbrough, Rossrs, Secretsqurl, Seedlessgrapes84, ShortShadow, Sophie means wisdom, Spencerz, Stenvenhe, Techboy776, Tesi1700, The Shadow-Fighter, Thunderbunny, Tom5467, Traveler45701, Treybien, Typhoon966, UKER, Wackjum, Walkiped, Wasted Sapience, Zombie433, 157 anonymous edits

Shall We Dance? (2004 film) *Source*: http://en.wikipedia.org/w/index.php?oldid=467679097 *Contributors*: AAAAA, AN(Ger), Altenmann, Andycjp, Bayberrylane, Belle Equipe, Booth088, Bovineboy2008, Brettstout, Bunny-chan, Camw, Cbrown1023, Classicfilms, ConMan, Dammit, DanArmiger, Djk3, Dutchmonkey9000, Erik, Estrose, Fabrictramp, Freikorp, Froid, Gene Nygaard, Gilgamesh, H2g2bob, I have no pants but I sure like to dance, Jdobbin, Kbdank71, Kusma, Liftarn, Lucas Brígido, Maniago, MarnetteD, Mayooresan, Mayumashu, McNoddy, MegaChris123, MovieMadness, Ndugu, ObsessiveJoBroDisorder, Ozdaren, Phildav76, RLipstock, RattleandHum, Rebel-Angel-Hero, Revth, RicJac, Rjwilmsi, Roaring Siren, Samuelhww, Shining.Star, SnapSnap, Speciate, Stu-Rat, Suckstobeabum, Tassedethe, Tertiary7, TheMovieBuff, ThomasK, Tigerman81, Timbatron, Tony Sidaway, Treybien, Vmarshall51, Wasted Sapience, Wasted Time R, Woohookitty, Wtmitchell, Xezbeth, Yaksar, 61 anonymous edits

Bee Season (film) *Source*: http://en.wikipedia.org/w/index.php?oldid=471095985 *Contributors*: *drew, AN(Ger), AbsoluteGleek92, AlbertHerring, Andman8, Bhadani, Ccbanker, CoolKatt number 99999, Cybercobra, Darev, David Gerard, Dewey Finn, Dohanlon, DoubleCross, Dr. Blofeld, Edward, Erik9, Error, Feydey, Filll, FrankRizzo2006, Gaius Cornelius, Hondo11008, Horkana, Jeandré du Toit, Kevinalewis, Kollision, Kwamikagami, Laspezi85, Nehrams2020, Pegship, PiMaster3, Polisher of Cobwebs, Qaqaq, RattleandHum, Rich Farmbrough, SISLEY, Satchfan, Scolaire, SilkTork, Supernumerary, TEHodson, TheMadBaron, Treybien, Wasted Sapience, Wool Mintons, Yodaat, 38 anonymous edits

The Hoax *Source*: http://en.wikipedia.org/w/index.php?oldid=461686382 *Contributors*: AN(Ger), AaronY, Alansohn, Amonggiants, Andrzejbanas, Antaeus Feldspar, ArnoldReinhold, Artichoke-Boy, BD2412, Bahar101, BlastOButter42, C d h, ChefBoy6382, Chris the speller, Cliff smith, Clintong, Djflem, Donmike10, Easchiff, ElvisFan1981, Erik, Hegria66, ImperatorExercitus, JYi, Jadeonly, Jaydec, Jgm, Jonathan.s.kt, Kuralyov, Leflyman, Leroyinc, LiteraryMaven, Maegdalene, Michael Devore, Mostergr, Movieguru2006, N. Harmonik, NorthernThunder, Odikuas, Patrick, Pegship, Pepso, Polylerus, Purealex, RenniePet, Resident Evil Twin Guy, Rjmorris, RobNS, Rusted AutoParts, SLWalsh, Santryl, Smetanahue, Smgold92, Smyd286, TexMurphy, TheMovieBuff, Thumperward, Treybien, Truth is relative, understanding is limited, Verne Equinox, Viper007Bond, Waggers, Wasted Sapience, Webhat, Woohookitty, Wtwhitejr, Yancyfry jr, Yurivict, Зейнал, Четыре тильды, 28 anonymous edits

The Hunting Party (2007 film) *Source*: http://en.wikipedia.org/w/index.php?oldid=470190591 *Contributors*: AN(Ger), Akarkera, AlbertSM, All Hallow's Wraith, Alser, Analoguedragon, Ancient Land of Bosoni, Andrzejbanas, Ankur Banerjee, BalkanWalker, Bob3599, BosnianBoy123, C777, CWSensation, CiudadanoGlobal, Ckatz, DJ Bungi, DagErlingSmørgrav, Dans, Dchall1, Derelk, Descartes1979, Downwards, Elmschrat, Eluchil404, Enpitsu, Erik, FMAFan1990, Fickmich, Fortunecookie289, Garion96, General Epitaph, Grandpafootsoldier, Imbris, JPG-GR, Jack Upland, Jeff3000, KBi, Kollision, LilHelpa, Logan, LtMuldoon, Lugnuts, MaGioZal, Madgerly, MadocDoyu, Malcolmxl5, Matt91486, McGR, Melly42, Mhym, Mike Babic, Morpose, Movieguru, Njj4, OlEnglish, PRODUCER, Patrick, Peccafly, Pixelface, Rakesh00, Rama, Rjwilmsi, RoadDogXVIII, SAWGunner89, Santasa99, Serbian Defense Forces, Skier Dude,

Article Sources and Contributors

Slysplace, SpikeJones, TheMovieBuff, Themarcuscreature, Timbouctou, Tohd8BohaithuGh1, TracyLinkEdnaVelmaPenny, UberCryxic, VandalCruncher, Vladimir Prelog, Wasted Sapience, Xleax, Xoxomcdreamy, Zec, Zombie433, Zvonko, 250 anonymous edits

I'm Not There Source: http://en.wikipedia.org/w/index.php?oldid=470064161 Contributors: 650 Norton (1951), 96T, @pple, AN(Ger), AbsoluteGleek92, Adamrush, Adh 1000, Ael 2, Aesopos, After Midnight, Aitias, Akamad, Akmenon, Alexius08, Alison, Amire80, Andrea Cioffi, AnmaFinotera, Archetypo, Arno Matthias, Asbestos man, Balthazarduju, Bdburako, Beardo, Behdad, Bender235, Berenlazarus, Bigelectric, Binarypower, Bjones, Blackjanedavey, Blukens, Bomac, Borkdog, Bovineboy2008, Brian Kendig, Bruce1ee, BubonicLou, Californian Treehugger, Capchoirgirl, Caspian blue, Cbing01, Cdop, Chantessy, Chicopac, Childzy, Christian Roess, Chupon, CieloEstrellado, Cloonmore, Conman33, ConradKilroy, Cop 663, Coresus, Cstella23, Dancemotron, Dankeezer, Darth NormaN, Denstat, Dhartung, Discospinster, Donking3, Downtownstar, Drummondjacob, Dureo, Easchiff, Elembis, Erik, Espoo, Esprit15d, Eumolpo, Extraordinary Machine, FMAFan1990, Feudonym, Fred Bradstadt, Frostlion, Gabbo, Gary King, Geniac, George cowie, GoingBatty, Goodnightmush, Grmanners, Gyrofrog, Hl, Hmrox, Icarus of old, Inoculatedcities, ItsTheClimb17, J.delanoy, JK-MD, JaGa, Jayjg, JesseRafe, Johnblow1, Joshdboz, JustAGal, Jwk3, Kammerice, Katharineamy, Kbrian, Kingboyk, Korah7106, Kuhutanvir, L3afyGr33n, Lafe Smith, Lilac Soul, Lockesdonkey, LostLikeTearsInRain, Luna Whistler, M.Naff, Matterson52, Meisam, Melinoe, Melty girl, Merryjig, Mick gold, Mike Eder, Mjj808, MovieMadness, Mrblondnyc, NWill, NYScholar, Not-So-Funny-Comedian, Notdedyet, Oanabay04, Ode2joy, Omerasta, Password16, Phil Bordelon, Phocks, Pinchofhope, Pixelface, Pyanth, Quadell, Quentin X, Razorflame, Red dwarf, Richhoncho, Right4, Roberta F., Robixsmash, Ron whisky, Saltywood, Sandhillcrane, Senseofsurreal, Ser Amantio di Nicolao, SethTisue, Shamrox, Skier Dude, SkyWalker, Slowhand934, Sonhomeu726, Spacini, Spongefrog, SpyMagician, Squirrelisland, Sstteevvee, Stogdad, Stolengood, THEN WHO WAS PHONE?, Tabletop, TashTish, Tomdobb, Torstein, Travelbird, Treybien, Trogga, Tsungwei, Tyler Barlass, Tysto, UJohnnyZephyr, V-train, Warchef, Wave of Mutilation, Wildroot, Wool Mintons, Writtenright, Yamanbaiia, Yellowbounder, Zasderfght, Zepheus, Zombiebaron, 368 anonymous edits

The Flock (film) Source: http://en.wikipedia.org/w/index.php?oldid=423650731 Contributors: AN(Ger), Baa, Bopo, CiaPan, Cit helper, CyberSkull, Dahamsta7, DanielDeibler, Darth NormaN, Discospinster, Eekerz, Extraordinary Machine, Fdgsdgdfggvx, FrankRizzo2006, Gordon Liu, GrahamHardy, Histrion, Hoverfish, JM.Beaubourg, Kintetsubuffalo, Kramertron, LtMuldoon, Millahnna, Mushroom, MysticBlue, NBbeauty, Nehrams2020, Patrick, Pearle, Pegship, RadioKirk, Radosław10, Rich Farmbrough, Rje, Robertvan1, Rosalbissima, Sander Moholi, Skier Dude, SkyWalker, Sreejithk2000, Tanger123, The Hungarian, The Wordsmith, Totie, Treybien, Tubeyes, Xompanthy, YUL89YYZ, Ὁ οἶστρος, 61 anonymous edits

Nights in Rodanthe Source: http://en.wikipedia.org/w/index.php?oldid=462724764 Contributors: AN(Ger), All Hallow's Wraith, AndrejD, Andy Marchbanks, AnmaFinotera, Annasibs, BillFlis, Blehfu, Captain-tucker, Chantessy, Chase172, Cliff1911, Commander Shepard, Cperrott2, Decltype, Dgmoran, Dragonmara, Ecasbarro, Efe, Equendil, Erik, Everyoneandeveryone, Flyinhawaiian, FrankRizzo2006, Gamer007, Garion96, GastonGirl08, GeneralBelly, Greendesk, HawkeAnyone, Joeysaad, Johndburger, Liquidluck, Lugnuts, Muso99, Nirigihimu, Nupe 11, Nwbeeson, ObsessiveJoBroDisorder, POTCfan99, Pamskiii, Patrick, Paulmlieberman, Penbat, Pinkadelica, Quentin X, RODERICKMOLASAR, RepliCarter, Roaring Siren, Rudisnell, Salvio giuliano, Ser Amantio di Nicolao, SkyWalker, Sreejithk2000, Starkiller88, Stetsonharry, Suckstobeabum, Tassedethe, Taty2007, The Rogue Penguin, Tigermilked, Tim!, TracyLinkEdnaVelmaPenny, Treybien, Umiami09, WaldoJ, WhisperToMe, YUL89YYZ, Yaminator, 101 anonymous edits

Amelia (film) Source: http://en.wikipedia.org/w/index.php?oldid=469844921 Contributors: 1Matt20, Ahunt, Al3xil, All Hallow's Wraith, Aquila89, Babbage, Beemer69, Bencey, Bhall87, BigBang616, Bovineboy2008, Brutaldeluxe, Bzuk, CXCV, Cheddarjack, Christianster94, Colin Douglas Howell, Contributor777, Dawynn, DeWaine, DerHexer, Djbj16, Doctorfluffy, DoubleCross, Drbreznjev, Easchiff, Elendil's Heir, Emilynothing, Fierce Beaver, Freshh, FromtheWordsofBR, GG The Fly, Gamaliel, Garion96, Gothicfilm, Goustien, Grandpafootsoldier, Gunculture, Gwen Gale, Horkana, InfamousPrince, JamesAM, Lugnuts, Luke4545, Mamoa, Maryloo2002, MathewBrooks, Merriment™, Momopop, Movieguru2006, Mwatts23, Ndboy, Nhl4hamilton, Packinheat2u, Petiatil, Prathik911, Pricer1980, Redmond Barry, RobNS, Shining.Star, Skier Dude, SkyWalker, Softlavender, Spstaff, Tassedethe, TheLastAmigo, Thismightbezach, Timeineurope, Treybien, Varlaam, Vkil, Vrenator, Warreed, Watts23, ZXXLawAbidingCitizenXXZ, Ὁ οἶστρος, 71 anonymous edits

Hachi: A Dog's Tale Source: http://en.wikipedia.org/w/index.php?oldid=471519152 Contributors: 10metreh, A3oertENG, Agustinaldo, Andycjp, Bcistudio, Beirne, Belle Equipe, Bendono, Bfigura, Billy Hathorn, Bovineboy2008, Briantw, CharCharOverOver11, Coaster1983, Commander Shepard, Djbj16, Doglover33, Donmike10, Easchiff, EchetusXe, Ed Poor, El Monterrey, Emily Jensen, EoGuy, Erud, Etr906, Fear Itself, Freshh, Hai Tien, Hankengine, Ian.thomson, Idonotlikebabies, Ilovedogsrayna, Irrational pi, Itzuvit, JCGDIMAIWAT, Jerem43, Jimp, Jojhutton, Knee427, KoshVorlon, Litalex, Logan, LtMuldoon, Marek69, Martin451, MasterDamian394, Materialscientist, Mtl2la, Nardog, Ndboy, Nobart, Oda Mari, Oscarcom, Oshowski, P.PradeepRaj, Patrick, Paulmas, Peorth, Pig2008, Rahulzerg, RainbowOfLight, Ralaring807, Ravave, Rawfrijoles, Robzz, Rogue11, Ronhjones, Rror, Salvio giuliano, Simple Bob, SirCadogon4, Skier Dude, SkyWalker, Smetanahue, Staka, Stdumjb, Steam5, The Thing That Should Not Be, The White Duke, TheMage25, TheMovieBuff, Tommy2010, Tony1, Tora-dono, Tos42, Typhoon966, Vanjagenije, Viatheway, Wayne Slam, Wnick99, Редмонд Барри, Ὁ οἶστρος, 193 anonymous edits

Brooklyn's Finest Source: http://en.wikipedia.org/w/index.php?oldid=467110964 Contributors: 91nacho, ADwarf, Andrzejbanas, Applause2.0, Artoasis, BD2412, Bender235, Bjones, Blue387, Bovineboy2008, Bridgefan09, Cavie78, Cmart514, Coasterlover1994, Commander Shepard, CommonsDelinker, Coolhawks88, Crazy4metallica, Dali.s47, DepressedPer, Dhabolt, Dhartung, Djbj16, Downwards, Elvis1977, Ely1, Fabish Boaitey, Fierce Beaver, FrankRizzo2006, FreakFett, Girolamo Savonarola, GlassCobra, Great entity, Horkana, InfamousPrince, Jngnyc, John, John of Reading, JohnInDC, Joswargo, Kidlittle, Kwiki, Life of Riley, LtMuldoon, MDowdal, MR.HJH, Malke 2010, Martarius, Marychan41, Merlinsorca, Mewnumber2008, MrsPhoenix91, NBbeauty, Nono64, Ohconfucius, Overturefilms, Paulturtle, Planecrash111, R'n'B, Rayhunt3r, Raymbala, Roaring Siren, SGGH, Schizodelight, Shadowjams, SkyWalker, Solatha, Swliv, Theburn77, Thismightbezach, Tide rolls, Tinton5, Tkynerd, Tobias truvillion, Tony1, Treybien, Trumpetrep, UESParules, Varlaam, Who then was a gentleman?, Winston Spencer, Woohookitty, Yankees10, Zombie433, 京葉車両センター, 156 anonymous edits

The Double (film) Source: http://en.wikipedia.org/w/index.php?oldid=471639342 Contributors: Bbb23, Bovineboy2008, Debresser, FollowGuard, Freshh, InfamousPrince, LtMuldoon, Noclador, Obi-WanKenobi-2005, Peppage, Sama724, Theburgen, 23 anonymous edits

Arbitrage (film) Source: http://en.wikipedia.org/w/index.php?oldid=470916217 Contributors: Bovineboy2008, Klemen Kocjancic, Krevans, LtMuldoon, SILICON-POWER, Wilhelmina Will, 2 anonymous edits

Image Sources, Licenses and Contributors

File:Richardgere.jpg *Source*: http://en.wikipedia.org/w/index.php?title=File:Richardgere.jpg *License*: Creative Commons Attribution 2.0 *Contributors*: spaceodissey from Parma, Italy

File:Loudspeaker.svg *Source*: http://en.wikipedia.org/w/index.php?title=File:Loudspeaker.svg *License*: Public Domain *Contributors*: Bayo, Gmaxwell, Husky, Iamunknown, Mirithing, Myself488, Nethac DIU, Omegatron, Rocket000, The Evil IP address, Wouterhagens, 18 anonymous edits

File:DalaiLamaRichardGere.jpg *Source*: http://en.wikipedia.org/w/index.php?title=File:DalaiLamaRichardGere.jpg *License*: Creative Commons Attribution 2.0 *Contributors*: Sneakerdog

Image:Richard gere2.jpg *Source*: http://en.wikipedia.org/w/index.php?title=File:Richard_gere2.jpg *License*: Public Domain *Contributors*: Original uploader was WacoJacko at en.wikipedia

File:Power movie poster.jpg *Source*: http://en.wikipedia.org/w/index.php?title=File:Power_movie_poster.jpg *License*: unknown *Contributors*: AvicAWB, Quentin X

File:Star full.svg *Source*: http://en.wikipedia.org/w/index.php?title=File:Star_full.svg *License*: Public Domain *Contributors*: User:Conti from the original images by User:RedHotHeat

File:Star empty.svg *Source*: http://en.wikipedia.org/w/index.php?title=File:Star_empty.svg *License*: Creative Commons Attribution-Sharealike 2.5 *Contributors*: User:Conti from the original images by User:RedHotHeat

File:Unfaithful.png *Source*: http://en.wikipedia.org/w/index.php?title=File:Unfaithful.png *License*: unknown *Contributors*: ariya shookh

Image:Kittanning Citizen's Bridge.JPG *Source*: http://en.wikipedia.org/w/index.php?title=File:Kittanning_Citizen's_Bridge.JPG *License*: Public Domain *Contributors*: User:Mvincec

File:Director and actors of I'm not there at the 64th Venice Film Festival-01.jpg *Source*: http://en.wikipedia.org/w/index.php?title=File:Director_and_actors_of_I'm_not_there_at_the_64th_Venice_Film_Festival-01.jpg *License*: Creative Commons Attribution-Sharealike 2.0 *Contributors*: Mireille Ampilhac

File:Nights in Rodanthe house south side 2009.jpg *Source*: http://en.wikipedia.org/w/index.php?title=File:Nights_in_Rodanthe_house_south_side_2009.jpg *License*: Creative Commons Attribution-Sharealike 3.0 *Contributors*: Captain-tucker

License

Creative Commons Attribution-Share Alike 3.0 Unported
//creativecommons.org/licenses/by-sa/3.0/

CPSIA information can be obtained
at www.ICGtesting.com
Printed in the USA
BVOW07s2038061217
502135BV00007B/345/P